Great Failures of the Extremely Successful

D0863266

Great Failures of the Extremely Successful

Mistakes, Adversity, Failure
and Other Steppingstones to Success

Steve Young

Tallfellow®Press

Los Angeles

2004

Published by
Tallfellow® Press, Inc.
1180 S. Beverly Drive
Los Angeles, CA 90035

Visit www.greatfailure.com
www.tallfellow.com

Designed by SunDried Penguin Design

ISBN 1-931290-19-9

Printed in the United States of America
by Berryville Graphics

1 2 3 4 5 6 7 8 9 10

Dedication

Dedicated to my dad,

Reuben,

whose only failure

was to die much too young.

Preface

fail·ure': 1. the state or fact of being lacking or insufficient. 2. a losing of power or strength; weakening, dying away. 3. not doing; neglect or omission. 4. not succeeding in doing or becoming. 5. a person who does not succeed.

Babe Ruth spent his childhood years in an orphanage and then struck out 1,330 times on his way to 714 home runs and baseball immortality.

In 1954, **Elvis Presley** was fired from the Grand Ole Opry after only one performance and told by the manager, "You ain't goin' nowhere, son. Better get y'all job back drivin' a truck."

Oprah Winfrey didn't let getting fired from her reporter's job and being told, "You're not fit for TV," keep her from becoming one of the most beloved and successful women in television.

In 1933, **Walter Cronkite** failed an early audition in local radio and was told by the radio station manager that he would never make it as a radio announcer. He went on to become one of America's most recognizable and trusted voices.

Being unable to hear, speak or see didn't shut down **Helen Keller**'s world. It opened her up to a life more full than most able-bodied people might experience in a lifetime.

All these people have one thing in common. They refused to let hardships stop them on the road to victory. They learned that every triumphant discovery resulted from many unsuccessful experiments; that every home run has been tempered by a multitude of missed swings; that every great book was built on the back of endless rewrites; that every top performer has been humiliated by more than one performance; that many a scrumptious recipe found its way to the dinner table through burnt and bruised trials; that failure is part of the process that breeds success.

Sir Edmund Hillary wanted to climb Mount Everest and, after three failed attempts, finally succeeded. People said, "You've conquered the mountain," and Hillary said, "No, I've conquered myself."

The greatest commodity our planet possesses is the human race. The greatest resource...ourselves. If this were a world of constructive and positive reinforcement, we need go no further. Our children would grow up to be successful adults, brimming with confidence, continuing to spread the word of a world full of endless possibilities. The cycle of enthusiastic affirmations would renew itself throughout the generations, and we would all live and die, happy and content. Only I would be miserable because there would be no need to write this book.

Alas, most people, at some point in their lives, have been the object of the not-so-tactful judgments of those in a position of authority or so-called *superior* knowledge, who have been shown to be, for the most part, dead wrong. Those who can, do; those who can't, become critics.

Parents, teachers, coaches, business supervisors, religious authorities and critics of all sorts, inadvertently or not, have been responsible for dulling aspirations and destroying dreams. Many mistakes have been proclaimed failures and subsequently punished, leaving many of us afraid to take risks or even to try again. All too often these disciplines and evaluations have been brought about in a misguided attempt to correct and improve the individual. More than likely, however, the opposite has resulted.

There are others who have been born physically or mentally challenged, or became so through sickness or accident. They may have been told that they were not capable of doing what they had done before, or that they should not even try something for the first time, lest they be disheartened or hurt. Thank God for the likes of Stephen Hawking and Christopher Reeve.

Many whose unique thoughts and deeds are deemed too radical or too odd for "more reasonable" minds are not taken seriously. Yet it is these same enterprising and original thinkers of every generation who end up leading the charge into a new period of growth and discovery.

Whether well-intended or absolute evil, the result of conservative reactions to anything out of the norm has been a society of doom and gloomers; those who say "I can't" without ever saying "I'll try." Even worse, these skeptics will pass on this hapless message to their children and colleagues. The circle of learned apprehension will grow unless we understand that the circle can be broken. AND IT CAN!

The objective is to appreciate the fact that our life is a process, a process made up of infinitesimal experiences and moments all fashioning us into who we are today. And if we continue to breathe, our missteps, errors and misunderstandings are absolutely necessary for growth. They are the life-lessons that are essential for progress and enrichment. Without them, we would stagnate and whither away. Why? Because we learn nothing from being perfect. It feels good for the moment, but it doesn't teach us a dang thing. Never did. Never will.

Do babies come out of the womb walking and talking? Not many. Are they criticized for falling down when they begin to walk? I hope not. They are in fact cheered and, with major huggies all around, encouraged to try again. After innumerable tumbles and assorted boo-boos, they're soon up and running everywhere. Does a baby feel that it should do better or learn faster? No, because a baby has no expectations, except maybe for the anticipated tranquillity a well-placed thumb brings. What a child did was what it did and when it did it is when it was done. And that, ladies and gentleman, is how it works best. When did we begin to deem it appropriate that devaluing ourselves by not meeting some quasi-standard was the proper way to live? And why can't Dr. T. Berry Brazelton be here for us, too, the over-five generation?

We may want to haul off and flatten the next person who says, "What doesn't kill us makes us stronger," but Mother Nature handles failure and obstacles...naturally. We call it evolutionary adaptation. As organisms evolved, the stresses faced by our ancestors caused the human body to change in order to handle environmental needs. In effect, our bodies know how to react to adversity intuitively. It would make sense that our brains and our hearts are equipped to do the same...as long as we choose to get out of the way. Biologically, while *pain* would seem to be anything but good news, we would never know there was something wrong in our bodies if it weren't for the pain. It's nature's wake-up call.

Life's solutions don't come down the chute, gift-wrapped and ready to be opened any time we decide they should be. We have no idea if the very next effort won't provide us with our success. So why do we decide to quit before we reach our objective? Why do we let a single failure stop us? If Thomas Edison had quit because coal, carbon and other tested materials didn't ignite his bulb, you might only be able to read this book by day or by candlelight. He stuck with it and each attempt brought him closer to the discovery that tungsten would do the trick.

But stuff does happen and we sometimes must suffer through our failures, right? Not necessarily. *Any situation stops being a failure as soon as we attempt to learn from it.* And we don't even have to actually learn something. The attempt alone is enough. Once you've taken the action, the constructive process begins. And that activity begets more activity. And here's a profound thought: *When you stop or quit, nothing happens.*

What occurs when you receive a negative evaluation? It probably feels lousy. But if your desire is to enhance your life, dig through that review to see if there's something in it that can help you improve. Even if the reviewer is a fool, he might stumble onto something of relevance for you. After you take what you can use, THROW OUT THE REST! It serves no purpose. Do not give it any power. Take the lemons and make lemonade. Take the leftover lemon rinds, grind them up in your food processor and use them as fertilizer, 'cause ladies and gentleman, there just ain't no going back. What happened, happened. But what is changeable is how you treat yourself. Acceptance plays here. Since you have no control over the past, embrace it and trust that it happened for a good reason. How? Here's the good news *and* the bad news. First the bad news: If you can't figure out some positive rationale for your seemingly negative situation, I wouldn't even venture a guess as to what good it serves. The good news? You don't have to know.

There are some people who believe that everything, good or bad, is for a good reason. It's not an easy concept. Sometimes you have to *fake* the idea or *act as if*. That is, *act as if* things are good. It takes some practice and, in many cases, a lot of faith. If you have a god in your life, this is where you can make good use of Him/Her. And what if, at the end of your life, you haven't discovered the "good reason"? Well, all you did was waste your entire life feeling good when all along you could have felt miserable. Not much of a risk, huh? Is this just a case of kidding ourselves? Not if we want to live a positive life. *Carpe diem! Seize the day!* Nowhere does it say that the day has to be a good one— only that we can make it good if we choose.

Failure is not always of our own making. Other people and events disappoint us, too. Even our own bodies and health fail us from time to time. But no matter the source of the failure, it is our attitude toward the situation that makes all the difference.

And so we come to the reason for the next 300-plus pages. It seems that advice does not make as much of an impact as sharing one's experience with another. In the stories that follow, well-respected and well-known individuals share their heartbreaks, flops, misfortunes and botched opportunities. You'll hear in their own words, and with the emotions we all share, how they relentlessly pursued their dreams past roadblocks and crushing rejections and turned their seeming liabilities into steppingstones to triumph. They reveal how they overcame their personal demons and humiliations to come to believe in themselves. And they are more than happy to tell of those who told them they would never succeed. The anecdotes are meant to encourage us all to learn from their setbacks, to push on, and turn every "I can't" into an "I will." Misfortune will come, but it need never bury you.

Our subjects come from all walks of life—business, science, sports, entertainment, art, education and politics. After all, no one is immune to failure. The difficulties they've dealt with come in all sizes and degrees. While you may not be able to relate to a particular event or circumstance, most likely you'll connect with the feelings. No matter your social standing or on which part of the earth you reside, it's the feelings that are universal, that make us one.

As you read on, be aware that not only are we accused of failures, but we can often be the accuser. If we are in a position of authority or power, teacher or coach, employer or supervisor, parent or friend, we can learn to disregard our inclination to chastise, no matter how delicately, no matter how *right* we think we are. Rather than tear down or humiliate, we can use the same incident to inspire and encourage. The results for you and the rest of humanity can be a windfall of untold good.

So it is, I chose to compile the information for this book. For if we all attempt to change our attitude toward imperfection, Webster will be forced to add to their definition of failure: *6. a steppingstone to success.*

Lincoln's Road to the White House

Failed in business in 1831.

Defeated for Legislature in 1832.

Second business failure in 1833.

Suffered nervous breakdown in 1836.

Defeated for Speaker in 1838.

Defeated for Elector in 1840.

Defeated for Congress in 1843.

Defeated for Congress in 1848.

Defeated for Senate in 1855.

Defeated for Vice President in 1856.

Defeated for Senate in 1858.

ELECTED PRESIDENT IN 1860.

Acknowledgments

There are so many people I'd like to thank. Most of them have no idea that they played such a great part in my life because I've never met them, only their rejection letters. The ones I do know include:

My overly supportive wife, Diana, who allowed me to remain basically unemployed while she weeded through my terribly structured first drafts in order to make this all readable by someone other than my mom.

My editor, Claudia Sloan, for not hammering me when I had no idea what I was doing. Laura Stern for answering my many phones calls without once letting on that I was being a pain in the neck. Leonard Stern and Larry Sloan for taking a chance on a book that thousands (at least six) others had passed on. The legendary Larry Gelbart for getting me to Tallfellow and for every other wonderful thing he's written. *Written By* magazine editor, Richard Stayton, for printing the article that led me to Larry Gelbart who sent me to Tallfellow. Whew!

Margie Beziat for turning me down to dance when I was 14.

My mom for always believing in me and my sister Joy for always believing in me except when I made fun of her. Jackie and Harold Praw for letting Josh play baseball with Billy Idol's son.

My kids, all of them - Michael, Donna, Ryan, Kelly and Casey— who continuously told me how proud of me they were, even when I wasn't.

Those who went out of their way to help get me to people I never would have reached without their help: Bill Plaschke, Susan Shapiro, Pat O'Connell, Tony Gleeson, Larry Merchant, Gil Stratton, Jean Sarabia, Judy Toll, Trina and Mark York, Marc Dellins, Richard Rosen, Binyamin Jolkovsky, Nanci Cone, Karen Kalensky, Andy Goodman, Shelly Mellot, Leslie Levy, Bob Myer, Bob Young, Dick Blasucci, Rod Mitchell, Gail Stocker, Jayne Meadows, Bill Allen, Sarah Haberman, Arlene Leib Kurtz and Bryan Byun.

All the assistants, secretaries and publicists who didn't hang up on me. And all the ones who did.

Mike Sund for making this book look like…a book.

Janna Wong, Janis Uhley and Michi Fujimoto, whose proofreading helped me to be grammatically gooder as well as spel well.

Bill W. for the tools of life.

My IRA for lasting just long enough.

The bidding war for my first screenplay that never happened.

All the people who were so willing to open up their hearts to me and share their experiences.

I'd list all the agents who passed on me, which I can't afford the ink to print, though I'd like to give special mention to the literary agent who told me that I had some nerve thinking that I could write.

Most important, I want to thank those people in my life who let me down, didn't return my calls, and ignored my charming gaze from across the room—for giving me the idea for this book. The list is too long to mention here.

Steve Young

Table of Contents

Chapter 1

In the middle of difficulty lies opportunity.
  —Albert Einstein

Chapter Two

*Failure is good. It's fertilizer. Everything I've learned about coaching,
I've learned from making mistakes.*
  —Rick Pitino

Chapter Three

*Success isn't built on success. It is built on failure and frustration, sometimes catas-
trophe, and learning to turn it around.*
  —Sumner Redstone

Chapter Four

Men succeed when they realize that their failures are the preparations for their victories.
   —Ralph Waldo Emerson

Chapter Five

Problems are to the mind what exercise is to the muscles, they toughen and make strong.
   —Norman Vincent Peale

Chapter Six

Failure is a detour, not a dead-end street.
   —Zig Ziglar

Chapter Seven

Don't cry when the sun is gone, because the tears won't let you see the stars.
　　—Violeta Parra

Chapter Eight

*Just because something doesn't do what you
planned it to do doesn't mean it's useless.*
　　—Thomas A. Edison

Chapter Nine

*You don't drown by falling in the water;
You drown by staying there.*
　　—Edwin Louis Cole

Chapter Ten

What is defeat? Nothing but education.
Nothing but the first step to something better.
   —Wendell Phillips

ART BUCHWALD

WASHINGTON, DC 20006

Dear Mr. Young,

In answer to your question concerning success, I attribute mine to an unhappy childhood, when I decided at an early age it was me against the world. I had no role models, so I made mine up. I love to write, and that was my saving grace. I put everything on paper and then, when I grew up, I sold it.

Good luck,

Art Buchwald

In the middle of difficulty lies opportunity.

−Albert Einstein

Erin Brockovich

"Each disaster became a steppingstone for growth."

It's very difficult to hear the name Erin Brockovich and not think of Julia Roberts' Academy Award-winning performance in the movie of the same name. But there is a real Erin Brockovich. With two failed marriages, three kids, a cramped house filled with roaches, a bare cupboard, jobs that didn't last and an empty bank account, her life went from bad to worse. A car wreck left her with a herniated disc. Desperate for work, she begged Ed Masry, the Los Angeles attorney she had hired to handle her personal injury claim, for a job as a legal secretary. Her life began to change when she learned that the residents of a small California desert town called Hinkley were slowly being poisoned by chromium VI, a cancer-causing chemical that Pacific Gas & Electric added to its plant to reduce corrosion. Although inexperienced in investigative work, her energy and tenacity won the support of 630 residents, more than enough to institute a class-action lawsuit. Her grit and determination paid off and PG&E settled the suit in 1996 for $333 million—the highest pollution lawsuit ever settled in U.S. history. Difficulties started early on, but it may have been a childhood injury that actually helped make Erin Brockovich the person she finally became.

Kites rise against, not with the wind. No man has ever worked his passage anywhere in a dead calm.
—John Neal

At 5 years old, I received a serious head trauma. My parents began to notice that I started putting my shoes on the wrong feet and transposing numbers. I was labeled retarded, a slow learner, and ended up in special education classes. I was actually dyslexic, though no one knew it back then. I always felt like the underdog. Since I didn't learn like the other kids, I had very low self-esteem. I couldn't keep up. There were times I thought I was stupid or retarded, but in my heart I knew I wasn't. The other kids made fun of me in elementary school. Kids tend to tease anyone who's different, but looking back I see that being different can be the very thing that actually makes you special.

In order to deal with the problems I was having, I put on a mask, became the "actress" and learned to rely more on my instincts. I used charm, wit, and I made sure I wore the greatest outfits. I was always the fun one in the group, which got me into fun places and made me forget about the "F"s I was getting on tests.

To avoid criticism do nothing, say nothing, be nothing.
—Elbert Hubbard

We're usually taught to think with our mind and intellect, but you have to listen to your heart, too. I listened to mine in the Hinkley case [PG&E's water contamination]. My heart and gut guided me when I first reviewed the case. It didn't make any sense that those people would lie and make up such sad, frightful stories. There was an innate sense that allowed me the opportunity to go to the water board to look at the county records. The clothes I wore became a symbol that said, "You can't label me." That charm, as well as the cleavage, worked the way academics never have. Sadly, there are corporate heads who possess superior intelligence yet have no sense of their effect on other human beings. Many companies pay no attention to how inner values can be applied positively in business.

I got my sense of pride from Mom and Dad. They instilled in me deep-rooted values, morals, honor, dignity, pride and respect. They taught me that it's so easy to walk away, so hard to stay and fight. Doing the right thing may not always be popular but it pays off. If something didn't go my way, I thought about what Mom and Dad would say. My mom and dad were my inspiration. So were the people of Hinkley.

I once lied and was severely grounded by having an important school trip taken away. My dad made a decision not to argue or butt heads with me. I was so angry and resented the way I was being treated. The next day, without saying a word, my dad went on a business trip. On the road he realized he needed to communicate to me why he had made his decision. He wrote a letter to me sending along a newspaper article about President Jimmy Carter and the reality of lying. He wrote, "Last night tore you up and it tore me up, too. When you're old enough, you'll understand that if the family cannot honestly communicate with each other, then we have lost everything. Someday we will look back and laugh at what took place. I used to do the same with my parents. Accept your punishment as an adult and resolve it will never happen again. The loss is not that great. The loss of respect is greater. We love you so much." My heightened state of anger over having the trip taken away from me subsided. I felt a strength from my dad and realized the importance of family. I saw that I had let him down, but I knew that he would still be there for me.

The ultimate measure of a person is not where he or she stands in moments of comfort and convenience, but where he or she stands at times of challenge and controversy.
—*Martin Luther King, Jr.*

My mom taught me that mistakes should be accepted and learned from. On another occasion, I really crossed the line and again I was punished. This time it was a letter from my mom that brought me to my knees.

"In view of your latest report card, your parents have decided the following course of action is necessary. You will have no personal phone use. Your grades can be no less than a "C." You may not partake in after-school activities. Television will be limited. We are not happy having to restrict your social life, but you have to cut out time-wasting habits. You haven't been able to discipline yourself or adhere to proper study habits. You must have self-discipline and self-determination. You have wonderful natural abilities. Face up to the fact that you and no one else can put in the time. Don't pass on the blame. Apply yourself each day to the task at hand. Try to not be easily distracted by monkey business. Don't worry about popularity. You're fortunate to have friends and you will still have them. Give schoolwork a good hard try and you will be surprised at what you learn. Stick-to-itiveness is important. You have to develop the habit of perseverance. Take this with the right attitude. We love you and care about your development. Use all your potential to grow into a mature person. We love you and who you are, but we need assurance that you're doing your best, and it is our responsibility to see that you do it."

> *The only failure one should fear is not hugging to the purpose they see as best.*
> —George Eliot

I could have perceived the letter as horrible or I could have decided to change and show my parents I could do it. These were parts of the lessons that I was able to apply when I stumbled onto Hinkley. I was able to communicate honestly, exercise stick-to-itiveness and believe in myself. I had nothing else to go on. The whole time I kept hearing my mom and dad's voices. What I got back from being of service to those people was empowerment and the feeling of complete satisfaction with who I was. Everything I believed in got me to where I am today. I had no special talent, but for the sake of my children and what my parents gave me, I could do what I did. It was those values that became my ticket in life.

Sometimes we forget to believe in ourselves. Everyone has the power and ability to become whatever they want, and you can use street smarts instead of beating your head against the wall in school. I had a learning disability, but I got to step back and perceive it for what it was. I found another way to go, another way to get things done. There are always options, always other opportunities. When one door closes another opens.

The pain and strife that resulted from my car crash in which I was injured and received no just compensation became a turning point in my life. Without it, would I have gotten my foot in the door

> *Only in winter can you tell which trees are truly green. Only when the winds of adversity blow can you tell whether an individual or a country has steadfastness.*
> —*John F. Kennedy*

of the law office? Would I have gone to and accomplished what I did at Hinkley? Probably not. Karma becomes one's fate. There's a lesson here. In each bit of imperfection there is something to be learned; the trauma to my head, the dyslexia, my inability to cope academically, the masks I chose to wear, the discipline problems, being grounded and the admonitions from my parents—each *disaster* became a stepping-stone for growth.

So many times, failure and success are mislabeled as normal and abnormal. The fact is, they are both normal and often the same thing, but in different forms. It is important and essential to adjust the perceptions to reverse the pejorative meaning of and approach to failure.

Any negative situation can be perceived of as either horrid or a learning tool. Whether it is a problem with school, the loss of a baseball game or a loss of a friend, you can take it as the worst that can happen and be despondent, or you can use it as an opportunity to better yourself. The best thing is, it's always up to you.

ADMIRABLE ADMISSIONS

"If I had thought about it, I wouldn't have done the experiment. The literature was full of examples that said you can't do this."
–Spencer Silver on the work that led to the unique adhesives for 3M Post-It® Notes.

 *Jim* *Marshall*

"Face the music. Make things right. The rewards are unimaginable."

Minnesota Viking football great Jim Marshall, part of the feared Purple Eater defense, played in 282 National Football League games [an NFL record] and has been faced with many adversities off the field. At the age of 16, he watched his mother die in his arms. He once had a simple tonsillectomy, lost nine pints of blood and died twice on the operating table. He broke almost every bone in his body in an airplane crash. But it was on a windswept October 25 of 1964 when he learned the true meaning of failure. It may have been the single most embarrassing moment in the history of professional sports.

We were facing the San Francisco 49ers at chilly Kezar Stadium and I was having my best day rushing the passer. In the second quarter of a close game, San Francisco quarterback George Mira dropped back and tossed a short pass to running back Billy Kilmer. He fumbled and there I was…staring at that ball rolling on the ground. Nothin' looks better to a defensive end than a free ball, except maybe if you could score a touchdown with it. Without missing a beat, I scooped up that ball and looked up to see nothing but daylight and an end zone some 62 yards away.

I ran for that goal line as fast as I could, protecting the ball from any 49ers' player who I know must have been breathin' down my back. And that crowd was cheering. Cheering louder than I'd ever heard before, which, I might add, is kind of strange because we're playing in Frisco. But so what, five more yards to go and TOUCHDOWN! I score! The fans are goin' wild and I'm being congratulated…by Bruce Bosley, the San Francisco center. "Thanks a lot, Marshall. We could use more of those." Huh? I look toward the sideline and our quarterback, Fran Tarkenton, yells out to me, "Jim, you ran the wrong way!"

It was the most devastating moment of my life. I was only 24 years old and I scored for the wrong team in front of millions of people on national television. My heart dropped. The only saving grace at the time was that it was right before halftime and I could hide in the locker room.

During halftime, the players were all supportive and Coach Norm Van Brocklin, who was normally anything but sympathetic, said, "Beanpole, don't worry. If it wasn't for what you did we wouldn't have done zip, 'cause no one else out there did a damn thing!"

I was real down. And I was terrified. I hurt the team and I knew when I went back out on the field I was going to be faced with ridicule and humiliation. It was then that I remembered what my father and grandfather taught me: "Be responsible. If you make a mistake, you got to make it right." I realized I had a choice. I could sit in my misery or I could do something about it.

He who never makes mistakes, never makes anything.
—English Proverb

I tried to focus on the second half. I ran out there and, instead of the usual cheering or booing, there was an eerie buzz going through the stands. Real weird. People were talking and pointing. But by this time I had anesthetized myself. I could not let it affect my play. I was intent on making things right.

I don't know if it was due to my first-half blunder, but I ended up playing one of my best halves ever. I hurried the passer into three interceptions by linebacker Roy Winston, and thank God, I caused the fumble that Carl Eller picked up and ran in for the winning touchdown.

After the game, I knew I was going to get a battery of embarrassing questions. I still had so much hurt and shame. But, once again, I had to face the music.

For months after the game, the barrage of questions continued, almost as much as they reran that play on television, which they continue to do to this day.

Following the game, my friend asked me to speak at a Monday morning quarterback club. I tried to get out of it but my friend wouldn't budge. Once again, I was full of dread. To my surprise, when I walked in, I received a standing ovation. It meant so much to me. Once again, I had faced the music and it came out okay…more than okay. I hadn't given up.

Almost immediately, the calls and letters started coming in, from people I never met, who told me of their various embarrassments and shame. Most of them said they had never told another person, but what I had done gave them the courage to finally admit it. It freed them from their dark secret and they felt better for it. My mistake had actually helped others. What a gift.

On the field, I worked hard to concentrate on every moment to become a better player. Because of the shame and embarrassment I suffered from that play, I became more aware of other people's feelings. I was becoming a better person. Who would have figured that there was anything positive to be gained from something so outright humiliating?

The support and love I received from fans, teammates and others was unbelievable. The solid foundation that my family had given me was affirmed. "Face the music. Make things right." The rewards are unimaginable.

"Crises" can help us discover much about ourselves and enrich our lives. Another wonderful experience that can grow out of a seeming disaster is the joy of appreciation. AIDS patients who relearn how to walk, for example, are often delighted at being able to take two or ten steps again. They appreciate tremendously something that they took for granted their entire lives. How many "healthy" or "normal" people are grateful that they can walk or talk? My guess is, very few. But how much value is there in something taken entirely for granted? If "disaster" enriches our lives with gifts that would otherwise have been taken for granted, is it really a disaster? Or is it a gift in disguise?
—Elisabeth Kubler-Ross

As life went on I faced many more crises, always testing my faith, and teaching me life's lessons. When I saw that kids were facing similar difficulties, I knew I had to do what I could to give back what I had so generously been given. I realized I wanted to spend my life helping kids. Along with Vikings running back Oscar Reed, I opened the Professional Sports Linkage, which later became Life's Missing Link. Over the past 11 years, we have helped inner-city youth, incarcerated kids, seniors and new immigrants let go of their past mistakes and shown them how to make the right choices so they can become responsible citizens.

Failure is an event, never a person.
—William D. Brown

I've learned that kids can do anything they want, but first they have to learn how to dream. How? It's like making a movie. First you have to imagine where you would like your life to go. Then you write it out, and don't shortchange yourself of the possibilities. Now, to make it into a movie, you have to think, "Who would be the best person to produce, direct and star in that life?" The answer is YOU. But YOU have to be the one who initiates the dream. Now, go out there and make a movie. Make a life. Have your dream.

MOUTH-WATERING MISCALCULATIONS
In the 1930s, Ruth Wakefield attempted to create chocolate butter cookies by cutting up a chocolate bar into her recipe. Instead of melting in as a flavoring, the chocolate chips remained intact, producing the world's first chocolate chip cookie.

Mike Espy

"If you put things in perspective, you will find that it's not as bad as you think."

Mike Espy became the first African-American from Mississippi to serve in the United States Congress since the Reconstruction era of the 1860s and 1870s. He became the youngest secretary of agriculture and the first African-American named to the post when President Bill Clinton appointed him in 1993. His success in public office was unparalleled. Yet it was in that very position that he was confronted with his greatest challenge, as well as the darkest period in his life.

In the spring of 1994, while serving as secretary of the Department of Agriculture under President Bill Clinton, I began to hear rumors stirring that I was under scrutiny. I would receive anonymous e-mails and demands that I resign almost every Friday. No one, including the Republicans, my adversaries or the administration was calling for my resignation, so these messages were merely an annoyance and I dismissed them.

The accusations became stronger as each week went by. I continued ignoring them, figuring it's just one of the burdens that comes with the job. That was a mistake. If I had paid serious attention to them at that time, I probably could have nipped it in the bud.

The rumors were twofold. One, that I had accepted so-called gifts from entities and individuals regulated by the United States Department of Agriculture. And two, that I had somehow compromised my office and given favors to these individuals. I knew that the rumors were completely untrue, which gave me the confidence to ride out whatever storm that would come about. Any discrepancies were easily explainable and I thought no one would pay attention to them.

I believe the overarching goal was to try to retard Clinton's entire administration. One of the ways to "get him" was to get his surrogates.

I just kept moving forward, but soon the rumors bloomed into full-fledged allegations. I was blindsided. I was asked to be interviewed by the OID, the internal investigative arm of the USDA. They then turned it over to the FBI.

Because I had nothing to hide, I agreed to two FBI interviews. I never asked my personal attorney on staff or the counsel at the USDA to sit in on them. I did it alone.

None of it was recorded for my benefit, which came back to bite me later at my trial. I had to use the report from the two FBI agents without having any contradictory witnesses on my behalf. But I had been looking at this from a political standpoint. If I called an attorney, the word would be that I had to have an attorney, and I thought that lent itself to suspicion of guilt. I thought that by going into the teeth of the lion alone, I would essentially prove my innocence. That was also a mistake.

Once in those FBI meetings, I knew I was in trouble. I would answer their questions completely, but it seemed they weren't very interested in my explanations. At that point I went to outside counsel for help.

The press continued to hammer me. I began to have cameras set up outside my home. The daily stories were, in the main, inaccurate. I tried to mount a media defense by compiling a list of my accomplishments, a list of answers to all the allegations, explaining all that could be explained. I then met with several members of the print media in private, where I allowed them to ask any questions they wanted to ask. *The New York Times, The Los Angeles Times, The Washington Post* and others came in one by one and had at me.

This had all started over allegations that I had attended games paid for by Tyson Foods and that I had flown in their private jet. I explained that I did attend a couple of events and I did fly in their plane, but it was well within the rules for cabinet officials to fly in corporate planes. It was only required that you reimburse the owning entity equal to the cost of a first-class air fare ticket plus $1. I provided copies of the invoices and receipts. I thought that would quench their thirst. But it did not. The stories continued being written, and in October of 1994, I had to respond to these allegations at the White House, in front of the White House counsel and Leon Panetta, the President's chief of staff.

Things had certainly passed the annoying stage. There was now a clear and present danger. A danger to me and my career. I really thought that my career could be over. To leave my position under these circumstances would taint me forever. It would certainly not be a good career move.

Again, I had nothing to hide, so I complied with all requests to appear before them to answer these questions. My lawyer and I appeared before them once, and the next time it was just me and Panetta. I was asked very pointed questions. I answered them thoroughly and with great clarity. I didn't want to leave anything out. I wanted them to know that any questionable situations could be explained and were well within the code of ethics. There was nothing criminal about anything I did.

All of us have bad luck and good luck. The man who persists through the bad luck—who keeps going—is the man who is there when the good luck comes—and is ready to receive it.
—Robert Collier

Mr. Panetta allowed me to go through it all. I answered all the questions that had been brought up in the media. I reminded him that the president was under continuing scrutiny and that his enemies were my enemies. I told him that no one, at that point, including the Republican Party, had called for my ouster and that I remained very popular among the farming constituents. I thought I had done a good job in every respect, especially in food safety, many times against the wishes of many in the food industry. I told Panetta that if I was indicted, I would resign. Therefore, I didn't think there was any cause to take any type of action to "force me out." His response shocked me.

He said he knew that everything I said was true. That at any other time, under any other president, in any other administration, I would have received only a reprimand. But because the president's poll numbers were low, and the Democrats were about to lose the House and the Senate for the first time in several decades, they just did not have the time nor the inclination to help me out of the morass I found myself in.

I reacted on two levels. First, I was shocked that I was not receiving the benefit of the doubt or a willingness to work with me. In effect, I felt somewhat betrayed. But some of what had happened was a perception problem, and one of the cardinal rules of politics is that you have to guard against even the perception of wrongdoing. I had violated that rule and I couldn't overcome it. At the same time, I knew that I was a political appointee who served at the will and the pleasure of the chief executive. My fortunes would rise and fall based on his desire. There would be no help from the White House.

I was asked to resign and to clear my desk out within a week's time. To me, that was totally unreasonable. If I left that way, I thought the public would feel I had no defense. I refused to leave in a week. I told them it would be more orderly and less onerous to leave at the end of the year. They agreed and I resigned that afternoon.

After that the administration actually gave me more work to do. Like I said, this wasn't about the job I was doing, it was about perception. Before I left office, the president told me that he had hoped they would be through with me before they were through with him. He said that I had been the best Secretary in the history of the country.

Sunday morning talk shows had Newt Gingrich commenting on my situation, saying all this was not so much directed at me as it was directed against the administration to be used as fodder to take the House.

At the end of the year, I left the USDA and I was faced with the proposition of trying to survive. I was a divorced father of two, with mortgage payments both for my house and the house of my kids and ex-wife. I had child support payments to make, none of which I missed. Phone calls that used to be returned immediately weren't being returned at all. That was no surprise, after all, this was Washington. The members of Congress who I had known were of no help, though I did hear from staffers. I was deep in denial. I was angry and I was sad. I felt very sorry for myself. Depressed, I just laid around the house for a couple of months. My depression was so bad that when my daughter was named homecoming queen at her high school and I was supposed to escort her across the field to be coronated, I felt so embarrassed about my situation, I didn't even want to go. It took a lot to suck it up and go.

At first, there was nothing good that I could see coming out of this entire situation. I was being turned away by people I thought were friends. But there were a number of calls from Mississippians, from old college friends, from family and people I'd met during my course of public service, whom I'd not heard from before. That was gratifying. They were calling me when I needed them, not when they needed me.

Then, one Sunday morning, out of nowhere, I had an overwhelming desire to attend a particular church. Never being there before, I called for directions. I had missed the services, but the pastor there said the Lord told him that I was to call. He asked if he could come visit me.

I don't measure a man's success by how high he climbs but how high he bounces when he hits bottom.
—George S. Patton

We sat in my home for three hours. He explained to me that all this had been a test. The Lord had put this obstacle in my way to show me that what I had achieved was not done by myself but because He allowed it to happen; that since He had put me in prominence, He could take me out of it just as easily. In Washington, egos are quite high. Here I was the secretary of agriculture, the youngest ever in the history of the country, the first African-American, the first black Mississippi congressman since the Reconstruction, the youngest congressman at that time. I had worked very hard to get where I was. I had a $62 billion budget, a 10,000-person staff and I thought I was doing a good job. Perhaps I thought I had more to do with the results than I actually did.

If I could pass the test, the travail would be over. I decided to pass that test. In the grand scheme of things, this was just a bump in the road. It might have been a very large bump, but it was just a bump nonetheless. I decided to become more prayerful and ask for guidance. I definitely became more religious. You read about David and you read about Daniel and you see people who were in much worse circumstances and came out of it.

I decided to increase my physical fitness regimen. I was going to put things in order. I'm talking about body, mind, soul and agenda. I sat down, got a piece of paper and decided what I needed to beat the prosecutor and beat the odds of life such as they were at that time. I had already been a Tae Kwan Do black belt, but I had fallen off my regimen. I began to go to classes, do morning workouts, lose weight and help my lawyers. I decided that I was going to beat that prosecutor in every way possible.

The prosecutor, Donald Smoltz, during one media interview, was said to have done 60 or 70 pushups for the reporter. I said, well okay, if he's doing 70, I'm doing 150. And that's what I did every morning.

I reached out to some friends to discuss how to recoup a career. I created a copious, detailed plan. Every morning I would make a list—read the next three chapters of the Bible, read 25 FBI reports, read a book, get that third-degree black belt, see my children.

I started to see that all I lost was a cabinet job. I wasn't destitute. I was healthy and I was a lawyer. I had the tools to use to come back. I formed a commodities company to trade on my knowledge selling bulk goods to various countries. I also solicited legal jobs in Washington and Mississippi. I traveled throughout the world meeting with presidents and prime ministers and discussing the issues affecting their countries. With some I succeeded, others I didn't, but I was already making more money than I ever made in my life.

I still never thought I would be indicted. At best, these were minimal charges and in no way did I compromise my office. In fact, I had been a thorn in the side of those in the industry who wanted to maintain the status quo on many regulations. I was the agent of change and the reform proponent at the USDA and I just figured people knew that. There might have been smoke but there was no fire. I thought that if a credible, independent counsel would sort through the allegations, they would find that this was a case that should not be continued.

But I was wrong again and I was indicted. Surprisingly, once I was indicted, things became easier for me. It seems ironic, but that was the first time I could sit and read what I was being charged with. Up to this point they were only allegations, innuendo, rumors and media stories. But finally someone with the ability to put me in jail was coming up with concrete charges. Once I read the 39 counts against me, I actually said, "Wow. This is nothing. They'll never prove any of this." I became very confident.

> *There is no failure except in no longer trying. There is no defeat except from within, no insurmountable barrier except our own inherent weakness of purpose.*
> *—Elbert Hubbard*

During the three years of the case, I never heard from the prosecutors. I began to hear that they were after others. They were subpoenaing Tyson documents and going after friends of the president. It was very clear after the first year of activity that they had not set their sights on me, but on bigger game…the president of the United States. I was never even asked to appear in front of a grand jury. They never asked me to come to their office to talk with them. Not even off the record.

The trial went our way the entire time. At times, the jurors would laugh at the prosecutor. The jury took a day and a half to decide. The reason for even that short delay, I was told later, was that there was a battle to decide who would be foreman because each wanted to announce me not guilty. The foreman said, "You were as not guilty as anyone we ever heard of."

I went home and, with the people there who had given me the benefit of the doubt and support, I was redeemed. Today I work full-time in a law firm spreading my time between Mississippi and

Washington. I am now well-received in Washington with most telling me that it was all a political witch-hunt. It was biased, should have never happened and was a prime reason for why the independent prosecutor statute was not reauthorized.

I found that whenever you have to face adversity, you have to gauge how much of it was beyond your control. In my case I had to be realistic and understand that some of this was my fault. I discovered I could respond successfully to a crisis. That is empowering. But you must prepare yourself in all ways. My fight was a legal one, but I did not confine myself to accomplishing legal goals. That would not have been enough. I had to fight to gain more spirituality, a better body mass, to improve my psyche and personal spirit and, at the same time, gain income. All of that aided my battle in the legal arena. You cannot segregate one aspect from the other. You have to work in unison. Most important, if you put things in perspective, you will find that things aren't as bad as you think, and you can make it.

Storms purify the atmosphere.
—Henry Ward Beecher

RIDICULOUS REJECTIONS

"We don't like their sound, and guitar music is on the way out."

–Decca Recording Co. rejecting the Beatles, 1962.

Nanette Fabray

"I was actually trying to be someone I wasn't and that wasn't anywhere near how good I could be by being myself."

Multi-Emmy winner and Tony recipient Nanette Fabray has been far more than a stage and screen star. Handicapped for most of her adult life by a hearing problem, she has spent much of her time fighting for the rights of all disabled people. A founding member of the National Council on Disabilities, she participated in the creation of the Americans with Disabilities Act. Among her many laurels, Ms. Fabray received the President's Distinguished Service Award and the Eleanor Roosevelt Humanitarian Award. She and Helen Keller are the only women to receive the Public Service Award from the American Academy of Otolaryngology. This woman of great accomplishment in so many fields spent a great deal of her life unaware of just how much she had to give.

My mother started me into dancing when I was 4 years old. I hated it. I felt my mother loved me only if I performed. It's terrible for a child to have to compete in an adult world, made to conform to time schedules and performance schedules. It wasn't until my fourth or fifth Broadway show that I thought, "Hey, this isn't too bad."

Around the age of 12, I began to experience the effect of a hereditary condition known as otosclerosis [hardening of the tiny ear bones that transmit sound]. I was gradually losing my hearing and I didn't even know it. Seated in the back of the classroom, when the teacher would turn to the blackboard, I had no idea that she continued speaking. I was too shy to say I didn't understand what she was talking about. By the time I was in my senior year in high school, I was flunking everything. My conclusion was that I was stupid.

I later attended Los Angeles Junior College where I hoped my education would lead me to become a doctor. Months later, with terrible grades, they asked me to leave. This certainly didn't help my already flagging low self-worth.

Nevertheless, after my lack of success with school, I went to New York with the show, *Meet the People.* Arthur Rodzinski, the great conductor of the New York Philharmonic, saw my show one night. I sang "Caronome" from the opera *Rigoletto* and finished the aria with a tap dance. Rodzonski wanted to sponsor me to study opera at Juilliard. He had never sponsored a singer before so this was a big deal. Yet, here I was, I couldn't read a note of music and didn't have a clue on how to audition. So, when I auditioned in front of the faculty with "Caronome," I did as I had done in the show. After singing I went into my tap dance. They were just appalled. They were appalled, and since it was too difficult for me to go to Juilliard at eight in the morning and do a Broadway show at night, Juilliard was not to be in my future plans.

The only way to discover the limits of the possible is to go beyond them into the impossible.
—Arthur C. Clarke,
Technology and the Future

Still, I was working! I was called to audition for Richard Rodgers in a new Ray Bolger show. I did so well that Rodgers said, "That was the single worst audition I've ever seen." But he also said he had seen me on stage before and gave me the job. That's the way it went. I would go from one stage show to another. Good things just kept happening and still, I didn't have a clue what I was doing. In fact, one night after a performance, Laurence Olivier came backstage and told me, "You have something very special. You don't know it yet, but you have contact with the audience. The audience loves you. You will learn to love the audience and after a while you will begin to feel it." For the next three months, I tried to love the audience. It was disastrous. Finally, the director came to me and said, "Whatever you're doing, stop it." I was actually trying to be someone I wasn't and that wasn't anywhere near how good I could be by being myself. This all made finding out I had a hearing problem all the more distressing.

I have relative perfect pitch, so even if I missed cues I could still sing and perform. I would just go to the musical key I knew the song was supposed to start with. On stage, with people speaking louder than normal, I never knew that I had anything wrong. I thought everyone heard the same way I did. Then, one night in Chicago, the orchestra was situated under the stage. I realized I wasn't hearing the orchestra at all. Afterward I told the conductor that I hadn't heard the music. When he said they were playing the same as they always had, I decided to look up an ear, nose and throat doctor. After an examination, he told me that I would "lose my hearing in five years and when you lose your hearing, you lose the ability to speak soon after." I would be deaf and dumb.

Up until then, I had lived my entire life in a world of fantasy. I might have been 20 years old, but in my mind, I was 9. I had never faced any real crisis. I decided that going deaf was something I must keep secret. In those days, you'd fall down an open manhole before admitting you needed glasses. To me, wearing a hearing aid was out of the question.

My self-image was sagging even lower. I was terrified. I believed that if anyone found out about my problem, it would mean the end of my career. Where would I go? What would I do?

I decided to go to a lip-reading teacher. At the end of six months she told me that I wasn't very good at it. This was a turning point for me. What seemed like the only way to deal with my hearing problem was not going to work for me. So I went on to learn sign language, still not telling anyone what was happening, including my first husband. How

For a long time it had seemed to me that life was about to begin—real life. But there was always some obstacle in the way, something to be got through first, some unfinished business, time still to be served, a debt to be paid. Then life would begin. At last it dawned on me that these obstacles were my life.
—Father Alfred D'Souza

could I? I felt it would devastate my marriage, as well as everything else in my life. My career would be in the toilet, nobody would love me. Meanwhile, the reality was, my career was progressing just fine.

Judy Garland was ill, so I was signed by MGM to replace her in her upcoming films. Now I was going to become a movie star. The reality? I made one movie and, because of the advent of television, all the studios basically closed down. I was out on the street. I had no job. I thought I had no future and my hearing was getting worse. At this point I had bought a hearing aid, but I did what most people with hearing problems do...buy a hearing aid and never wear it. I was ashamed of it. I was in my mid-20s and I felt like I had no future. I felt if anyone knew that I didn't hear well, I would never work again. Not wanting to subject my husband to what I was going through, I divorced.

I went back to New York and one day I found myself in a coffee shop where I saw a man at the counter acting oddly. I thought to myself, "This man is mentally ill...but I'm just fine." I went back to my room and called the person who I was supposed to meet with and said, "I can't do this anymore. I can't face the world anymore. I can't make any more decisions, ever." Then I called my friend Dave and said, "No more. No more..." Dave immediately ran over to find me, still on the phone, still repeating, "No more. No more..." Dave called my doctor and they took me to High Point Hospital.

I had had a mental breakdown. I was overwhelmed. I was physically, emotionally, and in every other way, unable to handle any more problems. I simply couldn't do anything more. Still, my mother and the rest of my family would not admit I had a problem. They said, "You're alright. Just pull yourself together and come home."

As horrid as that moment was, that breakdown and being in the hospital turned my life around. Most important, my doctor helped me understand that I wasn't stupid. I stayed in High Point for seven months, getting better each day.

When I got out, I called my agent and said I was ready to work again. Sid Caesar's *Caesar's Hour* was having some problems finding a replacement for Imogene Coca. I met with Sid and told him that I had just gotten out of the hospital and wasn't sure I could do this. He took my hand, looked me in the eye and said, "Don't worry. I've been locked up, too." Sid was honest with me and that was the very first time I was actually honest about who I was and how I was feeling.

I was hired for one week. In show business, every so often, magic happens. That's what happened between Sid and me. It was as if we had worked together forever and I was asked to come back. Working there was both very hard and very exciting. It was really quite an extraordinary time for me. *Caesar's Hour* was the high point of my theatrical life. The most creative, the most inventive, the most self-discovering. Just think of who Sid's writers were—Neil Simon, Larry Gelbart, Mel Brooks, Woody Allen, Mel Tolkin. In all, the show had 10 of the top writers in the world. I was given wonderfully creative things to do, things that I didn't even know I was able to do. Sid gave me the opportunity to be a risk taker. He would let me try new things. It was a great time of experimentation and growth. One never knows, but if it wasn't for the breakdown and hospital stay, I probably wouldn't have been physically, emotionally or mentally able to do Sid's show.

They have seen but half the universe who never have been shown the house of pain.
—Ralph Waldo Emerson

By this time, since they had become small enough, I resigned myself to wearing a hearing aid. Once I made that decision and admitted the problem to myself, I never hid it. I was the first celebrity to stand up and admit that I wasn't perfect, that I had a problem. In those days it was very tricky. I was attacked by the press. They thought I was looking for sympathy or publicity. They didn't understand that it was therapy for me to admit I had a problem, that speaking out to help others who were going through the same thing could help them and me. I felt that if I could help one person, my speaking out would be worthwhile. You can't imagine how much mail I received. Mary Switzer, who was the director of rehab for the Department of Health, Education and Welfare, took me under her wing and brought me to Washington. She taught me what went on in Washington, and how to raise money, and the ways to help the hearing impaired. She put me on councils and introduced me to Senator Jennings Randolph, who was the head of the Senate Subcommittee on the Handicapped. He also took me under his wing and taught me how to deal with senators and members of Congress.

It was a very important time in my life. I grew emotionally and intellectually. It was great for my self-esteem. I was seeing how my service to others was coming back to me manyfold. I had a presidential appointment as a founding member of the National Council on Disability. We wrote the Americans with Disabilities Act. What that did for my self-esteem! Before, I thought my hearing problem could only be a catastrophe. It turned out to also be something profound and good. I was learning from my misfortunes, but I found I had still more to learn.

Prosperity is not without many fears and distastes; and adversity is not without comforts and hopes.
—Francis Bacon

In 1978, I was making the movie, *Harper Valley PTA*, when I was attacked by an elephant. I was knocked down and received a brain-stem injury, a serious concussion and was hospitalized for a month. I attempted to finish the film, unable to remember lines and with my face partially paralyzed. I believe that injury caused my breast cancer. Once again, back then, breast cancer was something not to be talked about, especially in show business. After the movie, I was doing a play in Chicago and found a lump. Another problem. I decided to wait until I returned home to have it checked. Three months later I was in front of a breast cancer specialist who scared the daylights out of me. He said that I had a serious problem and he proceeded to show me horrific pictures of mastectomies. I went into the bathroom and threw up.

Even though the doctor told me that I had a rapidly advancing cancer and must have surgery, I immediately checked with another doctor and found that there was a new procedure called a lumpectomy. I asked for the truth about my chances and he said I had a less than 50 percent chance of survival. I went ahead and had the operation as well as massive doses of radiation. A very small percentage of those who have the radiation will have their bones become brittle as glass. Unfortunately, I happened to be part of that small percentage. Months later, one by one, all the ribs on my left side broke.

The worst thing a victim of circumstance can do is become a victim of life.
—F. Cooper

My doctor said that as a result of my condition, for the rest of my life I could no longer sing, dance, run or exercise. I couldn't lift anything over five pounds. To me, that was a death sentence. I could not live my life that way.

I spoke with my ear specialist, Dr. Howard House, who looked into it and found that a study was being done on the use of fluoride and calcium to help people with osteoporosis. They had never used it for my condition, but we gave it a try and they placed me on massive doses of calcium and fluoride. After a year or so, my ribs were healed. They called it a wonderful breakthrough for those who had problems after radiation. Here again was my opportunity to contribute to the world, not because of some hardship that I would have chosen to go through, but because I could either live with my problem or take a chance and hope to get well.

I don't know what I can say to someone who is struggling that would make it any easier. I can only share my own experience, which led me to believe that I have two choices in this life: I can live or I can die. Dying, though some may choose to, doesn't seem like a very good choice to me. If I choose to live, then I have two more choices: I can just exist or do something better; make each day a bit better than the day before. I figure that I will be Nanette Fabray only once. I will never come back as me again. And if that is so, then even with all my limitations, I should try to make everything as worthwhile, giving, loving, fulfilling and as important as I possibly can.

INDEFENSIBLE INSINUATIONS

"Professor Goddard does not know the relation between action and reaction and the need to have something better than a vacuum against which to react. He seems to lack the basic knowledge ladled out daily in high schools."

–*The New York Times* editorial about Robert Goddard's revolutionary rocket work, 1921.

Norm Pattiz

"You'd have to be incredibly shrewd to think I would have gained such an advantage out of seemingly so negative a situation. But I did."

Called "The Ted Turner of Radio" by *USA Today*, Norman Pattiz founded and runs Westwood One, America's largest radio network and syndicator. In 2000, President Clinton named him to the United States Broadcast Board of Governors. He sits on California's 21st Century Infrastructure Commission and perhaps even more impressive, he has courtside seats for all Los Angeles Lakers home games. But in 1973, Pattiz found himself without a job, with little money and no idea what to do with his life. He was unexpectedly fired from a job he felt he had done well and he was devastated. But life had other plans for him and his seemingly inopportune dismissal turned out to be one of the best things that ever happened to him.

My firing as sales manager at KCOP-TV [Channel 13 in Los Angeles], which I was totally unprepared for, blindsided me. It happened three days before I was to be married. At the very least it was a stunning occurrence. I had originally planned a short honeymoon, so sudden unemployment gave me a chance to take a longer one while thinking over what was really going on in my life.

My thought processes were, in the least, muddled. I really didn't know where to find a job or know what kind of job I wanted to do. Did I really want to go back and work for another television station and conceivably face this type of situation again?

And boy was I pissed. At first it became a primary motivating factor. In the early stages of Westwood One, there was a great bit of "I'll show you." Once the business showed itself to actually be a business, that became less of a factor. The day-to-day problems of building a business became more important than trying to prove someone wrong in having made a decision about me that then turned out to be one of the best things that ever happened in my life. The reality was whomever I was interested in trying to show was not interested at all in what I had to say anyway.

Up until the firing, my ambition was simply to become a general manager in the television business. I had no notion that I would be creating a business of my own. That was until circumstances, unwanted as they were at the time, created opportunity.

Following my firing, I was just hanging with a buddy when I heard a local radio station doing a 52-hour Motown weekend. Being in television up until then, I was curious as to whether radio ever syndicated their programming like television did. I took a meeting with the general manager of KGFJ radio in Los Angeles. Two weeks later I'm putting together a 22-hour special called *The Sound of Motown*, which was the first I ever produced. That was a good example of circumstances creating opportunity. In no way did I plan to get fired and sit around with nothing to do but listen to music with a buddy. But today I've come to learn that so much success comes from taking negatives and turning them into positives.

In the early stages of Westwood One, my largest customer was Warner-Lambert. Approximately 75 percent of all my advertising came from them. I was sitting in my office in Westwood and I had some people there wanting to do business with me. At that moment I received a call from the media buyer at Warner-Lambert's advertising company who informed me that they were canceling all of their advertising with me, which meant that, effectively, I was out of business...again. I don't remember what happened to those guys sitting in my office. I just remember getting on the phone and making plane reservations to go to New York to meet the new head media buyer who was taking over the W-L accounts. I got to New York

> *Avoid having your ego so close to your position that when your position falls, your ego goes with it.*
> —Colin Powell

and sat for hours in the lobby of the media buyer's office until he would see me. Our meeting lasted far into the evening, including a large quantity of beer, and we ended up making a deal. I would give him three months free of charge if he would stick with us for the balance of that year. I would have to find a way to get through 90 days, but I had a yearlong deal. By the time the year was over, we were back in business. The fact was that he was so impressed with us willing to work with them while other creditors were holding them to original contracts and commitments, we had established a relationship that ended up lasting for years. That kind of relationship, that bond I was able to forge with Warner-Lambert, would never have happened if not for the fact that they first canceled their business. You'd have to be incredibly shrewd to have ever thought I would have gained such an advantage out of so seemingly negative a situation. But I did.

> *"Quit now, you'll never make it." If you disregard this advice, you'll be halfway there.*
> —David Zucker

My first regularly scheduled program for Westwood One was one called *Star-Trak*, a 90-second rock news and interview feature. At the time, my advertiser, Warner-Lambert, told me that if I could clear 50 percent of the U.S. and either station KHJ in Los Angles, WABC in New York or WFIL in Philadelphia, they would support a daily feature, which would make me a few thousand a week, while making this a real business. Chances of getting on either WABC or KHJ were practically nil. So my only option was WFIL in Philadelphia. The program director at the time was Jay Hook. I bet I called this guy a hundred times and couldn't get through. I sent him letters and didn't get an answer. I sent him demo tapes and received no response. Finally, I found that he worked late. So I began to make my calls after the switchboard closed and I got him on the line. I can't tell you what I said, but I said a lot and I said it quickly and found a responsive note. He said they didn't carry syndicated programming, but by talking we came up with an idea in which we would make a special *Star-Trak* feature with a hostess being identified as WFIL's California girl…a seeming California correspondent.

I had failed on the first hundred or so calls to reach the program director, but I didn't stop calling. And once I did reach him, I stayed on the line even while he was telling me he would not use syndication until I found out how he would. It was in the failing that I learned what it would take to succeed.

It is a mistake to suppose that men succeed through success; they much oftener succeed through failures. Precept, study, advice and example could never have taught them so well as failure has done.
—Samuel Smiles

When I speak to people about working for my company, I make sure they understand that you must give people the room to fail. While we can learn from our success, the opportunity to fail is far more likely, so it is wise to learn from those disappointments. They're a part of any journey, but the most important event that takes place is the last one. It's up to you to make the last one a success.

KELVIN'S KRAZY KONCEPTS
"Radio has no future."
–Lord Kelvin, president, Royal Society of London, 1897.

Clive Cussler

> *"If good books get roses, and bad books get skunks,*
> *Cussler's book would receive four skunks."*
> The New York Times Book Review *of* Raise The Titanic

Author Clive Cussler is known to many as the Grandmaster of Adventure. His best-selling Dirk Pitt novels have sold over 70 million copies. Working with the National Underwater & Marine Agency, a nonprofit group begun by Cussler, he has helped find over 60 shipwrecks, including the long-lost Confederate submarine *Hunley*. He has been honored with the Lowell Thomas Award for outstanding underwater exploration and belongs to the Royal Geographic Society and the American Society of Oceanographers. With all this success, it still took getting fired to get Cussler to sit down and write.

I hated the classroom. I was the dreamer. During algebra, I would be looking out the window. I was a million miles away on some pirate ship. My grades were all "C"s and "D"s except in English, which came easy for me, though at the time I just thought I was lucky. When people ask me what teachers inspired me, I'd say, "None." They just wrote me off. In those days teachers had a tendency to concentrate on the smarter kids. They didn't see anything in me whatsoever. So I just did what I had to do to get by.

When I first started to write, I threw my first manuscript in the wastebasket and said, "This is ridiculous. I can't do it." Then, in my mid-30s, I took a creative writing course. The teacher, Pat Kubis, told me that I could be published. I think that's the only time I was ever given encouragement. I was quite happy. I remember this one

> *Mistakes are a fact of life. It is the response to error that counts.*
> *—Nikki Giovanni*

> *Never confuse a single defeat*
> *with a final defeat.*
> *—F. Scott Fitzgerald*

gal in class, Helen, who ripped apart everyone's work. When the teacher read what I had written in class and then asked Helen what she thought, Helen only said, "It was good." At that point I knew I had arrived. In fact, it was back then that I actually received an award for my writing. I finished second in a writing competition and got this little trophy that still sits on my desk.

My wife worked evenings at the local police department. I would sit at home with nothing to do. I figured, "Gee, I think I'll write a book." I had been in advertising for so many years, writing quick, snappy copy, I couldn't write anything literary. I didn't have the Great American Novel burning inside of me. So I thought it would be great fun to do a paperback series. I went out and studied Sherlock Holmes, James Bond, Philip Marlowe and Matt Helm. To be different I thought I'd put my hero in and around water. And that's how Dirk Pitt came about.

We moved to Colorado and I had three books finished that had yet to be published. I got a job as a copywriter at a small agency. I had been very successful with some larger agencies in Los Angeles, but I couldn't tell them that, otherwise I would be considered overqualified. I ended up sitting at a little desk, near the restroom, writing newspaper ads. One day they came to me to ask if I could work on a deal that they were having trouble with and I came up with something that won a Cleo and all sorts of awards that put this little agency on the map. But I got so busy, I wasn't writing anymore.

At the same time, the literary agency I was with wanted to drop me. Luckily, my agent there stuck with me. Finally, one of my works was published as a paperback and another one as a hardcover and only 3,000 copies sold. Now, a signed copy of *Iceberg* in pristine condition sells for about $2,000.

Around that time, the ad agency brought in a new executive vice president. We shook hands and there was instant dislike. In three months he got me sacked. I looked at all the awards on the walls and left.

I didn't look for another job. I figured I had already wasted three years. I was 43 and I now felt that I had this book in me. It took me nine months to write it. I figured if nothing happened, I'd go back to advertising. That book was *Raise The Titanic*.

I sent the manuscript to my editor and it was turned down. He said, "The book is too long and the cost of paper has gone up. We just feel it's not a viable work." I kept writing and *Raise The Titanic* kept making the rounds. It went to Putnam and the editor there wanted a massive rewrite and I refused to do it. Then it went to Viking and they bought it for $7,500, but with great trepidation. One editor thought it was a stupid buy. Everyone was telling me that a series hero never sells.

Fortunately, an editor from the British branch of MacMillan was visiting Viking when the purchase was made. He asked for a copy of the manuscript and read it on the plane back to England. A bidding war in England ensued for the paperback rights, and when U.S. publishing houses got wind of the interest, the bidding went international. My wife went to work the next morning and I jokingly told her that when the bidding reached $250,000, I would call her and she could quit. I was able to call her at 10 a.m. and she gave her notice. Ultimately it went up to $840,000. At that point we never looked back.

When someone wrote a book on "critic's reviews," I always thought they made a big mistake by not calling me. The first review I ever received from *The New York Times* said, "If good books get roses, and bad books get skunks, Cussler's book would receive four skunks."

Making a living can get in the way of writing a good book.
—Joseph Sacco

That was about *Raise The Titanic*. I asked my publisher if that guy had to be so nasty and he said, "If we started getting good literary reviews, we'd be in big trouble," meaning that books with good reviews don't sell.

A critic from the *Christian Science Monitor* reviewed my book, *Dragon*, and ripped it apart. I thought, "Who is this asshole?" When I get to the bottom of the review, I find that it was one of those reader-submitted reviews. This one was from Charlie Jones, the city superintendent of Muncie, Indiana.

Reviews don't really bother me. If someone says, "You got a bad review," I say, "That's okay, just keep the checks rolling in." I think I got used to criticism while I was in advertising. I'd pour my heart and soul into a campaign and think it was the greatest thing since peanut butter and then the client's wife would say it sucks and throw it in the wastebasket. So I was used to rejection. You can never tell how someone else is going to receive something. One time a bunch of us were having a difficult time with a campaign so we went out and got bagged. We came up with something that was meant to be a joke. We laid it on the account exec's desk and the next day he tells us he shot it to the client who loved it. The client was Ajax and the campaign was the Ajax White Knight and the slogan we came up with was "Stronger Than Dirt." *Newsweek* and *Advertising Age* spoke of the great, in-depth, psychological research that went into our campaign's development. In truth, the in-depth, psychological research was six guys getting bombed one night.

Failure calls out for a need to change direction or keep going in the same direction or to stop altogether. But sometimes you have to try each before you hear which one it is.
—Dr. Howard Dansky

At this point, I knew I could write, but I didn't really know how good I was. Then one day I received a letter from The Mystery Writers of America. I thought it was an invitation to join. When I opened it I found a note that read, "Dear Mr. Cussler, Congratulations. Your mystery novel, *Mediterranean Capers*, was nominated as one of the best paperbacks of the 1970s." I went numb. Up to that point I was just published and I didn't know if I could do it or not. But this letter and this congratulations meant that my peers thought I could write.

There are friends who have said, "If Cussler can do it, anyone can." What they neglected to add was that it was the determination and obstinacy of a hardheaded man who refused to listen to the cynics and who refused to give up.

RED-LETTER REJECTS
Robert M. Pirsig's *Zen and the Art of Motorcycle Maintenance* was rejected by over 100 publishing houses before being published in 1974 and selling over four million copies.

Failure is good. It's fertilizer. Everything

I've learned about coaching, I've learned from making mistakes.

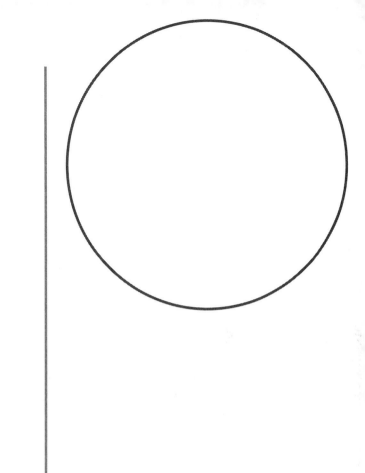

−Rick Pitino

Jane Goodall

"Overcoming challenges strengthened my faith in God and myself."

As the world's foremost authority on chimpanzees, Jane Goodall, living with the chimpanzee community in the jungles of Africa, has studied their behavior for over 40 years. Her research and writing have revolutionized the way in which the world now regards evolution and the relationship between chimpanzees and humans. But it was her relationship with other humans in which Jane Goodall found that friendships can fail just when you need them most.

When I was a child, I wasn't very good at math and I wasn't very good in languages. But I was lucky to have a mother who said as long as you do your best, you'll be fine. When I was 16, I wanted very much to have a career working with animals. A career advisor recommended taking photos of pet dogs. When the advisor found that I planned to travel to Africa to study wildlife, she told me that it was "inappropriate"; that I would have no chance doing anything like that. Everyone who knew what I wanted to do thought that I should look into more practical work. Everyone, that is, but my mother. Whatever I felt I had to try, she fully supported me.

What does not destroy me makes me stronger.
—Friedrich Nietzsche

I have had young people write and say, "I read your book. You were so lucky to have a wonderful mother. I don't have that, but I've found you and your book." When you are young you must try to find someone who can be your mentor. If it's not a parent, then it can be a teacher or someone from an extracurricular project. You can learn from their experiences. With chimpanzees, it's the early family life that establishes self-confidence.

Still, most of the time you have to learn on your own. Even if they're lessons you'd rather not have to learn.

In May of 1975, 40 armed men from Zaire raided our Gombe camp and kidnapped four of our college students. Because my house was set farther away, I was not told of the kidnapping until after the armed men left. We were stunned. When someone reported hearing four gunshots, we were afraid that they had been killed. It was sheer terror and a number of weeks passed before we knew what had happened to the students.

Don't worry about those who jump off the bandwagon at the first bump in the road. Who needs the extra weight?
—Pearl Sklar

While we found that they were still alive, it was a nightmare, and even after one of the students was released, there came an excessive ransom demand. As much as it was hell for all of us that were waiting, how horrifying was it for the victims themselves, not knowing whether they would live or die? When the ransom was paid, they still held on to one hostage. I was sure they would kill him. Two weeks later, much to my relief, he was released.

I tried to put the nightmare behind me, but when I returned to the United States, I discovered it was far from over.

After two weeks, I was back teaching at Stanford. To my utter surprise, it was "suggested" that I leave school. There were absurd rumors of my husband Derek saying that the death of the students would be preferable to payment of the ransom. There were also questions concerning why I did not give myself in place of the students who were taken hostage that night. At the time, I was not aware of the kidnapping until after they had all left. This did not seem important to my accusers. I was shocked. Shattered. The kidnapping itself had been devastating, but now the many people who I thought were my true friends turned out to be of the fair-weather variety.

I felt angry. Still, as the Bible says, I "girded my loins." I traveled from place to place telling many of the same people who were now avoiding me what had really happened. It was all quite distressing and difficult, but finally, most of the rumors had been calmed.

So utterly unexpected, so bizarre and so challenging as it all was at the time, it taught me so much. I learned that human nature was much more difficult to understand than I had thought. I learned that if all this had not happened, I would not have found out who my real friends were and what a wonderful support those true friends turned out to be. I learned that if all this had not happened, I would not have the faith I have in God today. Most important, if all this had not happened, I would not have nearly the strength nor confidence in myself that I have today.

Learn from the mistakes of others. You can't live long enough to make them all yourself.
—Eleanor Roosevelt

[*For more information on the Jane Goodall Institute and the Roots And Shoots program, an international environmental and humanitarian program for young people, go to www.janegoodall.org or write to Jane Goodall Institute, P.O. Box 14980, Silver Springs, MD 20911.*]

BAD BUSINESS
"This telephone has too many shortcomings to be seriously considered as a means of communication. The device is inherently of no value to us. "
–Western Union internal memo, 1876.

Pat Croce

"...take whatever obstacle you run up against and figure out how to turn it into an opportunity."

Pat Croce might be the most positive man on the planet. He certainly seems like the happiest. He rose from a local fitness therapist to become an owner of the Philadelphia 76ers professional basketball team, taking them from a bottom-of-the-barrel laughingstock of a franchise that no one came to see, to one of the best and most respected teams that now plays to regular sellouts. Croce had some serious "no's" in his career that transformed into some powerful "yes's." Rick Pitino rejected Croce's attempts to be the Sixers' coach in 1997. Pitino's saying "no" permitted Larry Brown to say "yes." Sixers forward Matt Geiger said "no" to a trade that would have resulted in Allen Iverson leaving the team. Iverson ended up becoming the league's Most Valuable Player in 2001 and helped return the Sixers to the NBA Finals for the first time since 1982–83. In fact, Pat Croce began his inspiring career with a door unceremoniously slammed in his face.

My dream was to become a professional football player. Unfortunately, I couldn't even start for my high school football team. I wasn't physically mature enough. Even when my body started catching up, I realized I wasn't big enough or fast enough and even if I did play, I'd probably get killed. I had no choice but to change my dream. I revised my entire career path so that I could become a physical therapist. If I couldn't play for the Philadelphia Eagles, I would work for them as a conditioning coach.

I tried to get into school but I received nothing but rejections. I kept applying and finally

If the world should blow itself up, the last audible voice would be that of an expert saying it can't be done.

—Peter Ustinov

got into the University of Pittsburgh's School of Physical Therapy. Concurrently, I received a degree in athletic training. Remember, at this point, my goal was to be the physical therapist for the Eagles. I was so ready. I went to their office, confident, chest up high, and knocked on the door of the Eagles office and told the man at the door:

"I'm here to apply for the job of physical therapist for the Eagles."

"Sorry, we don't need anyone."

And he slammed the door in my face. I knocked again.

"Look, I told you we don't need anyone."

And for good measure, he slammed the door again.

Our greatest glory is not in never falling, but in rising every time we fall. —Confucius

I obviously needed more to learn. From that day on, every chance I had, I took additional courses and learned as much as I could about sports medicine. In 1976, I realized that there were no sports medicine centers in hospitals. There were some in college institutions, but nothing in a hospital setting for the public. So I came up with the concept and in 1976, I opened the first sports medicine center situated in a United States hospital.

In 1980, I received a call from the Philadelphia Flyers. They needed someone to help with conditioning problems. With my therapy education and karate background, they hired me as a consultant. The next year, they hired me full-time as their conditioning coach. I continued running the sports medicine center.

In 1983, I left the sports medicine center to open the first privately owned sports medicine center called Sports Physical Therapists. By 1984, with the help of Mike Schmidt and Gary Maddux of the Philadelphia Phillies, we were able to expand to 40 centers.

In 1986, the Philadelphia 76ers came on board and soon after, professional teams across the United States were using my facilities. In Atlanta we took care of the Braves and the Hawks, in Orlando the

Magic, in Green Bay the Packers, in Cincinnati the Reds. I was building centers and with the help of a great staff, my dreams were coming true. Not in the way I first imagined, but still, great things were happening.

I've learned that just because one door slams that doesn't mean your life is over. I've learned that you take whatever obstacle you run up against and figure out how to turn it into an opportunity. You have to take a look from different perspectives, and continue to try your best. Luckily for me, that door to the Philadelphia Eagles training room never opened. I say luckily, because if it had, I'd probably still be the assistant trainer or trainer instead of the owner of two franchises.

To expect defeat is nine-tenths of defeat itself.
—Francis Crawford

In my first year of ownership of the Philadelphia 76ers, we won only 22 games. Not exactly what I expected. I had hired an inexperienced general manager who in turn hired an inexperienced head coach. But at the end of the year, I had to release both of them. Now my mistakes were not personal. They were public. I decided to go to the people of Philadelphia and apologize. I told them I had made mistakes and I planned to correct them. I don't think most people would have publicly apologized, but that's what I felt I had to do. People were depending on me to bring a winner to Philadelphia. Today, I realize that experience was worth its weight in gold...and wins. Now we have Larry Brown, one of the winningest coaches in the league, and along with general manager Billy King, we brought in the right players.*

Because of their courage, their lack of fear, creative people are willing to make silly mistakes. The truly creative person is one who can think crazy; such a person knows full well that many of his great ideas will prove to be worthless.
—Frank Goble

I admit I wear rose-colored glasses. I've always had a very positive attitude toward life. I got it from my mom. She was the dreamer, the optimist, the person who kept telling me to keep trying and things will work out. The Little

Engine That Could, that was my mom. It's stayed with me to this day. If you go into things with open eyes, open ears and an open mind, anything, whether positive or negative, can become a learning experience. I used to do daily fitness tips on the radio, not to help my business, but because I believed in the mission of fitness, wellness, health and nutrition. In the end, it helped promote my business.

I truly believe one of the foundations of my success is having a fit body, therefore a fit mind. The mind and body are one, so that a fit body will bring a fit mind. It's difficult to feel great if you're injured and in pain. You can't feel great if you're tired. If your body is in shape through physical fitness, sports or outdoor activities, you'll have that much more energy with which to follow your dream; more energy to work harder, play harder, study longer and fulfill your goals.

People of mediocre ability sometimes achieve outstanding success because they don't know when to quit. Most men succeed because they are determined to.
—George Allen

Charles Barkley stands only 6 feet 5 inches but had to play against all kinds of seven-foot-plus guys. Still, he believed that he should get every rebound. One would think that is a physical impossibility, but in 1987, he won the NBA rebounding title. That's because the mind has such a powerful influence. In Barkley's case, it was particularly powerful.

I believe that everyone loves to watch people make lemonade out of lemons. One of the guys I liked reading when I was young was Zig Ziglar. A top motivational speaker, Ziglar was a big influence on me. He said that you get everything you want by helping others to get what they want. By lifting them up, they will in turn lift you up. People have to realize that it can't be *me, me, me*. We have to do it together. The 76ers reached out to the public. We created a 76ers basketball league with about 10,000 inner-city kids involved; a 76ers backboard restoration program, putting new 76ers backboards on all the playgrounds. We showed how much we cared and eventually the crowds came out. As we built a winning team, we became part of their community, part of their family.

It's important for all kids, no matter what their situation, to do their best. I promise, God will take care of the rest. I'm spiritual as well as religious. It's part of my optimism. I believe that if something is not to be, then it wasn't meant to be. If something you try doesn't work and the door slams shut, that's okay. Just never stop trying.

When I spoke with Pat, he had no idea that his Philadelphia 76ers would reach the 2001 NBA championship finals.

WEIGHTY WRONGS
"You want to have consistent and uniform muscle development across all of your muscles? It can't be done. It's just a fact of life. You just have to accept inconsistent muscle development as an unalterable condition of weight training."
—Comment made to Arthur Jones,
inventor of Nautilus Fitness Systems, 1969.

Morton Downey, Jr.

"I was a kid who was a rebel with a cause, but I didn't know what the cause was."

Morton Downey, Jr. became a household name as the hard-driving, opinionated TV host of one of television's most popular talk shows, *The Morton Downey, Jr. Show*. He was also a successful businessman, author, radio host, singer and songwriter. He taught political science at the University of Notre Dame and was recognized by Pope Paul VI for his refugee work. Downey soon found that being born of special privilege didn't necessarily equate to being treated as such.

At the age of 12, my mother and father divorced. My reaction was to write these song lyrics:

"My love has left and gone away,
Ain't got nobody no more,
Like a bird sprouting wings she's flown out to sea,
And I'm left alone on the shore.
I've got money, marbles and chalk, sweetheart,
But I still feel like I am poor.
'Cause my money won't spend and my marbles don't roll,
My chalk won't write anymore."

When my father read those lyrics, he sent me to a psychiatrist. He thought that anyone at my age who expresses himself with that kind of depth has something drastically wrong with him. I did. I was a kid who was a rebel with a cause, but I didn't know what the cause was.

My father's best friend was a man by the name of Joseph Kennedy, who was the father of the soon-to-be president of the United States, John Fitzgerald Kennedy. We were raised together in Hyannisport. Once Jack became president, our family home was used as the summer White House because it was easier for the Secret Service to protect. I was never known for being stylish, always mismatching my colors, which I found out later was actually my color blindness in action. I showed up at the world famous Stork Club for my 16th birthday party and all my friends were there – my father, Joe Kennedy, Sherman Billingsly, the owner of the Stork Club, Gordon and Sheila MacRae, Walter Winchell and a young man named Edward M. Kennedy, who was 17 years old at the time. I was wearing red socks and brown shoes. Joe Kennedy said, "My God, was the boy dressed in a closet by a blind man?" Of course everyone got a laugh at my expense. Mr. Kennedy's next comment was, "Today I interviewed a man whose qualifications were such that you thought you'd want him for the job. But he came in dressed in red socks and brown shoes. Morton, I don't know anyone I've ever met in my life wearing red socks and brown shoes who ever succeeded. Young man, let me tell you now, you do stand out, but you don't stand out in a way that people will ever admire you." My father agreed. I was pretty hurt. I was always trying to prove to my dad that I was as good as the Kennedy boys.

Failure is the condiment that gives success its flavor.
—Truman Capote

The next day, to show my disdain for Kennedy, I again put on my red socks. To this day, every morning I put on red socks. There were still times that I thought Joe Kennedy might have been right.

When I was 21, I went to work at Holly Sugar as their advertising manager. The third day I was there, my boss said to me, "Red socks and brown shoes? Where the hell did you get dressed, a dark closet? Don't wear them again."

I was more than a little irritated to have someone tell me what I should or should not wear again. I told him that I wear red socks all the time. He said that I'd be better off cutting off my feet at the ankles than wearing something like that. I wore them again the next day, and the day after that I was fired.

I was beginning to think that what Joe Kennedy had said might be true, but something inside me said that I should continue to wear those socks. I wore them, and I wore them, and I wore them. And in the course of wearing them, I became I.T.T. Salesman of the Year, three years in a row. I then became their manager of the year, two years in a row. I helped found the American Basketball Association and was president of the New Orleans Buccaneers, the first Western Division Champions of the ABA. I helped found the World Team Boxing Association. I then became the first in-your-face talk show host, and finally, became a success with *The Morton Downey, Jr. Show.* And I still wear red socks.

However, being successful doesn't mean you aren't susceptible to life's roller coaster. When you are young, you are immortal. I was indestructible, and I was sold a bill of goods. I was told that more doctors smoked Camels than any other cigarette. I'd walk a mile for a Camel. Lucky Strike Green has gone to war.

The pessimist sees the difficulty in every opportunity; the optimist sees the opportunity in every difficulty.
—Winston Churchill

I had heard all the positive things about this product. It was ingrained in me by the time I was 13, and so it was perfectly alright for me to smoke. Later on it became quite a compassionate friend. When they finally put the Surgeon General's warning on cigarette packs in the '60s, I thought it was all political. When I found out that I had lung cancer and I had about six to eight months to live, I was really some kind of pissed off, not at the cigarette companies, but at myself.

I was the heaviest smoker since Bette Davis. I had kids asking me to sign their cigarette packs. By the time I discovered I had cancer, I felt like Bette Davis. I could no longer make excuses for smoking. I had to be honest. That's always worked for me.

I came out publicly and said, "I was a God-damned fool. I was an idiot. I was a moron. For God's sake, don't be as stupid as I was."

I went on *Larry King* six hours before my operation. I smoked my last cigarette 10 minutes before I was anesthetized for my operation. Never had one since. Never had the desire. Fear was a great motivator. I am living my second life now. And even though it would seem that smoking was a complete negative, I see the good that's come from it.

Every problem has a gift for you in its hands.
—Richard Bach

I have been able to tell my story. I have been able to relate the stupidity of trying to emulate the habits of great people when what they are doing is stupid. At one time, it was great to be a smoker. Edward R. Murrow was a great person and a smoker. How ironic that I ended up receiving an Edward R. Murrow Award.

Usually when you get bad news you tend to hang your head. I found that if you choose to do that, it makes it very difficult to see what's in front of you. If I had just hung my head, nothing would have been accomplished. I would have never been able to put the word out about what cigarettes had done to me.

Negatives you feel about others, as well as what others feel about you, can hold you back, too. I discovered that when people speak negatively about one another, it is a reflection of what they believe about themselves. That belief has helped me turn anger into compassion. I find that it helps to say, "I don't know what it is, but there's something about you I really like." Sometimes I have to fake it, but faking it soon becomes reality. More likely than not, it will cause the other person to let down their guard, their defense mechanism that keeps them from liking you. It's very difficult to dislike someone who likes you.

I've achieved a lot. Yet there's not a kid who's taken a breath who isn't smarter than I was. Don't ever let anyone tell you because you've had one or two failures that you are a failure. When my father and his friends put me down, it ended up working for me. Other seeming

Who has never tasted what is bitter does not know what is sweet.
—German Proverb

negatives did, too. I had buckteeth. One of my trademarks became my teeth. I have always tried to take negatives about my persona and pushed them forward, red socks, teeth and all.

People tell me I've had a lot of failures. I tell them, "No, I've had a lot of lessons."

[A man of many and varied talents, Morton Downey, Jr. died March 12, 2001.]

TENACIOUS & TIRELESS

Debbi Fields, embarrassed by the host of a party for mispronouncing a word, was inspired to launch her own business, if for no other reason than to show this man up. In 1977, as a young mother with no business experience, Mrs. Fields opened her first cookie store.

Judy Muller

"It's terrifying when something that works for you so well becomes exactly what you have to lose."

Emmy Award-winning news correspondent, Judy Muller, spreads her time over *ABC World News Tonight, 20/20* and *Nightline*, and is also a regular commentator for NPR's *Morning Edition*. The best-selling author of *Now This*, recounting her life in and out of the news business, had to first survive the loss of a job, a marriage and the possible loss of her daughters before she was able to gather the strength to succeed big time.

It's almost too easy to talk about my failures since self-deprecation comes easily to me. On any given day I can consider myself a failure. That's how fragile my confidence level is. All it takes, for instance, is forgetting that I was supposed to do this interview and I become a piece of *you know what* for a good couple of hours. This comes from growing up as a Navy brat, moving every two or three years and developing survival mechanisms to quickly adjust to my new environment. I would survey the scene, check out who's in and who's out; where do I want to fit in; adapting a persona that worked for the situation. Making friends and being popular was very important. Doing all those things took an amazing amount of role-playing, which I believe led me to become a theater major in college. It wasn't until later that I realized the damage. I had a hard time letting down all those masks. I still do to this day.

That's been the toughest thing to learn, letting down my guard. It was either, *you'll be leaving* or *I'll be leaving*, so what's the use of getting close to

> *People's best successes come after their disappointments.*
> —*Henry Ward Beecher*

you? It has been so hard for me to believe that people would like me for my genuine, authentic self; that I'm just a hair's breadth away from the fear of being discovered for something less than what I'm putting forth. It's taken a long time to discover that people actually like it when you're authentic.

It's terrifying when something that works for you so well becomes exactly what you have to lose. It's always been a struggle for me because I grew up in a family where you didn't talk about your accomplishments. I still have friends today who say, "What is it going to take to convince you that you're a success? You've won an Emmy, you've written a book, you're at the top of your profession, you have two wonderful children." It's not about arrogance, but at some point you've got to claim your successes.

I got married too young, right out of college. I couldn't believe I chose a marine, and neither could my dad, who was in the navy. It was a terrible mismatch. I felt trapped in a loveless marriage, always biding my time. Journalism was my salvation. In terms of getting out of myself, it was about as close to the theater as you could get. The very process of writing made me happy. It carried me.

I did morning radio in Denver for a local station where the legendary Alan Burke was a talk show host. I later became a talk show host and I was terrible. I didn't want to interrupt any of the callers. I would get all the shut-ins who would drone on and on. It was about that time that I couldn't take it any more and I finally left my husband. I moved with my two children, 6 and 7 years old, into a condominium called Happy Valley Road condominiums, which was anything but. It was traumatic and hard on all of us. My husband cut off all of our money, hoping that I would bring the kids back to him.

Ninety-nine percent of the failures come from people who have the habit of making excuses.
—*George Washington Carver*

One day, I got a call from the owner of the

radio station telling me not to bother to come in to work because the station was closing down. There were now five talk show hosts, including Alan Burke, out of work in a small market. I was out of work with no money and two little kids. I didn't know at the time, but I was depressed. I couldn't get out of bed in the morning. I had a mattress on the floor with a rainbow quilt, which was the opposite of how I felt. I was terrified. The depression was like a huge, heavy blanket that I couldn't lift off. I just couldn't get up. The kids would come in my room in the morning telling me, "Mom, you've got to get up. You've got to look for a job today." I would look at their eyes and see the fear that mirrored my own. I couldn't let them feel that way. I had been their rock.

Don't fear failure so much that you refuse to try new things. The saddest summary of a life contains three descriptions: could have, might have and should have.
—Louis E. Boone

I went back to the radio station where I was a reporter. They made me take a pay cut, almost out of spite. They called me "Newsette." I was so miserable there. Unbeknownst to me at the time, this would actually become a godsend. My unhappiness was the stimulus to send a resume and tape to CBS in New York. They didn't have any openings, but they passed my tape on to the network. I got a call to come to New York for an interview and test. Soon thereafter, I got hired—at triple my salary. I thought this was it. I had made it. I wouldn't ever have any troubles again. Of course there was the fear that I wouldn't be up to it. I had jobs in television and radio before, but my husband would belittle them by calling them "my hobbies" and saying that all they did was put us in a higher tax bracket.

I was in New York looking for a place to live while my husband watched the kids. Without warning, without telling me, he sued me for custody. He decided that, even though he had an office in New York, he would fight to keep the kids with him. I got the word on the phone. My daughter said, "Daddy said we can't live with you until we're 18."

My husband then told me that I would soon be served with papers. Here I was, 2,000 miles away, alone, and he had my kids.

My world stopped. I remember every detail in the room during that call. I had thought that everything was going to be fine and then to be shot in the back like that…I really wanted to kill him. I can't remember ever feeling such rage and fear. At that moment I understood domestic violence. I told CBS that I had to go back to Denver for the court hearing.

All profoundly original art looks ugly at first.
—Clement Goldberg

Once I arrived back in Denver, my lawyer asked if I was ready to give up the job in New York, because if they said you can't take the children out of Colorado, that would have been my choice. I could keep my kids if I stayed in Colorado. There was no way that I was ever going to lose my kids. I was ready to drop the job. There has never been anything, before or since, that had been so uncompromising in my life. There was nothing else I could have done. I had to fight for them, and I did.

In the hearing the judge said, "This is crazy. You're telling this woman who finally found a job that allows her to support her children that she can't take them with her? Tough. She gets to take them."

Fear is okay. Accept it and courage will follow.
—Joy Little

I had won. I had my kids and I had a job. I probably wouldn't have had the guts to stand up to my husband if I hadn't gone through all that I did on my own. The day I lost that job was the beginning of all those doors opening for me. When I look back, I can't remember how I did what I did, but I was finally becoming the real me.

I knew that I had really achieved something special when my daughter got a job as a producer at *60 Minutes* and she wrote me a postcard saying:

"Dear Mom, Here I am in a plane descending into Newark, and am completely terrified about screwing up my new job, but with all my anxiety I can only guess that it pales compared to your move to New York. To think I'm stressed with movers, I can't conceive of adding two children and an overnight shift to that mix. When I think of what you did and how effortless you made it seem, I can't help but think that I'm the luckiest kid in the world. It's not hard to think of how I've gotten to where I have. Thanks for everything up to this point, and in advance for the support you'll have to provide when I start flooding in tears.
I love you."

The suffering and adversity we deal with become touchstones in our lives. I've actually been very lucky. Obviously some people go through much greater suffering than others, but for me, it was nearly losing my children, going through those days and weeks literally feeling sick to my stomach every day. If the path were easier, I could not have achieved what I did. I needed to lose the job and I needed to be divorced to really say, "Okay, you've got to get off your butt and you've got to do something very big here." That meant applying to a big place...CBS.

Our doubts are traitors,
And make us lose the good we oft might win,
By fearing to attempt.
—William Shakespeare,
Measure for Measure

It's important to accept that we're not perfect. It's very difficult for me to surrender and just accept things the way they are. Why I can't remember that it works against me I don't know, but I will swim upstream as long as I can until it's obvious I'm not going to win this way. Eventually the river's going to take me, anyway. Every time I surrender to it, it gets easier.

I now know that the way you choose to go isn't necessarily a forever thing. I was a teacher, a newspaper writer and I did radio. I didn't go into television until I was 43 years old. Who *starts a* television career at that age? I wrote my first book at 52. This was not my plan and yet each happened when I decided to go for it.

I found that we can be whatever we want to be whenever we want. You just have to go inside, get rid of all the voices that aren't yours, the shoulds and shouldn'ts, and hear yourself. That's when you'll hear the truth. That's what we have to listen to.

TENACIOUS & TIRELESS

At age 17, Fannie Farmer suffered a stroke. As she was recovering, she took up cooking as a hobby. In 1896, she wrote *The Boston Cooking School Cookbook*, though her publisher, Little, Brown and Company, would only publish it if she paid for the printing. She agreed. It has sold over four million copies and is still in print today.

Dr. W. French Anderson

"It's the experiment that fails that tells you the most."

Known as the "father of gene therapy," Dr. W. French Anderson is the director of the Gene Therapy Laboratories at the University of Southern California Keck School of Medicine, where he also serves as professor of biochemistry and pediatrics. Dr. Anderson headed the team that carried out the first approved human gene therapy clinical protocol and is recognized as an ongoing innovator in the research area of human gene transfer. He is also known as a leading ethicist in the field of human genetic engineering. It was during his long effort to prove his protocol where he was met with continuing failure and near ostracism in the scientific community.

I had been wanting to go into the molecular study of disease ever since I was a senior in high school. As a senior in college, I got the concept of gene therapy; a technique of treating disease by putting genes into human cells. It was obvious that the way a body functioned was because of its molecules, and if you could understand those molecules and their behavior, you should be able to understand normal function as well as disease.

Unfortunately, after a year or so of finally getting it down, I soon had the reputation of being off the wall, beyond maverick, and really strange for thinking that something as bizarre as gene therapy would work. The combination of pushing forward in a way that bordered on arrogance antagonized sufficient people. I have never done the things that are politically appropriate, so I spent two years being assaulted by the public and press. When

If there exists no possibility of failure, then victory is meaningless.
—Robert H. Schuller

I finally proposed gene therapy as a concept, it became the most reviewed clinical protocol in history.

It was evaluated by seven different regulatory committees at the national and local levels. Fifteen different hearings, 28 hours of testimony, all of it in front of regulatory committees, some in front of TV cameras, and much of it in front of activists and lawyers. I am still listed as controversial because of that. And everyone predicted it would be a failure.

I don't know if that experience was actually devastating to me. Certainly it wasn't the kind of devastation in which one totally fails at an experiment. This was more of a matter of a wake-up call. I understood it simply wasn't time to prove my protocol. So instead, I was going to lay as much of the groundwork as I could. I never thought I knew when it would happen. I just knew it would happen and I would make a future contribution to it. There were other things we could try, and in time we did just that.

We learn more by looking for the answer to a question and not finding it than we do from learning the answer itself.
—Lloyd Alexander

As we continued our effort, we tried to get gene transfers into monkeys because we couldn't get it to work in mice. I did the counterintuitive concept thinking that it might work in primates. There were a number of technical reasons I thought it to be possible. Though it was considered somewhat bizarre, I was convinced that it might very well work. So we kept working on it for two or three more years. But every experiment failed and finally my group was starting to come apart. Nothing was happening, nothing was being published. I had six to eight young people working with me whose whole careers were dependent on publications and having some success. The labs I run are basically training labs. If the students come for three years and get nothing, they can't move on. I asked them to stick with me for one last try. We agreed we would try one other way and if that didn't work, then they could all move on to other projects. If it hadn't worked, I still would have kept going, but I would have lost my team. I would stay with it because I was convinced one day it would work. The next morning one of my team called me and said, "I think you should come in." What we found was a human protein in the monkey's blood. The system was a go. It was the first time it had ever been done. The years of failed experiments had led to a worthy result.

The team stayed together and the rest is history. We fought to make it applicable to humans. It worked brilliantly and we revolutionized medicine. Billions of dollars a year are now being spent on gene therapy, compared to zero before that. Of course, because it did work, it's much easier now to be humble and gracious.

It's the experiment that fails that tells you the most. You do the experiment and get the result you don't expect. You get something different and it tells you something new. If you get what you predicted, you haven't learned anything new. All you've done is confirm your previous thinking. If you want to do pioneering work, you don't want to just confirm; you want to look for something that's different from what you expected. Sometimes you can't succeed because you've overshot. The ones who are successful are the ones who rise a little bit higher and make the greater effort. That requires a certain drive and dedication. It doesn't just happen. Up to that point you can succeed because you tried, but beyond that point there has to be something that really drives you, that gives you that extra energy. Failure, especially humiliating failure, can hand you that extra drive. Unless you're Jim Thorpe with extraordinary physical abilities, or Einstein with his extraordinary mind, failing is almost what gives you the wherewithal to exceed beyond where you would have arrived naturally, because it can force you to work harder than other people. It will depend on how hungry one is; on how much fire in the belly.

Nothing fails like success because we don't learn from it. We learn only from failure.
—Kenneth Boulding

If an experiment works, something has gone wrong.
—Finagle's First Law

Since I was a little boy I believed that I was destined to do what I am doing, and so long as I worked as hard as I could, I would be a success.

Not everybody can become an Olympic champion, but you can be successful enough to be proud of yourself, to be comfortable with making your life the best you can. Don't use other people's standards to gauge what your standards should be. There's a poem that applies here. "If you can't be an oak at the top of the tree and the only thing you can be is a little pine, be the best little pine you can be."

COCKEYED CONCLUSIONS

"Louis Pasteur's theory of germs is ridiculous fiction."

–Pierre Pachet, professor of physiology at the

University of Toulouse, France, 1872.

Larry Gelbart

"What matters is how I behave in any given situation, not the result of that behavior."

Tootsie, Oh, God! A Funny Thing Happened on the Way to the Forum, TV's M*A*S*H*, Barbarians at the Gate—they all came from the fertile mind of Larry Gelbart. Called by Mel Brooks "the fastest of the fast, the wittiest man in the business," the Emmy and Tony award winner wrote for Bob Hope, Jack Benny and Danny Thomas before he joined the legendary writing staff of Sid Caesar's *Your Show of Shows.* It was Larry Gelbart's lack of academic prowess that helped produce his classic wit and a fertile future in the world of comedy.

I remember the first joke I told. I was 5. Right away I saw that people liked to laugh.

My mother gave me that sense of taking a bad situation and finding a way to turn it into a funny observation; the ability to be biting and sweet, and simple at the same time. She would say things like, "Your next mother won't be so good to you." If I asked to go out on Saturday, she would say, "Wait, you don't know if you'll live to Saturday." And this was Friday. I was about 6 years old and I had done something that really displeased my mother, and she hit me…hard. I said, "Ma, I'm not made out of rubber." And she said, "I wish your father had used one." She could decompress a very pressured moment and take the sting and fear out of it. M*A*S*H* was filled with those types of moments. That is the business of comedy and writing. We try to make life more palatable.

> *The game of life is not so much in holding a good hand as playing a poor hand well.*
>
> *—H.T. Leslie*

I didn't do well in school so instead I would

show off. I didn't have a schoolteacher who inspired me. I don't think I ever had a schoolteacher who I didn't try to con with comedy because I hadn't done my work. Since I had two left feet, two left hands, two left everything, there were no sports coaches to encourage me. Since I didn't perform favorably, I was always trying to figure out how I could cover myself. I did it with humor. Comedy became my sword.

My father, who was my real influence, was a barber who stood on his feet from the age of 12 until he turned 89. So I was used to watching somebody doing their job, sometimes two jobs. That's the attitude I took into my work.

Remember your past mistakes just long enough to profit by them.
—Dan McKinnon

My father was always showing me off. On Sundays he would cut hair in our bathroom home. He would have me sit on the toilet and play my clarinet for the customers. When I was 16 and had yet to ever think of becoming a writer, my dad, who just happened to cut Danny Thomas' hair, talked Thomas into hiring me to write jokes for his radio show. Sixteen years old and I was a professional writer.

Some weeks you had good shows, some weeks you had bad. No matter what, you always came back and did the next show. *You don't kill yourself over a failure and you don't pop a cork over a success* became part of my professional DNA. In television, you would do 39 shows a year and, believe me, they weren't all gems. But you always had the next show. It's different in film because you don't write a new show every week, unless you're Neil Simon.

Film has probably been the least successful medium for me to write in. It's a minefield. There are so many ways to get your heart broken. You really have to hand it over to someone else. I've had some major public embarrassments. You get a lot of those in film. You not only lose control, but you also lose contact with the work that has your name on it. For example, the film *Bedazzled* was terrible. I was hired to write it, but there was a point where I realized I wouldn't be able to deliver what the director had in mind. He realized it, too. He got someone else to work on it, but my name is still on it and it embarrasses me. A few things in it I find offensive and in terrible taste. That's an example of work taken away from you for which you will forever bare some responsibility. There's a line in my play *City of Angels* in which the screenwriter says, "Am I supposed to run up and down every theater aisle in America and say I didn't write that?" You just can't. If I do films now, I try to do them with HBO.

It may not feel great all the time, but you do need people to question you, to keep you honest, say, "Hey, that's not very good." I love the story of King Philip VI of Spain who was burned to death. He fell asleep in front of a great roaring fire and, because you were not allowed to touch the King unless he told you to, no one pulled him away.

Theater is less excruciating, although it's still risky. My play *Mastergate* was previewed in Cambridge, Massachusetts. Frank Rich, theater critic of *The New York Times*, came up to Cambridge to review it. He gave it a rave review. It motivated us to bring it to New York. Rich encouraged us to first take the show to Washington, D.C. because he said it would be the best civic lesson that town could ever have. We submitted it to The Kennedy Center in Washington and they turned it down because it was "too political." So we brought it to New York and this time Rich gave it a rather tepid review. The show played 69 performances. No business. It was an odd piece and you can't wait around for people to acquire a taste. So we closed. I felt very attached to that show. I had put up a great deal of money. That was a first for me. While I had other shows close, *Conquering Hero* and *My L.A.*, both in four days, they were with someone else's money. Even though it was my money, I still had no control of the results. Once the public says *we don't care*, you can't get 'em in.

> *If you try to fail, and succeed, which have you done?*
> —George Carlin

At the same time *Mastergate* was closing, my *City of Angels* was previewing in New York. The first line of Frank Rich's review in *The New*

York Times was, "When was the last time you heard a joke stop a show?" Extravagant praise. I certainly couldn't moan about another show closing when this production was obviously going to be so successful. I had worked on *City of Angels* for eight years. It's a lot easier to deal with something that didn't work when you've got other projects already in the works.

I think I can take failure as easily as I take success because neither really matters to me. What matters is how I behave in any given situation, not the result of that behavior. Was I honest? Did I get my point across?

You have to live every day as if it's your first. You get up, if you're lucky, and you retain some sense of naïveté, a sense of wonder, curiosity, optimism. You don't want to go around with an attitude of *just my luck, there'll be life after death*. In writing, especially speculatively, you have to forget the hurts, the broken promises, the betrayals. You have to dream. That's your job, committing your dreams to paper, to the screen. You have to say it's a new ball game every day of your life. I don't have a post-it that says that, but I wake up with the notion that I'm starting all over again today. It may be foolish in some way, but I don't believe time flies. I believe time doesn't exist, that each day is Monday, that nothing went before, that even if we do remember the past, we still seem doomed to relive it. It's okay to remember your mistakes, but don't remember everybody else's. It doesn't pay to have a chest filled with mistakes done upon you because if you had the time or interest, you would see how you actually collaborated in your own undoing. I think you'd find that it doesn't take two to tango, but by the time you die, it's probably about 2,000 and you also played some part in the process to screw it up. If you can isolate that, you can make a different choice. You can have a failure that you don't consider a failure. If I am able to write successfully for me, whether it's commercially successful or not, I'm happy. When I do fail it usually has to do with

Obstacles will remain obstacles until you use them.
—Anonymous

something I did wrong very early in the process. Even so, if I have a real passion for something and believe in it, I'll have an easier time if it does happen to fail. If I really believe in what I do, the chances are, I'll do a better job.

> **NONSENSICAL NOTIONS**
> "The abdomen, the chest, and the brain will forever be shut from the intrusion of the wise and humane surgeon."
> -Sir John Eric Ericksen, surgeon-extraordinary to Queen Victoria, 1873.

B

Success isn't built on success. It is built on

failure and frustration, sometimes catastrophe,

and learning to turn it around.

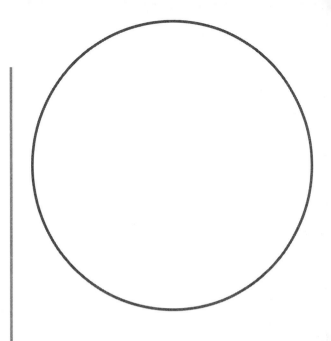

—Sumner Redstone

3

Jamie Goldman

"You don't appreciate how precious life is until it's almost taken away."

Jamie Goldman is a vibrant motivational speaker who draws crowds, cheers and great admiration. She displayed that same effort on the track when she set a world record in the 200-meter run. Adidas shoes showcased Jamie's talents in the widely acclaimed commercial that had the sports world buzzing. While outstanding, none of this would even be on her resume if not for a simple wrong turn that changed her life forever.

I was just your average kid. I didn't excel in any way, shape or form in anything. There was nothing that tickled my fancy. I felt I'd go to college, then into some sort of business. I had no passions, as yet. The only thing I really loved was skiing. I was otherwise not athletic.

It was the week before Christmas, 1987. I was 19 and living in Arizona at the time, having just finished the first semester of my sophomore year in college. My boyfriend's sister, Lisa, and I decided to drive to my boyfriend's place in New Mexico, then go skiing in Colorado.

After two days of skiing, we dropped off my boyfriend in New Mexico, and on the morning of December 23, 1987, Lisa and I headed back to Arizona. She had to work that day, so we left around 8 a.m. hoping to return home by 3 p.m. We had handwritten directions, which we had followed when we first drove to New Mexico. Unfortunately, when we crossed the border into Arizona, we turned southwest instead of southeast. I have no idea how or why we did that. It was just a mistake.

After another couple hours of driving, we realized we weren't where we needed to be. We stopped at a gas station to ask for directions and a map. They didn't have a map and the fellow who worked there had a very thick hillbilly accent that was very difficult for us to understand. He told us just how far offtrack we were and gave us directions that would bring us out near Sunrise, a ski resort in Arizona with which I was familiar.

There was still the possibility of getting back home in time for Lisa to make it to work, but it would be close. Another couple in the gas station agreed with the directions, and they were easier to understand than the gas attendant. "You go 273 and you'll come out behind the resort."

I knew how to go home from there.

Lisa and I felt quite confident and we left from there. We drove about 10 minutes and saw a sign that read "273." Turning on to it, we drove for a while before it started to snow. And then it snowed harder. Hard enough that we had to put the car in four-wheel drive. Nothing unusual there.

Every great work, every big accomplishment, has been brought into manifestation through holding to the vision, and often just before the big achievement, comes apparent failure and discouragement.
—Florence Scovel Shinn

After about a half-hour, the car just stopped. We discovered later that the car had hit a snow bank, slid and became stuck on ice. We were in the middle of a blizzard.

We got out and tried to rock the car back and forth. We tried to break up the ice under the tires with our ski poles. But nothing worked. I was frustrated, Lisa was worried about losing her job, and the car wasn't going anywhere.

On our way out to Colorado we remembered seeing snowplows, so we figured we could just wait for the snowplows to get us out. We waited and waited, but no one showed up.

We later found out that what those people at the gas station had told us was to go "to 73," not "273." The "73" was about two miles further down. And the road we took by mistake was one that had been left open for Christmas tree cutting only. After we had gotten stuck, and the snow hit hard, they closed the road. Unfortunately, while the county would normally close one gate, ride through the entire length of the road, then close the other side, this time, each side was closed separately and no one drove through to check for stragglers. It was a 15-mile long road with a gate at each end and both were now closed. We were locked in.

By the time our parents and the police started looking for us, we had two strikes against us. We were so far offtrack from the way we should have gone home that no one would have expected us to be where we were. And the road we were on was closed.

My parents started looking the next day, December 24. But because Lisa was 18, I was 19, and it was right before Christmas, the police response to my parents was just awful. Nobody wanted to look for us or help our parents. The police thought we could be runaways. The fact was, I had planned to go on a trip with my parents and there was no way I would miss that.

Defeat should never be a source of discouragement, but rather a fresh stimulus.
—Robert South

After a day or two of looking, my parents went to the media. Four or five days later, the police joined in. My father and uncle traveled every foot of the road they thought we should have driven.

Lisa and I spent days wondering why no one had come by. Where were the snowplows? At that time we had no idea that we had misunderstood and taken the wrong road entirely.

In the beginning, there was more frustration than anger. As days went on, when I would get very upset, sometimes thinking that my parents had left on vacation without me, Lisa would calm me. When Lisa would become discouraged, I would support her. I believe that more than anything else, we got our strength from each other. We never broke down at the same time. Helping each other was the key.

There were times I felt hopeless. The car's engine had died the first night. It snowed so long and so hard for the first three or four days, the only way I knew whether it was day or night was from my glow-in-the-dark watch. Inside that car it was dark all day.

After four days, the snow finally stopped. We had nothing to eat or drink the entire time. We knew we had to get out of there.

Our shoes had gotten wet the first day, so we put on our ski boots and, with the help of one ski stick each, we started out. I went first and I immediately sank down to my knees. Lisa followed in my footsteps. After we were some hundred feet away, Lisa collapsed. She started crying and saying that she couldn't go on anymore. She was so weak and was spitting up blood. It really scared her.

We didn't know where we were and we didn't know where we were going. We didn't know where the road was or if we might walk off the side of a hill. The car had been a safe haven. We talked it over and neither of us wanted to leave the other, so we decided that we would stay with the car.

By this time, I began to get mad that we couldn't get anywhere and no one had come. My faith would go up and down. But every day I woke up, I felt some hope. And with the sun coming out, there was something we could do. We could melt some snow to drink.

We found anything that could hold liquid. We used my contact lens case, Baggies, lens-cap solution receptacles. Anything. We would fill them up with snow and place them on the dashboard. The snow would melt enough for us to drink. We learned just how much to drink of the melted snow to get the most benefit from it.

Success is not measured by the position one has reached in life, rather by the obstacles overcome while trying to succeed.
—Booker T. Washington

It was about then that our feet, which were frozen, began to thaw out from the sun. That's when the pain set in. That's when we first actually looked at our feet and saw that they had turned a strange purple color. And they hurt. From that point, to get some relief, we would massage each other's feet. I don't think I felt hopeless, except for the days that my feet were so swollen I couldn't get my boots on.

We became creatures of habit. We'd do our jobs. We'd wake up in the morning. Melt our snow. Every day we'd get outside and wipe the snow from the car so we could be spotted. Sometimes we'd talk. Sometimes there were long periods of silence. But at no point did we quit. I might have questioned the possibility of dying, but for some reason, deep in my soul, I always thought I'd see my parents again. I might have gotten upset and cried, but I never thought I would die. After the first week, there was a lot of silence. We spent Christmas and New Year's in that car, but there was no celebration.

On Saturday, January 2, at 10 or 11 in the morning, suddenly, out the front window, we saw two people on snowmobiles, a man and his 12-year-old son. It was as if they appeared out of nowhere. The man was able to open Lisa's door, and in a real sweet mountain accent asked, "Are you those two girls from the news?"

You may be disappointed if you fail, but you are doomed if you don't try.
—*Beverly Sills*

We had no idea of the extensive search that had been going on. Lisa just cried and hugged him. He had a Snickers and a Dr. Pepper. We started eating and we almost got sick immediately. He said he had to go back and get "the law." I was a bit startled, but I began to pack. Lisa just wouldn't let go of him. He calmed her, left, and returned about an hour later, without the police. They didn't have the vehicles necessary to get us out.

With one bag each we climbed on their snowmobiles, leaving our feet exposed to additional damage. Waiting at the gate at the end of the road was our rescuer's wife and the police. I tried to move from the snowmobile to the car, but fell, unable to walk. The sheriff had to carry me to the car. At the time, we had no idea how damaged our legs actually were.

I remember my father coming to the hospital and I was so mean to him.

"Why couldn't you find us?! What were you doing?! We were right there!"

I think that was the hardest part to understand. We knew where we were. Why didn't they?

We'd never know how high we are till we are called to rise, and then, if we are true to plan, our statures touch the sky.
—Emily Dickinson

I had pretty severe frostbite. For three weeks they treated it. My body was getting better while my feet were getting worse. I had developed an infection and my feet became gangrenous. They were very painful. I was alive, but very sick. The decision was made to amputate.

About three days before the surgery, my parents brought in an amputation specialist who worked with a specialist in prosthetics who would fit me with legs during surgery. As I said, I wasn't an athlete. I never exercised, so that didn't bother me. It was more important for me to be able to walk into Macy's and buy myself a pair of shoes. How can I fit back into society? That was what was important to me.

The night before the surgery, I finally became upset. I still had my feet. Granted they were black, they made me sick, I couldn't eat and I was miserable…but they were still there. I think that was the only time I thought I had gotten a raw deal. Within 48 hours after the surgery, I was feeling better and I was able to eat, though it took me a good two years before I got my appetite back.

They told me I had to exercise. I was going to lose about 25 percent of my body: half of my calf and foot on each leg. I needed to strengthen my body to uplift myself to get by. At first I balked, but I figured that if it would get me out of this hospital, I would do it. I was up using a walker within 48 hours.

My grandfather became my coach, but ultimately if I was going to get rid of that walker I would have to do it myself. No one else could do it for me. I used the walker for the first six months. What really helped me was walking in the pool without the walker.

I started working out and I found that I liked it. I was becoming strong, and I had never known what it was like to feel strong before. It gave me another outlet. I was able to go to the gym. Incredibly, I became a runner. Odd as it seems, if I had not lost my legs, I would not have. I certainly would not have been as strong as I am today if the accident had not happened.

I started running seriously about four years later, in 1997. My goal was to run in the 2000 Paralympics in Australia. In fact, that was my entire reason for running. In 1999, in an attempt to film a commercial of disabled athletes having a softball game, Adidas contacted my athletic association to shoot a commercial. They ended up wanting to shoot one around a single runner, and that runner was me. I was so proud of the result. Here I was on the screen, a close-up on my face. I'm running hard and as I finish and check my time, they open up the shot, revealing that I had been running on prosthetic legs. Not a word was said. Quite dramatic. An amazing piece. I've gotten wonderful feedback. I've been able to make connections with many parents of children with prosthetics.

Challenges make you discover things about yourself that you never really knew. They're what make the instrument stretch, what make you go beyond the norm.
—Cicely Tyson

After the commercial, I continued to train for the Olympics. I had trained for three years. But in the end, I didn't make our team. I could blame it on a lot of things, but the point was, I just wasn't fast enough. I believe that everything happens for a reason. I didn't die for a reason. Because of my running I have been able to do amazing things. I got to run in Japan, Germany, England, Spain and, in fact, I did run in Australia and broke the world 200-meter record for my disability class.

I found that I needed a new challenge. For the Avon Walk for Breast Cancer, I had to walk 60 miles. I'm a runner. I had to learn to walk. It wasn't easy. I trained, I trained and I trained. I had to walk five hours a day. It was harder than I ever expected, but when the time for the walk came, I did it. And I finished. The last seven miles of that walk was the hardest thing I've ever done. I was alone, in the rain, crying. It was so difficult, but I did it.

So many people don't understand their own mental strength. They give up because of the negative voices in their head. Before a negative thought comes out, people must force themselves to make it positive. We can have wonderful support groups. I feel very fortunate to have friends and family who have helped me. But ultimately, how I feel and how I conduct myself depends on me.

If not for the accident, I would have never met my husband nor had the life I have today.

If not for the accident, I would not be as accepting of other people. I would not be as patient with them. I have no right to pass judgment on anyone who is different from me. Before, I judged people from the outside, not for who they were on the inside. I'm even more accepting of myself.

Everyone has bad days. So do I. It's normal. But the fact is, I have my life. You don't appreciate how precious life is until it's almost taken away. Appreciate what you have today. Take time out for the simple things. Tell your family you love them every day. If you're a kid in school and you're having problems academically, find out what puts a smile on your face. It doesn't have to come from a textbook. Focus on that. Bring that to school in some shape or form.

Would I want my legs back? Right now, no. My prosthetics define me. They are part of who I am. And today, I am exactly the person I want to be.

DEFECTIVE DEDUCTIONS
"Human flight is utterly impossible."
–Simon Newcombe, astronomer, 1905.

Gabriel Ruelas

"Some people are born with confidence. Some only need to prove it to themselves one time. But me, I was forced to learn it over and over."

Gabriel Ruelas admits he has had it all. He had stunned super featherweight champion Jesse James Leija, and the world, to capture the World Boxing Council Championship. He has had wealth, family, adoration of his fans. But Gabriel's life started on a cattle ranch in a horribly poor section of Mexico where children normally began working about the same time they started walking. Things most people take for granted, like electricity, telephones, TV and shoes, were only dreams. Even after he and his brother, Rafael, slipped illegally across the border into the United States, success seemed to be something only others could attain. A broken elbow nearly put an end to his boxing career. What he didn't know at the time was that break would be instrumental in making him a champion.

Even though life was hard here in the United States, it was different in Mexico. In Yerba Buena, I didn't have shoes. I had no socks. Kids who were 5 or 6 years old had work responsibilities. I had to wake up four or five in the morning before going to school to take the cattle, our donkey and horse from one water place to another. We were 10,000 feet above sea level. I used to cry in the morning because it was so cold. My feet used to go so numb working in the fields, I was afraid my toes would break off. It can get awfully cold in Mexico at 5 a.m. in the winter. I used to dream about shoes the way, I guess, other kids would dream about having bikes or baseball gloves.

Most people who come from Latin America don't have much, but in Yerba Bueno our life was even worse. The only goal in Yerba Buena was to find a job. That was it. Kids would get married by the time they were 14. There were no TVs, no radios, no news. I didn't even know what boxing was.

When I was 7, my younger brother, Rafael, and I came to America. My mother and father remained in Mexico. I didn't see my parents for the next eight years. I didn't even have a picture of them. After a while I began to forget what they looked like. At night I would pray that I wouldn't forget their faces. My brother and I saved enough money to send my parents a camera so they could take a picture and send it to us.

When I first came to the U.S., everything seemed so strange to me, especially seeing so many kids playing after school. It was hard to adapt. In Mexico, it was always work first. After school there was more work. I certainly didn't want to go back to that, but it did keep me from doing anything wrong. The discipline ended up helping me get to where I am today. I'm sure it kept me from even trying drugs.

We ended up living with my older sister. We had never met our other brothers and sisters who lived here, so I was pretty nervous around them. I was afraid to make a mistake or do anything wrong because I was afraid they would send me back to Mexico.

My sister could hardly pay the rent. Even though I was only 7, my brother and I had to earn money to buy clothes. We ended up selling candy door-to-door. Back then my brother and I were known as "The Candy Kids," but I was a horrible salesman. People who lived in big, beautiful houses would tell me that they didn't have any money to buy the candy. Kids can tell if you lie. I would call them liars and cheapskates. I never got fired because my brother was the best salesman they had. Having a younger brother who was the best at everything wasn't easy for me. He was an honor student. He took the most difficult classes and graduated a year early. I chose the easiest classes and it took me longer to finish school. I love my brother, but it made it a lot harder to deal with life. He was doing so well at the age of 12 that he could almost support himself, my sister and me. He made more money than ten other kids doing the same job.

> *Use the losses and failures of the past as a reason for action, not inaction.*
> —*Charles J. Given*

Until I met my trainers, Joe and Dan Goosen, I failed at every-thing I tried—school, learning English, finding a job. I went entire summers without finding a job. They wouldn't even hire me at McDonald's. One teacher told me that I would end up working in a car wash. But I couldn't even get that job. I filled out many applica-tions, but no one would hire me. Relatives would tell me I was a good-for-nothing. Sometimes you work harder to prove them wrong, but when your loved ones aren't behind you, it becomes that much more difficult. People kept telling me, "You couldn't do..." After you hear it so many times, you start to believe it. I would get so angry at myself. Why am I here? If I'm a failure at everything I try to do, why am I even living? I figured there had to be a reason, but God wasn't telling me what it was. Not yet, anyway. There were times I wanted to kill myself.

My great concern is not whether you have failed, but whether you are content with your failure.
—Abraham Lincoln

When I graduated from junior high, I didn't have enough money to buy anything decent to wear. The day of graduation I told my sister I had a headache and couldn't go to the ceremonies. My sister didn't have money and I figured that if I didn't go to graduation my sister wouldn't have to buy me a cake. I think a teacher found out and got someone to buy me clothes. At the graduation I felt like a beggar. I was never so embarrassed. Everyone could see how upset I was. That had a big effect on my life. To this day I don't know what happened to that diploma.

I managed to go to night school but didn't graduate. I went to high school for four years and didn't graduate. I flunked physical edu-cation. I didn't think it was important. I also think the whole junior high graduation experience still bothered me. I figured if I didn't grad-uate, my sister and I wouldn't have to spend the money for graduation. I would skip classes, sell candy, play video games or go to the gym, where I began to learn the basics of boxing. I had to sell my lunch ticket in school to be able to afford to take the bus to the gym. Again, everyone told me I'd never succeed, but I stuck with boxing because I finally found something I enjoyed.

As I became more and more involved in boxing, I started to win a lot of amateur fights. People were getting behind me. I slowly started to believe in myself. Not only did boxing help me believe in myself, but it made a lot of other people believe in me. The only way I ever received attention from people was when I fought. Nevertheless, it ended up giving me confidence in all areas of my life.

Even some of my relatives started coming to my fights. Still, I didn't dare dream of making a name for myself or becoming a top-ten contender. My trainer told me that one day I'd be fighting at the Reseda Country Club, which to me was the big time. I didn't dare believe him. But I ended up fighting there professionally over 20 times.

My first professional loss hit me hard. I was only 19 years old. People were expecting big things from me. I was fighting a guy who was a championship contender, and I was winning the fight. We got into a clinch, he grabbed my hand, twisted it and my elbow came out of place and snapped in two. I nearly fainted from the pain. I couldn't go on and the referee stopped the fight. Two days later, three screws were inserted into the broken bone. I was told to rest for six months. Then they discovered that two of the screws had broken off. A second operation was needed to repair the elbow with three new screws. A bone graft had to be taken from my hip. My arm ended up three inches shorter than it had been. Doctors told me I wouldn't be able to fight again.

If you're not big enough to lose, you're not big enough to win.
—Walter Reuther

I had just met my wife around that time and even though she hated boxing she kept telling me to not give up. Still, the doctors were saying I'd be lucky if I could even use my hand again. Once again I had failed. There was nothing to do but go back to Mexico and help my mom and dad with the land. But someone upstairs was telling me to be patient. When they took off the cast, the doctor told me to try it out. My arm never straightened out completely, but I could still hit hard, but not as hard as before the break. I was told that I'd never be the same, much less win the world title.

I started sparring in the gym and was about to learn something unbelievable. That horrible break in my arm would end up making me a better boxer. It forced me to become a smarter, more patient fighter. I couldn't brawl and survive anymore. I had to learn to box. I started to believe in myself once again. Some people are born with confidence. Some only need to prove it to themselves one time. But me, I was forced to learn it over and over.

He's no failure. He's not dead yet. —William Lloyd George

In my first fight back since that horrible break, I was pretty nervous about my elbow. Once the fight started, I forgot about my elbow. It was on national television and it was a very tough fight. I showed everyone, and more importantly, I showed myself that I could not only fight, but I could win. Even after I lost another fight, it didn't bother me one bit. I was stronger. I knew who I was and I knew who my real friends were. I had learned that no matter what happened I could always come back. And even though I lost my first championship fight, I knew I had what it took to become world champion.

What happened to me was a miracle. I didn't plan on getting rich. I only wanted to make enough money to live. Now, no matter what happens in the future, I've already made it. I won the world championship, but I know now that even before I ever fought for a world title, I had already gone farther than anyone ever, including myself, thought I would.

Today I still don't know why I'm here, I just know I'm happy I am.

DUBIOUS DIAGNOSES
"Men might as well project a voyage to the moon as attempt to employ steam navigation against the stormy North Atlantic."
–Dr. Dionysus Lardner, 1838, professor of natural philosophy and astronomy, University College, London.

Debra *Wilson*

"If I hadn't gone through what I went through, I would have not been able to do what I do with such force and conviction."

Debra Wilson has been a star on Fox TV's hit sketch comedy show *MAD TV* since its inception. She was also a regular on TV's *The Uptown Comedy Club*, a national spokesperson for Burger King and has appeared in numerous films. No one who knows Debra Wilson could ever imagine that this beautiful, strong, self-assured actress, who works tirelessly with kids to pass on a positive message, lived a childhood filled with self-hatred.

From the age of 11, I had contemplated suicide.

I grew up in a loving family with great parents. I was given the best of everything. Despite that, I grew up with low self-esteem because I was a chronic bed-wetter until junior high school. I told myself that I was an insult to my family, I hurt them, and as long as I was alive I would continue to embarrass them.

Trying to create a healthy self-image while developing breasts and hair in different areas of my body and accepting it as part of womanhood was hard enough. It was so much more difficult because my self-image was already poor. I hated the way I looked, the way I smelled, other people's reaction to me. As helpful as my parents were, no matter how undeserving, I felt unloved. I believed that they took care of me only because I was the *dog* of the family and they had to.

When a teacher asked what we wanted to be when we grew up, I told her I wanted to be a prostitute. At the time, my image of a prostitute was picking up middle-aged businessmen, and having someone to listen to their problems.

History is a relentless master. It has no present, only the past rushing into the future. To try to hold fast is to be swept aside.
—John Fitzgerald Kennedy

I had a vivid imagination, so instead of acting out in a negative way, my fantasy life took over as a comfort zone. To get people to like and accept me, I would act a certain way, tell a story, become characters from a movie. It was leading me to becoming a performer, an actress.

In college, it was overeating that became my comfort zone. I became extremely overweight. I went from one self-image problem to another.

I didn't withdraw socially but I would refuse to get close to people. I became *the clown* as a disguise. It soon became so natural that it wasn't a disguise anymore.

After college, I knew I had created a facade with men and that failure to deal honestly with them led me to purely sexual relationships. Manipulation was a game for me. It gave me control. I was spending time with men who were not worthy of my time. I had a *use me* stamp on my forehead. I continued to seek the comfort of strange men and the residual effect was emptiness. Still I kept coming back for more. It never dawned on me that if I kept doing this I would never feel good. It became my drug.

I would let men pick me up, hoping they would beat me and destroy me. I wanted to die the most painful way possible because my life was filled with pain. I loathed myself. I still had made no peace with my bed-wetting.

My relationship with my older sister was so conflicted. I was in my early 20s and I wanted to kill myself. I took a bunch of pills. I had so much angst that I wanted to die and blame her for it so she would feel guilty for the rest of her life. That's the same sickness I used with men. I just didn't care. I was such an unclean spirit. Not only was I unclean, but I was unsafe. By all accounts I should have contracted AIDS and died by now.

I would think, "At least I'm not alone tonight. At least someone wants me. I must be beautiful." I could make you laugh, I could make you feel good. It all was about having some control to make other people feel good. But I was incapable of making myself feel good.

One night, two men picked me up, took me to an alley in Howard Beach, New York, where I thought to myself, "This is where I'm going to die." Oddly enough, I felt comfortable with the fact that they might beat me to death. The only time I was scared and uncomfortable was after they took me home and I realized I was still alive. I stood staring in the middle of my living room for hours, thinking, "What was I going to do now? I have another day of trying to be responsible for my life and I know I'm a liar. I know I'm messed up. I know that there's something wrong with me." Outside, torrential rains fell. Inside, I was falling apart. I couldn't seem to fix it and I wasn't able to run from it.

I had hit bottom. I didn't want to go on living. While everybody still thought of me as the life of the party, I was 25 and I knew that if I didn't change, I would die. By all means I should be dead. With that, I had a revelation, one filled with anger toward God. I challenged Him to take me. To take over my life. It's not like I was doing a good job with it.

The anger subsided. I recognized that I must take a particular route to get to where I was going, though I didn't know where that was. I realized that I needed the grace of God and I had to do it with my own sense of spirituality, my own sense of prayer, my own understanding of my life's purpose. I then turned my life over to God, and the more I cried the stronger He held me.

I've learned that a blessing is not a blessing until you share it. If someone says, "Oh, you think you're something, huh?" I say, "Yes, and guess what? So are you."

Sweet are the uses of adversity.
—William Shakespeare,
As You Like It

> *When it is dark enough, men see the stars.*
> —*Ralph Waldo Emerson*

When you grow up with a legacy of shame, the adult responds to the shame as a child would. I remember weeping uncontrollably when my family came to visit me in New York. I brought up my bed-wetting. The shame, the fear, the sadness, the frustration. My mother and father looked at each other and my father walked out of the room. Turns out that my father was a chronic bed-wetter. And so was his sister. He never told me. It was a legacy of shame, a family secret, embarrassing to the neighborhood, embarrassing socially. Logically, he could have said, "I'm going to tell her that I love her and she's not alone. I won't allow her to isolate. I won't let her feel this way." But my father never said a word. Why would a parent, who wanted to save his child's spirit and heart, not say a word? Because he wasn't responding as an adult. He was responding as a child of shame, a legacy of the way he was raised. Later, he was able to pass on a loving message to my sister-in-law whose child, his grandson, was a bed-wetter. He said to her, "Whatever you do, tell him that you love him, forgive him and that it will be alright. Don't make the same mistake that I made with Debra because I will never get over that."

Today, I understand and embrace that legacy of shame, not to hold on to but as power. Today, I am aware of my weaknesses and use them as my strength. Today, I don't seek reparations from my parents. I often speak to kids and always finish by saying, "If you don't know, now you know. If you weren't told you were loved, I'm telling you that I love you. If you didn't know you could take responsibility, now you do. Once you are aware, you can't be unaware. If you weren't told that you are wonderful, great, blessed and beautiful, then I'm telling you that you are. Now it's up to you to take that journey, bust your ass and find out why you're here. What you have to offer the universe is unique. You can buy a Rolex watch with diamonds and platinum, but once the tiny mechanism breaks down, eventually, the larger things will fall apart. It doesn't matter what you do in life, the fact is you don't have to become the biggest or most important person in the world. You can change someone's life forever just by being yourself and then that person may go on to change another person's life."

How many people out there, especially kids, don't know that they are worthy? Although my family loved me, I still thought I was unworthy. So now I pass on to kids my stories and my legacy of shame. What I get back from many of them is how my own stories have changed their lives for the better. And for that I say, "Father, thank you for the blessings of my bed-wetting, my low self-esteem and self-image." If I hadn't gone through what I went through, I would not have been able to do what I do now with such force and conviction. I have been blessed.

ACCIDENTAL ACHIEVEMENTS

Thousands of years ago, some leaves fell into water being boiled by a Chinese emperor. Today, we call that tasty water...tea.

Jim O'Brien

"If you do the job you need to do in the short term, the long term takes care of itself."

Coach Jim O'Brien of the Boston Celtics is only the 14th man to hold that prestigious title in team history. Through 13 years as an assistant at six different colleges, as well as a stint under former Celtics head coach Rick Pitino with the New York Knicks and the Boston Celtics, O'Brien knew his destiny was to someday serve as head coach in the NBA. As head coach at the University of Dayton, he had turned around the program and led the Flyers to the tournament championship. As a player, O'Brien was a three-year starter at St. Joseph's University where he led his teams to three post-season appearances, was named team co-MVP his senior season and was elected to both the St. Joseph's and Big Five Halls of Fame. But it was with the birth of his daughter, Caitlyn, that he may have learned his greatest lesson.

Perhaps we shouldn't have, but everyone expects to have a perfect child. In our minds we already had two perfect children. We had no idea until the day she was born that our daughter, Caitlyn, would have Down syndrome. It was such a shock. Your first reaction is a knife through your gut. I'm married to a very strong woman. When our daughter was born they took her out of the delivery room. We had no idea that she had Down. While they were sewing up my wife, Sharon, they asked me to come out of the room where I was told by the doctor what Caitlyn's prognosis was. She asked if I wanted her to tell my wife. I said I would and the doctor came in with me. I will remember this conversation for as long as I live. I said to Sharon, "I don't know how to tell you this, but Caitlyn has Down syndrome." And I just lost it. The doctor began to explain *alternatives*. She said, "You don't have to accept this child. There are institutions…" The doctor didn't even get the next word out of her mouth when Sharon said, "Bring me my daughter." The doctor began to say something else. Sharon looked at the doctor, "I said, bring me my daughter." That was the greatest example I've ever seen of someone dealing well with adversity.

For us, it was the instantaneous shock that made a strong family even stronger. We found a network of extended family and friends that was overwhelming. At first, you look at this child's life in totality. You think, "Oh my God, look at all the things we're going to have to change," when, in fact, all you have to do is live in the present. If you do the job you need to do in the short term, the long term takes care of itself. It turned out that Caitlyn has been the greatest thing that has ever happened to us. Our other children are great but Caitlyn is a marvel. She is presently a wonderful, wonderful, 19 year old. She's full of life, intelligent, dynamic, never has a bad day and uplifts us in every possible way. She is a gem of a person.

I don't know if my wife saw Caitlyn and her situation as a gift at that first moment, but as a mother it didn't matter to her how difficult it would be. Soon thereafter, I saw what a special gift Caitlyn was. The lessons I've learned with Caitlyn helped me to deal with what happened at the University of Dayton.

I had worked myself up the coaching ladder. I was an assistant coach at Wheeling Jesuit College, Pembroke State College, University of Maryland, St. Joseph's University and the University of Maryland before returning to Wheeling Jesuit College as the head coach. I went on to become assistant coach with the New York Knicks under Rick Pitino, then landed the head coaching position at the University of Dayton.

During my first year at Dayton, we turned around a program that had won only 12 games the year before. We had the most dramatic turnaround of any college basketball program in the country, winning 22 games, and had a first-round upset win against Illinois in the NCAA tourney. Except for a tip-in in the very next game, we would have made it to the

> *A diamond cannot be polished without friction, nor a man perfected without trials.*
> *—Chinese Proverb*

Sweet Sixteen round. The next two years were a mix of injuries, rebuilding and playing in a new, tougher league. During that period, Tom Ferricks, who had originally hired me, died, and the new administration basically ran me out of town.

It was really the first time I had ever failed at anything. I was driving home from a recruiting trip, listening to a sports talk show on the radio. This sportscaster was ripping into someone. It seemed like he was talking about the devil. I wondered, "Who could be so horrible to be talked about that way?" That's when I heard he was talking about me.

It was a painful time for me and my family. People put "For Sale" signs on our lawn. It was very difficult. Dayton officials asked me to resign and I refused. I said you'll have to fire me and they said, "Okay."

When you get fired in coaching, it's very hard to get on track again. And though I wanted to keep coaching, I did consider a career change. But Rick Pitino, who had gone to the University of Kentucky, had an opening for an associate coach. We talked and it seemed like I had the job. When we finally got together, he said that the Kentucky job was probably not a good situation for me, and he wasn't going to hire me. He said that because of the difficult situation I had just been through, he didn't know if I still had the *fire* necessary for coaching.

Over the next 45 minutes, I made sure he knew my passion for coaching hadn't waned for one second. As a result, he hired me. It had been a test, one that was important for him to administer. No one wanted to hire someone who was beaten down and didn't believe in himself.

Many men fail because they quit too soon.
—Dr. C. E. Welch

Over the next three years at Kentucky, we went 95–12 and won a national championship. I was lucky to have a friend and a mentor like Rick Pitino. The next year he took over as head coach of the Boston Celtics. He wanted me to take over at Kentucky, but my goal had always been to be a head coach at the professional level, so I passed on the Kentucky job and moved with Rick to the Celtics as an associate coach.

When Rick decided to leave as coach and team president, the team hired me as interim head coach. Though we didn't get into the playoffs, we did a turnaround, and the owner negotiated a long-term deal with me to continue on as head coach. Seven years after being unceremoniously fired at Dayton, I had become head coach of one of sport's most historic franchises.

Dayton again taught me the importance of family. How good family and good friends can help you overcome adversity. It's extremely difficult to do it by yourself. I learned to force-feed myself positive literature, whether listening to tapes or reading books. I always wanted to have a positive attitude when I went in front of my team. I firmly believed that I would act the way I thought and I didn't want any negative thoughts in my mind.

> *The best gifts sometimes arrive in the most unexpected wrapping.*
> *—S. Young*

If I told you that I had the words that will give you the ability to succeed, be happy and overcome any obstacle in your life, you wouldn't believe me. But if those words were Earl Nightingale's *six magic words*, "You become what you think about," you'd find that what I said would be true. We are who we are for better or worse. It's our job to surround ourselves with positive people and information.

I have learned not to turn inward but to be of *service* to others, my family and friends, to serve my players and to not get caught up into a *woe-is-me* attitude. I learned that you take it one day at a time and you bust your ass each day. And whatever you do, you do it to the very best of your ability. It's a formula for success.

DEFECTIVE DEDUCTIONS

"Airplanes are interesting toys, but of no military value."

–Marechal Ferdinand Foch, professor of strategy,

Ecole Superieure de Guerre, Paris, France, 1911.

Teddy Pendergrass

"I was given a choice: live or die. I chose to live."

Known to many as "Teddy Bear," legendary singer Teddy Pendergrass went from a North Philadelphia ghetto to adoration by millions for his sensual song stylings. From his first hits as lead singer of Harold Melvin and the Blue Notes with "If You Don't Know Me by Now" and "The Love I Lost" to his own singles including "Close the Door" and "Turn Off the Lights," he has driven his fans into a frenzy that few have done before him. With a constant track record of Grammy nominations and multiplatinum albums, his stature in the music community continues to shine brightly. Though his near-fatal 1982 car accident left him in a wheelchair, it was a critic's destructive words and Teddy's fatherless childhood that were behind the perseverance that brought him back to the stage and the top of the charts.

I've had so many disappointments and hardships in my life it would be extremely difficult to pinpoint just one.

I didn't meet my father until the age of 10. I didn't know much about him and I wasn't very curious. I figured what happened between my parents was their business. I had no father; it was a simple and sad fact of life. Then my mother, who had raised me alone, felt it was necessary for me to meet the man who was part of bringing me into the world. We rode one of those Philadelphia trolleys to his house, which wasn't all that far away. The meeting felt odd. Here was a man who I didn't know, living with a woman who wasn't my mother, and he was raising a child with her and that child wasn't me. I don't remember if he actually said anything to

The person who goes farthest is generally the one who is willing to do and dare. The sure-thing boat never gets far from shore.
—Dale Carnegie

me, but I do remember clearly that before we left he asked my mother for 50 cents. How could a man who'd never given me anything dare to ask my mother for money? It seemed so wrong. That was the first and last time I saw my father. A year later, my father was murdered by a drinking buddy. I didn't know it at the time, but looking back it seems that from that point on I decided to never do without. So much of what I did was based on the strength I gained from not having a father there. With that loss, along with a strong and loving mother, I learned that I could persevere through almost anything. I had no idea how that perseverance would end up giving me the strength to deal with unimaginable adversity.

While I had faced many problems in my life, from inequality as lead singer of Harold Melvin and the Blue Notes to attempting to find my children from whom I had been separated, I don't think it would surprise anyone that my greatest challenges came from my near-fatal car accident and its repercussions.

By 1982, I was at the top. Platinum albums, sold-out concerts, Grammy nominations, my own line of designer jeans. I couldn't be happier with my family or prouder of my children. All the doors were open. We were readying a live HBO concert, product endorsements, a new album, another tour. I was truly blessed.

You gain strength, courage, and confidence by each experience in which you really stop to look fear in the face. You are able to say to yourself, 'I have lived through this horror. I can take the next thing that comes along.'
—Eleanor Roosevelt

On March 18, 1982, I was driving with one passenger along a notoriously winding road in Philadelphia that I had driven a hundred times before and knew well its dangerous twists and turns.

As we approached a particular curve, I braked to slow the car but it didn't respond. I instinctively gripped the wheel and hit the brakes again. Nothing. Then I heard a large crash as we hit the metal guardrail. After that, I remember my head hitting the ceiling of the car, then a terrifying blur before the car came to a sudden, violent stop.

My spine was injured and my spinal cord partially severed between the fifth and sixth vertebrae, at the base of my neck, right above my chest. In the very beginning, there was some small hope that my condition might improve, but it was not to be.

In one single stroke, my body had changed forever in ways that I could not even imagine. I felt a profound sense of loss. Everything I had, everything I was and everything I imagined for the future was utterly gone.

Having grown up in the ghetto, I knew that much in life is beyond our control. I'd lived my life working against the odds. I'd taken advantage of every possibility that ever came my way, because I *had* to be in control. For the first time in my life, I felt my whole world had come to an end. I was totally helpless.

From the moment they pulled me from the car that night, the question was whether or not I would ever sing again. And the real question for me wasn't whether I could live without singing, *but if I would want to.*

Then one day in August of 1982, an article appeared in the newspaper. There was my name in a front-page headline. I scanned the story and within seconds my heart stopped.

"Vacancy: In Search Of A New Pendergrass." Under my photo ran the caption: "Teddy Pendergrass, the singer-sex symbol who has left a void." My pulse quickened as I read: "The tall, bearded singer crooning flagrantly sexy songs in his gruff, powerful voice had"—had? "a devastating effect on females, from teenagers to women in their 40s. He was…"—was?—"…the cool, macho man with just a hint of sensitivity that seems to turn on many females. Since the late '70s he was the number-one black male singer-sex symbol. In March, the 32 year old was paralyzed from the chest

> *I have made mistakes but I have never made the mistake of claiming that I have never made one.*
> —James Gordon Bennett

down in a Philadelphia auto accident. According to the doctors, he will probably be able to sing, but it's unlikely that he will ever walk again, which means that he probably won't perform. If he sang from a wheelchair, it wouldn't be the same. His accident left a void. Who's going to be the next Pendergrass?"

> *Adversity has ever been considered the state in which a man most easily becomes acquainted with himself.*
> *—Samuel Johnson*

Tears welled in my eyes and a lump rose in my throat. I shouted, "What the hell are they talking about? They think I'm dead? No one's gonna take my place. I'm still here!"

If I sang from a wheelchair, it "wouldn't be the same." What the hell did that mean? I was stunned, enraged, hurt, devastated. To say this added insult to injury—literally—doesn't even begin to describe how diminished, worthless and inhuman those words made me feel. Who the hell was he to tell the world that it was over for me? That Teddy Pendergrass no longer mattered? For him, my accident was merely an opportunity for ranking every other popular black male singer, as if we were not individuals but interchangeable cogs in the hit-record machine.

"Let's consider the characteristics we're looking for," the writer continued. "He has to be black, reasonably young, good-looking, virile, aggressive and charismatic." I wonder which of these characteristics he assumed I no longer possessed.

I used to make it a point never to read reviews. I never cared what some writer thought of my show or recordings. In a way, it's ironic that it would be a critic—one who had reviewed and interviewed me several times before—who could hurt me in a way no one else could. My spirit collapsed under the weight of those words.

That wrenching moment proved to be a turning point. I've come to realize how painful it is for many people to see someone who has suffered a tragedy and how hard it is for them to understand that even though a person is now wheelchair bound, deep down inside, he is still the same man he was before the accident. The moment I finished reading the infuriating newspaper article, I vowed that nobody else would be "the next Teddy Pendergrass," and that I wouldn't rest until I was right back where I left off. Not long afterward, I sang for the first time since the accident.

Failures, repeated failures, are finger posts on the road to achievement.
—Charles F. Kettering

I had a choice: live or die. I chose to live. And if you choose to live you can't sit in the problem. You have to move past it.

I'd never been much of a talker, always keeping to myself, always keeping my deepest feelings to myself. My injury forced me to express my emotions; to say "I love you" instead of giving a hug, or "I'm hungry" instead of storming out of the room. And I had to learn to trust people I never would have—never could have—before. It wasn't all about me anymore.

I never fail to appreciate that every day I live in this wheelchair is a day I might easily never have seen. It's still a bitch, and it will probably always be a bitch, but I'm still here. I have learned to appreciate so much in life that I'd overlooked before.

My life will always be filled with uncertainty, but I refuse to die. I have so much to live for. Again, and forever, I am truly blessed.

TRULY BLESSED
(excerpt)
by Teddy Pendergrass

Now that I know just what I must face
And I see exactly what life can put you through,
Go through life now with a smile on my face,
Because there's nothing, there's nothing, there's nothing that I cannot do.
Now that I know that I'm not all alone,
He's there, and I know that He'll see me through.
I guess I'll sum it all up in one phrase:
I am truly blessed.

(Portions reprinted from TRULY BLESSED by Teddy Pendergrass and Patricia
Romanonski, copyright © 1998 by Theodore DeReese Pendergrass. Used by
permission of G. P. Putnam's Sons, a division of Penguin Putnam Inc.)
(Lyrics from TRULY BLESSED reprinted by permission of Teddy Pendergrass.)

SHORTSIGHTED SUMMATIONS
"While theoretically and technically television may be feasible,
commercially and financially I consider it an impossibility, a develop-
ment of which we need waste little time dreaming."
–Lee De Forest, radio pioneer, 1926.

Stephen J. Cannell

"Rejection is simply someone else's opinion, not everyone else's."

Stephen J. Cannell is regarded as one of television's most successful talents. The Emmy Award winner has created or co-created more than 38 shows, including *Baretta*, *The Rockford Files*, *The A-Team*, *21 Jump Street*, *Wiseguy*, *Hunter*, and *The Commish*. Cannell has also established himself as an exceptional novelist of thrillers with best-sellers *The Plan*, *Final Victim* and *King Con*. It may be hard to believe, but with all his success Cannell was once considered not all that bright.

I was always the stupidest kid in my class. "Stupidest" because of my learning disability, dyslexia; I flunked kindergarten. I was so young I really didn't even think twice about that. I flunked fourth grade and that one hurt. I knew I was the only one in my whole class who couldn't read. Whenever it was my turn to read, no matter how hard I tried to sound out the words, I just couldn't read. It was humiliating.

Because I was fairly verbal, there was never talk of any problem other than an academic one. They would tell me that if I applied myself I could do better. I thought that maybe I wasn't studying right. I could read to myself, but the next day I couldn't remember the information. At that time there was no awareness of dyslexia. Now we know that one of the symptoms of dyslexia is the inability to recall facts once learned.

After I flunked fourth grade, I was sent to a remedial school for a year, rejoining my class in the sixth grade. I was still the worst student, but at least I could read. Three years later I flunked ninth grade. In total, I ended up completing high school two years behind my original class. But even though I was flunking English, under my picture in the high school yearbook where it stated "ambition," I wrote "author." I guess that had a lot to do with the attitude I picked up in football. I was pretty good and had set records at my high school that still stand. I always thought there was no way that only one man could bring me down. Often one guy did, but my mind-set was that it shouldn't happen.

After high school, I went to the University of Oregon, graduating with only a 2.1 grade point average, but I had discovered writing. My English professor told me never to stop writing and I took that to heart.

Deciding to go into the movie business, I came to Los Angeles. I still believed that I would fail once I left school, that I wasn't very smart. But I didn't let that stop me. I became very good at shielding myself from negative thoughts. It really paid off in show business where there's much more rejection than acceptance. I learned that rejection was simply someone else's opinion, not everyone else's.

On weekdays I drove a furniture truck for my father and got home at 5:30. From 5:30 to until 10:00, I would write. Then I would write all weekend. I did that for five years. And for five years I failed to get anyone to read what I wrote. But I know now that failure is part of living. If you haven't failed, you haven't really lived. In show business, failure is the principle commerce. For every thousand pitches, 10 are bought, and most of those fail. Even though I was very successful in television, I, too, had my failures. I don't think you ever have success without failure. Probably the worst thing that could happen, career wise, would be that you were continually successful. It would become boring. Failures make success exciting. If you know how dark the hole of

NOTHING IN THIS WORLD can take the place of persistence. TALENT will not: nothing is more common than unsuccessful people with talent. GENIUS will not: unrewarded genius is almost a proverb. EDUCATION will not: the world is full of educated derelicts. PERSISTENCE and DETERMINATION alone are omnipotent. The slogan 'press on' has solved and always will solve the problems of the human race.
—Calvin Coolidge

failure is, yet continue the effort, victory becomes intoxicating.

> *I have always grown from my problems and challenges, from the things that don't work out. That's when I've really learned.*
> —Carol Burnett

During this time I just kept writing, but I was also reading others' scripts, some that were even being produced. I realized that I could write as well or better than most of those. That belief kept me going.

After selling my first television script, it took a whole year before I would sell another. During that time I continued to write every day. I finally sold a script to *Adam-12*. From then on, I was in.

Prosperity itself is difficult to define. In our society, money has become the goal. Money is not a joyous thing. It certainly beats not having money, but it shouldn't be the goal. For just when things seem to be as good as they could get, life changes everything.

At the age of 15, while playing on the beach in San Luis Obispo, my son, Derek, was crushed to death under a large sand fortress. Up until then, everything in my life went my way. I married the girl I wanted to marry, my career was going great, I had my own studio which my wife and I owned 100 percent and I had 1,500 people working for me.

All of a sudden, I don't have a son anymore and everything is upside down. I didn't give a damn about anything I had. It took Marsha and me five years to come out the other side. A five-year readjustment to life.

When you're running five shows at the same time and you're in a business of deadlines, there doesn't seem to be enough hours in the day. Whenever I would attempt to leave the office, 10 people would be lined up in the waiting room—every one of them with a heart-stopping problem that had to be solved immediately.

I realized that the only thing that was truly important in life was my family. I lost valuable time with them because I was constantly at work. I decided I wasn't going to let that happen anymore.

Prior to all of this, my dear friend and agent's wife had the bad timing to die during pilot season. I was up to my ass in casting, shooting and hiring directors when somebody came in and told me that Sam's wife had died. I didn't even stop working. I figured that Sam knew I loved him. But the fact is, I wasn't there for my friend. When my son died, everyone showed up for us. Dennis Weaver read a sermon. Ben Vereen flew in to sing at the funeral. Friends, network executives, everyone showed up. At times there were 200 people in our living room. Yet when Sam's wife died, I didn't even pick up the phone.

About a year and a half after Derek died, I thought, "Where am I coming from? What am I all about?" I had never picked up the phone to call Sam to tell him how sorry I was. I never wrote him a letter. I behaved in the most shallow and unfriendly way. I promised myself that I was never going to let that happen again. If I have a friend in trouble, I'm going to drop everything and be there. I don't care how much it costs me. I don't care if I lose a pilot. I will be there. I took Sam out to lunch and told him how ashamed I was of the way I had acted. And I told him that it would never happen again. I would pay Sam back by being a real friend to everyone I know.

I prioritized. I became a much better delegator. I would not put my own needs in front of others again. I'm a healthier and better person for it. It was a terribly difficult lesson, but one I needed to learn.

Asking for a different life or comparing one's life or work to another is a waste of time. I don't compare my work to Steve Bochco, David Kelly or David Chase. I root for them. You have to become a good critic of your own work and ask yourself if you are doing quality work. How well can I perform with the tools that God gave me? That's it. Whenever I hear myself denigrating a colleague, I know it's about one thing—my own insecurity. At that moment, I'm not believing in myself. Judging others is just as useless as judging the immediate value of your own efforts.

My first novel was turned down by the first five publishers I submitted it to. I sent it off to a novelist friend to see if he could find what might be wrong. Sort of a gut check. While he was reading it, another two or three rejections rolled in. He liked it though, enough to send it to his publisher. Ten days later they bought it for what I thought was too much money. It became a best-seller. Without those earlier rejections, my book may have never gotten to the right editor/publisher for me.

If at first you don't succeed, try, try again.
—Old Adage

It's important to remember that rejection is simply someone else's opinion, not everyone else's. It's your own persistence that will win out over all those rejections. If you don't quit, you can't lose.

OUTRAGEOUS OBSERVATIONS

"What can be more palpably absurd than the prospect held out of locomotives traveling twice as fast as stagecoaches?"
–The Quarterly Review, England, 1825.

Men succeed when they realize that

their failures are the preparations for their victories.

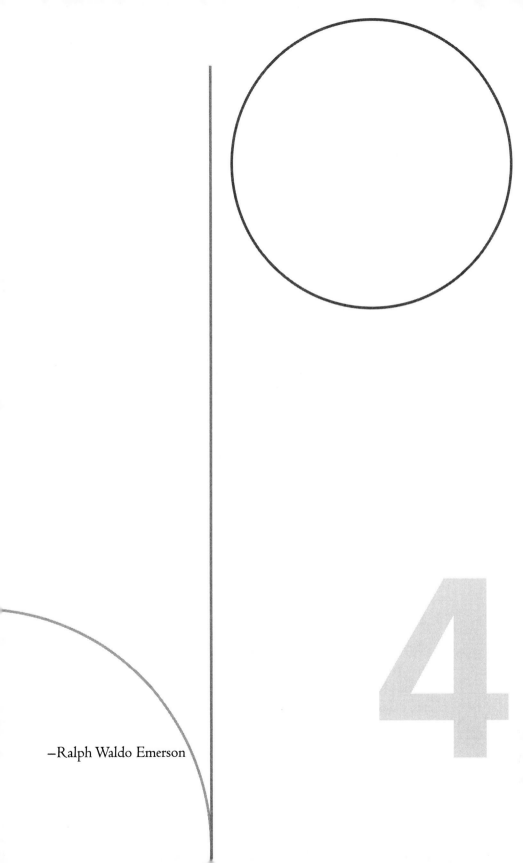

—Ralph Waldo Emerson

John Wooden

"Failure to prepare is preparing to fail."

John Wooden's career is one for the ages. From being an All-American player at Purdue University and NCAA Player of the Year, to coaching UCLA to an unbelievable 10 national basketball championships, four perfect seasons, and at one time, 88 consecutive victories, Wooden is only one of two people enshrined in the Basketball Hall of Fame as a player and a coach. John Wooden learned his lessons very early and has been spending the rest of his life teaching those lessons to others.

Though I lived on a farm through the ninth grade, I always wanted to be a civil engineer. I had dreams of building roads, bridges and things of that sort. It was the reason I went to Purdue University. At the end of my freshman year, I discovered that in order to gain my civil engineering degree, I would have to go to civil engineer camp every summer. I just couldn't afford it. If there had been athletic scholarships in those days or if my parents had any financial wherewithal, I would have become a civil engineer. That wasn't to be and ending that dream was quite a blow.

My dad taught me that if I couldn't get what I wanted, I must accept it. I changed my courses to liberal arts with a major in English. I knew from that time on that I would become a teacher and I would teach sports. Sometimes we get so involved in things over which we have no control that we end up affecting negatively the things we do have control over.

We also have no control over other people or what may happen to them. The most devastating thing that ever happened to me was the death of my dear wife, Nell. Yet in losing her I've lost all fear of death.

I got my positive attitude from my dad. He let me know that it's never about being better than somebody else. My job was to never stop trying to be the best I could be. There's nothing wrong with learning from others, but no matter how you perform, there will always be someone doing a better job than you. This is why we should never compare ourselves to others. You just do the best you can. When the game's over, you should be able to look in the mirror and say you made your best effort.

I've had players with a greater ability than how they performed. I don't expect perfect execution, but I do expect the effort to be there. My job is to teach a player how to bring out the best in himself. If I don't get that out of him, then, as a coach, I have failed that player. Was it just me alone? No. Let's suppose the player doesn't work hard enough. Is that my job to make him work harder? Perhaps he's not getting enough rest or hasn't practiced moderation in the important things. Is that my job to get him to do that? If I don't get him to what is necessary to perform at his own level of competency, then I have failed, but I don't consider myself a failure because I did make the effort. And out of that one situation I can learn something to help the next player through a similar situation, though it doesn't mean I can reach everyone.

It's up to each of us to decide for ourself if we have done our best. This is what I've always taught. I've never mentioned winning as it is normally defined. You can actually learn as much or more from being outscored by an opponent as when you outscore them. You can win when you are outscored and you can lose when you outscore someone. I know the alumni wouldn't look at it that way, but I did.

Success should be in the trying.
—Marcus Allen

I always felt the scores should only be a by-product of my ability to get this across to the team. As a coach, I wanted to win championships, but I didn't consider it a failure if we didn't. There were games that we lost because the players or myself were not making the best effort to outscore the other team, but we could always find something to learn from it. We gain strength through adversity.

Someone once said:

When I look back it seems to me,
All the grief that had to be,
Left me when the pain was o'er,
Stronger than I was before.

What is easily achieved or acquired seems not to be long lasting while what is more difficult to achieve is more worthwhile and enduring. Whether it's weightlifting where you increase weights to increase physical strength, or calculus where you start with simple problems, then increase the difficulty steadily, you get better by continuously building your strengths.

Losing is a part of winning.
—Dick Munro

We're continually tested morally and spiritually, getting stronger through adversity. Churchill said, "Failure is never fatal, but failure to act is." There is no disgrace in getting knocked down, but there is in not trying to get up. Ask yourself, "Why did I get knocked down?" There's always something you can learn from it.

Cervantes said, "The journey is better than the end." Robert Louis Stevenson said, "It's better to travel hopefully than it is to arrive." At UCLA, I always wanted the score to be a by-product of the practice. Try to improve a little each and every day. My dad always told me to make each day your masterpiece and the result will be one.

Failure to prepare is preparing to fail. With proper preparation you're going to perform to your level of competence, but not perfection. If you're shooting baskets and you miss one, from that point on your percentage is going to run a little higher because you're always going to end up shooting at your own level. So if you miss a shot, that's okay. It means you're going to have a better chance of hitting the next one.

The worst thing you can do for your loved ones is to do their work for them. This doesn't mean you don't help them with the necessities. The point is that by giving people their independence, you give them the opportunity to make their own mistakes, learn from them, and gain confidence. In the stock market crash of 1929, many people committed suicide. People who had worked hard to make their fortunes did not commit suicide. They knew how to make money. Most of those who committed suicide were those who received their fortunes from inheritance. They had no experience in building their wealth.

In order to learn you must start from where you are now. Alcoholics must admit to being alcoholics before they can be helped. If someone has an inferiority complex, he has to first realize it, accept the fact, and only then he can work to overcome it.

I always tried to get across to my players that ours was a team game. No individual can win it and no individual can lose it. It may seem so toward the end of the game. You may miss a shot that, if made, would have won the game, but that doesn't mean you lost the game. There were plenty of things that happened during the game, that if done better, would have made no need for your last-second shot.

I think the best way to teach is by example. We need models more than we need critics. Most of the time, just talking to kids who feel hopeless or helpless will not help. They need leadership by example. They must be referred to people, situations and examples that they can relate to.

In teaching or coaching, I always focused on the positive, not the negative. Though many coaches have had great success from the dictator style of coaching, I believe in the leader approach. I want to be out front and center, not in back with a whip. One of the greatest motivators is a pat on the back. Of course, sometimes your aim should be a little lower and the pat has to be a little harder.

There are some defeats more triumphant than victory.
—Montaigne

When I was in grade school, I remember seeing my dad hauling gravel out of a gravel pit with a beautiful team of horses attempting to pull the heavily weighted cart out. They were frothing from the mouth, sweating and stomping, but no matter how they pulled, it didn't budge. Then my dad walked over and stood between the horses. He started talking to them quietly and they began to calm down. As he talked, he gently grabbed the reins and the horses pulled the cart out of the pit. That's how I've tried to teach. Sometimes it was easier for me to get the attention of my team by speaking very quietly rather than screaming. I try to build on what's working, not what's wrong. Remember, when you disagree you don't have to be disagreeable.

Failure is the tuition you pay for success.
—Walter Brunell

The future welfare of our children all starts with the parents and effective parenting. And the most important part of parenting is teaching. Following that, it's the schoolteachers who are extremely important to the future of our young people. But whether a parent or a teacher, it is most important to remember that a leader should always be interested in finding the best way, not in having his own way.

MOLDY MISTAKES

It is said that long ago, a nomad traveling across the sweltering desert kept his milk stored in a pouch made out of the stomach from a sheep. After some time he reached into his pouch and found not milk but CHEESE! Unfortunately, crackers wouldn't be invented for three more years.

Dr. Audrey Manley

"If you take care of each day, each task, and do it the very best that you can, then the big picture will take care of itself."

College president, admiral, pediatrician, surgeon general. They're all Dr. Audrey Manley. President of Georgia's Spelman College, two-star admiral and former acting surgeon general of the United States, Dr. Manley became the first African-American female head resident at Chicago's Cook County Hospital. Coming from a poor, dysfunctional family, Dr. Manley learned early on that facing adversity as a youngster helped build inner strength and a faith that she would be able to use for the rest of her life.

My whole life has been an experience in overcoming adversity. We are a product of our genetics and environment. I was born to parents who were poor and grew up in a segregated Mississippi. There was a lot of family illness. When I was 10, my mother had what they called back then a nervous breakdown, which was later diagnosed as schizophrenia. As the oldest of three sisters, I was forced to grow up almost overnight.

I became the caretaker in my family. I was cognizant of the fact that I couldn't play like the other kids, but even though, at the time I might have *missed out*, as my life has unfolded, the joys and the pleasures of my achievements and awards I have received have been a great part of what has made me feel that this was all part of a divine plan. Those adversities made me strong, and throughout my life people have looked to me as a responsible and performance-oriented person.

I believe that my life is directed by some being greater than I, so I developed a very strong faith in God. Very early on, my parents brought us to church and taught us the value of education. I was raised in the church and the classroom became my home. My mother's illness only reinforced those values.

When I was 4, I told my maternal grandmother that I would become a doctor. That night, she passed away of a stroke. Since that time I have read everything I could about doctors and medicine. That's never changed. Throughout my school years there were mentors who came into my life. I had been a troublemaker up until fourth grade. I would finish my work quickly and then socialize or act out inappropriately. I'd get booted out of class and my paternal grandmother would have to come to school to get me back in. In fifth grade, that all changed. My teacher, Ms. Owens (who I learned years later was a Spelman grad), directed me to the library and the right kinds of books. My seventh, eighth and ninth grade math and science teacher, Mr. Caldwell, noticed my talents in his fields of study. Both teachers pushed me and challenged me to get ahead. They kept me too busy to get in trouble.

Students who have stellar talent or come from families with money will flourish. Teachers can help our society so much by recognizing the unique talents in each child and encouraging poor students who may need that extra push. If I hadn't had those teachers who were to give me that extra push, I know I would not be where I am today.

I received a four-year scholarship to Spelman College, pre-med. Then I earned a scholarship to medical school. At the time, for a poor black girl to work her way through medical school was unheard of. Again, when I look back, going through college and medical school without a lot of family support, while remaining my mother's caretaker, makes me believe that there was some *order* bigger than me that directed my path.

Trouble creates a capacity to handle it.
—Oliver Wendell Holmes

The next big impact on my life came during my residency at Chicago's Cook County Hospital. For the first time I saw poor people, black people, who were really sick. Our patient population was 99 percent black and our doctors were 95 percent white. I, in fact, was one of the first black residents at Cook. I would become their first black female chief resident.

I still thought that I would finish training, hang out my shingle, go into practice and make money. But I ended up visiting Nigeria and I realized my life was probably going to be different, though I didn't know how...until I got home.

The National Institutes of Health offer fellowships which provide selectees with research experience and living expenses for up to three years. At the time, no black person had ever received a fellowship and there were a lot of people who wanted me to *open the door*. I took the test and was awarded the fellowship. I spent the next three years doing research with newborns, and to this day, I consider myself, above all, a pediatrician.

Believe and act as if it were impossible to fail.
—Charles F. Kettering

While I was at Cook County, Dr. Albert Manley, the president of Spelman College, visited the hospital, and at 28, I was asked to become a member of the Board of Trustees at Spelman. I would end up marrying Dr. Manley, and when he retired his presidency, I was recruited into public health service.

I went to Washington and wound up having a 21-year career in the public health service, going from lowest rank to two-star rear admiral and deputy surgeon general of the United States, the highest rank you can attain in the service. At one time, I was not only the deputy surgeon general, but the acting surgeon general for the four years between the terms of Jocelyn Elders and David Satcher. It was a very trying time as Congress wanted to close the office of surgeon general. We had difficulty getting funding and support for the public health service. I was constantly on the *Hill* in front of new members of Congress who didn't really understand the service or its import to the public. By then I was so set in my ways that the good fight was second nature to me. I have a great deal of faith, and I felt if I just did things properly, it would all work out. If you take care of each day, each task, and do it the very best that you can, then the big picture will take care of itself. I think there's something about becoming a physician, about saving lives and dealing with life and death, that led me to take the actions I took on the *Hill.* You see something you have to do and you do it. In the last eight years of my tenure in the service, I held the four top positions. I was principle deputy, assistant secretary for health, deputy surgeon general and acting surgeon general. No one had ever accomplished this before or since.

As a 10-year-old child, I would never have thought I could have achieved what I did. Much of it was because I had people who were there for me, who gave me a stable environment, a *home.* Every child needs some kind of home in which to prepare them for life. Whether that's the classroom, the church or a boys or girls club, every child needs to find a place where they can just be, especially if things are not good at home, and believe me there are a lot of homes that are lacking in basic nurturing skills. Today, so many families are dysfunctional or disorganized. Children don't get enough early underpinning in terms of developing inner strength and the faith necessary to sustain them through life. You don't develop that in isolation. We all need help.

In every adversity there lies the seed of an equivalent advantage.
—Robert Collier

I would never go so far as to say that my mother's mental illness was a benefit to me, but much of my success was an outgrowth of it. I could have folded and withered away or stood up strong and proud to be the best person I could. I chose to be strong.

TENACIOUS & TIRELESS

In 1844, after drifting from job to job, William H. Macy opened a dry-goods store in California that quickly folded. His run of seeming bad luck continued when he opened another dry-goods store in Massachusetts, which also failed. It got worse. Macy moved to New York City, opened a store that was soon robbed and a few months later burned down. Not one to be easily dissuaded, he rebuilt the store, added new lines of merchandise and expanded. By 1869, the store was a hit, and today, Macy's Department Store continues going strong in malls and shopping centers throughout the country.

Tony Curtis

"There hasn't been a moment in my life, in anything that I've achieved, that hasn't involved some difficulty."

Screen legend Tony Curtis has enthralled the world with an unbelievable range of roles, from magician *Houdini* to the *Boston Strangler* Albert DeSalvo, from a circus star in *Trapeze* to a bootlicking press agent in *Sweet Smell of Success*, from an Oscar-nominated performance in *The Defiant Ones* to his starring turn with Jack Lemmon and Marilyn Monroe in Billy Wilder's *Some Like It Hot*. His appearances in *Operation Petticoat, Spartacus, The Great Impostor* and *The Outsider* have solidified him as one of the big screen's all-time stars. Through all his ventures, whether an actor, novelist, poet, painter or in just living life, Tony Curtis has always understood how to effectively deal with life's adversities.

There's no way I can point to a single experience or event and say that from then on, my life was changed. It's just the living of life itself. You cannot put that into words. It's too variable. Too changing. Every moment, every second we are alive provides so many inputs and impulses that it's so difficult to choose one and say, "That's what did it for me."

When you're younger, other people's judgment becomes your judgment. When you're a kid you don't have the ability to go out and do what you want, so you may end up taking on many of those judgments and suffering from them. You may face discrimination or be the object of name-calling. That happens because people try to even the score inasmuch as they don't feel that they compare to you. You have to stay out of the business of comparisons. I tried to ignore those things, saw what I wanted in my life, and then went after it. Every year, like an onion, another layer is peeled off and I see another thing I can go after.

If I was screwed up as a kid, it's because people took advantage of me. I grew up as a Jewish boy in New York City where there was a lot of anti-Semitism. You were treated like a slave, like a nothing, like you and your religion did not deserve to be on the face of the earth. It's made me open and conscious of what it means to be alive. If I had taken the anger that those people had heaped on me and heaped it back on them, before you know it, I would have been living in hateful relationships with family and friends. I'd have no way to get out of that cycle of anger. The joy of living is so powerful, there was no way that I could see my life that way.

I didn't have much formal education. After my first year of high school I joined the Navy. When I got out, I received the G.I. Bill of Rights high school diploma so I could go to an acting school. But I've educated myself. I speak six languages. I'm a painter, a writer, an actor, a poet. In whatever I do, I research it as deeply as I can. Then I'm able to do those things at an acceptable level. Acceptable to me. If I don't, I'm just going to end up frustrated.

Many of us grow up thinking of mistakes as bad, viewing errors as evidence of fundamental incapacity. This negative thinking pattern can create a self-fulfilling prophecy which undermines the learning process. To maximize our learning it is essential to ask, 'How can we get the most from every mistake we make?'
—Michael J. Gelb and Tony Buzan,
Lessons from the Art of Juggling

I try to think of the most structurally positive way to get things done. If I feel negative about something, I stop and examine it to find out why and change what is not beneficial. This has happened in marriages, marriages that I shouldn't have been in— almost every one of them.

I don't even remember the acting roles that I didn't get. For whatever reason I didn't get them, I just didn't get them. I wasn't available, I wasn't right for the part, they didn't offer enough money or I just wasn't in the right place at the right time. Someone not wanting to use me in a role didn't necessarily make me feel bad. There were certainly roles I wanted that I didn't get, but there were plenty of roles I did get that a lot of other actors wanted.

I feel like I've never made a mistake because I have done everything the way I wanted. If it didn't come through, then it didn't come through because I was personally not prepared for it. I never made the mistake of taking something, then thinking I should have taken something else. I took what I could when I could.

If you have tried to do something and failed, you are vastly better off than if you had tried to do nothing and succeeded. You must never regret what might have been. The past that did not happen is as hidden from us as the future we cannot see.
—Richard Martin Stern

You cannot live under pain, under anger. That's like living under a Hitler, under societies in which you have no say over what you do. Even in a free society you'll find yourself somehow brow-beaten by family or someone you work for, but you can't let it get to you. Today we need to reach out to kids without infringing on their privacy. Point out problems but don't blame them; make sure the environment is as stress-less as possible, allowing them to express themselves honestly. You can show kids by your own behavior how good life can be, hoping all the time that they might see things just a shade differently.

I don't go near anything unless it captivates me. I make sure that my own sense of values tells me what is right and wrong. If I do that, I don't vacillate, lie, become disagreeable, angry or frustrated. There hasn't been a moment in my life, in anything that I've achieved, that hasn't involved some difficulty. It comes with the territory. There is no way you can divorce the negatives from life. Envy, avarice and anger might keep you from accomplishing something quicker or easier, but in the end you have to get rid of the detriments around you so that you can work toward what you believe to be that best goal for you.

RED-LETTER REJECTS
Richard Bach collected 26 rejection slips before getting lucky with number 27. His book, *Jonathan Livingston Seagull: A Story*, went on to sell over 30 million copies worldwide.

Chris Crutcher

"When you are a trial-and-error species, you shouldn't go knocking the errors."

Chris Crutcher is an award-winning author and screenwriter whose novels are a reflection of real life as he sees it. His novels, *Running Loose*, *The Crazy Horse Electric Game* and *Stotan!* combine humor with difficult and serious situations. His book, *Staying Fat for Sarah Byrnes*, was praised by *School Library Journal* in a starred review as "a masterpiece by an award-winning novelist." Chris Crutcher's failure in school and teaching provided the road to his becoming a six-time ALA award-winning author.

I was a dismal student. I became the first *educational ecologist* because I recycled every bit of my brother's homework. I went through his closet and found it all. I had to go through his book reports and such, misspell some words and come to some bad conclusions.

I had a very short attention span, but when I was up against it, I would do what was necessary to get my "C." I read a sum total of one book the entire time I was in high school. I was assigned *To Kill A Mockingbird* and since it was new at the time, my brother had yet to write a book report on it. I had to actually read it. The next book they wanted me to read was *The Scarlet Letter*. I still remember that test. The only things I got right were the color and the letter.

Even though I didn't read or work hard, I guess I already had the writer in me. I had two teachers who thought I was funny, but they also thought I was out of control. As punishment, they would assign me 500-word essays. You couldn't get me to spend more than 15 minutes writing an essay for a grade, but I would stay up all night to come up with something to make these guys laugh, for no grade at all.

I wasn't sure whether I wanted to go to college, but my dad would ask, "Which service station do you want to pump gas at?" The only

"A" I received was in child/adolescent psychology. Though my academic prowess wasn't working at the highest level, my imagination was. I could take a look at headings in books and be obscure enough in my test answers to get a "C." I graduated college *summa cum lucky* and received a sociology and psychology degree, which qualified me to pour concrete bridge beams in Dallas, Texas, for $2.13 an hour. So I went back to school to get teaching credentials and became a social studies teacher. When I started teaching, I thought one day someone was going to figure out that I had no idea what I was talking about. I was pulling it out of the book as we went. I owe a class-action apology to anybody who took social studies from me.

I didn't like what I was teaching but I did like the kids. I was the magnet for the kids who weren't making it; the ones who hated school. I related well with kids. After about a year and half of teaching in public schools, I realized that if I had to do this all my life it would drive me crazy. I was in the wrong place. I had five years of college behind me, but I didn't want to get a master's degree and be a psychologist. I didn't want to put on a tie, I didn't want to go to an office, I didn't want to do construction.

I moved to the San Francisco Bay area and I found a glut of teachers in the public school system, though there were openings in the alternative schools. I went to work at Lakeside, a kindergarten-through-12th-grade school. I taught elementary classes and I was a miserable teacher. I sucked at it. I was funny and worse, you could get me off the subject in half a minute.

By virtue of just sticking around, I became the school's director. The fellow who was the money guy behind the school came around one day. I told him that the high school kids were coming to school drunk and spending much of their time dropping water balloons on elementary school kids during recess. I thought it might be a good idea if we got some of these high school kids in class. He liked the idea and I was made the school's

The only true failure lies in failure to start.
–Harold Blake Walker

head director, the guy who would handle all the problems. I agreed because it got me out of the classroom. It also gave me a chance to do a lot of *one-on-one* work with the kids. That was the place I became focused on the characters and stories I wanted to write. These kids had vicious stories with a lot of rugged upbringing. I was brought up in Cascade, Idaho, and my entire college had two black kids, and here I was in inner-city Oakland as director of a very diversified school.

A teacher's job is part teaching and part connecting. I was able to make the classroom comfortable for the student; comfortable enough that the student would be open to learn. I figure that kids, and most people for that matter, don't need advice. They need a witness. They need someone to look at their life without judging it. They need to be able to celebrate what they can and have some help to make the part of them that hurts, not hurt so much.

I always thought I had a sense of humor and could get along with almost anybody. But I didn't have a skill. I was 35 years old before I made as much as $10,000 in a single year.

One of the advantages of being disorderly is that one is constantly making exciting discoveries.
—A. A. Milne

When I left Lakeside I left teaching behind and went to Spokane, Washington, in hopes of selling running shoes. But when I arrived in Spokane, I found that running shoes had gotten way too complicated for me to sell. I saw an ad in the paper for child protection team coordinator. I called and asked what a child protection team coordinator was and he said, "We're not sure." I said, "That sounds like the job for me." I ended up coordinating a team of pediatricians, mental-health specialists, nurses and cops who give child protection workers advice on their tougher cases. There I learned the system and made good contacts with the mental-health therapists. At that time, with a bachelor's degree, you could get the necessary hours for a therapist's license right on the job. The job was all about connecting with people, tenacity, helping to bring a family together, among many other things. Success wasn't always imminent, but the belief in it was.

I knew author Terry Davis, who wrote *Vision Quest*. I would edit his chapters for believability. By the time his book was finished, I realized I could do what Terry was doing. I had my own story so I sat down and wrote it. It was the first time I ever remember being really focused about anything that required me to sit down. I sent it to Terry, who sent it to his agent, and in less than a week she said she would represent it. It sold quickly.

> *The only time you don't fail is the last time you try anything—and it works.*
> *—William Strong*

I had gotten a book published, but I still felt I pulled the wool over everyone's eyes. Even though my first book had done well, when I sat down to do the second one, I thought, "What do I do now?" I had no story and I had an editor who was waiting for one. So I went back into my swimming background and came up with some bizarre characters which became my book, *Stotan!*. Then I knew I was on my way. I never called myself a teacher. I never called myself a therapist. But I had no problem calling myself a writer.

As a teacher, I felt like a failure. But when I look back, teaching brought me to those kids and grown-ups on the outside; the ones who had to struggle. And that character trait has become the basis for my books.

There's a part of me that says no matter what would have happened in my life I would have eventually found my way to writing. I was always good with words.

All the things that I expected to happen in my life never did happen. I realized that you have to wipe away all expectations. Somebody else puts those in your head. You have to look at what makes you sing, what makes you fly, what makes you want to come back and check it out.

All your life people tell you how to proceed, giving you a recipe for your life. What you're supposed to do, what you're not supposed to do—when you're bad, when you're good. But it's not about people, it's about you. You have to find your passion and not let anyone tell you that you can't have it. You might not be able to have it the way you want it, but if you keep working at it you will have it the way that works best for you.

I wanted to be a writer a lot more than I wanted to write. That wasn't enough. You have to fall in love with what you do, not with what you want to be or with making a name for yourself.

When you reach for the stars, you may not quite get one, but you won't come up with a handful of mud either.
—*Leo Burnett*

I had no idea there was such a thing as *young adult* literature. For God's sake, I write for people who don't read. But by telling my stories, I've been told that I created a place and genre in which no one else was writing. I didn't do it by deciding to be a writer of that genre. I did it by research and I hung out with people who were beating the hell out of each other and trying to *get up* on one another; bouncing around from one foster home to another, having no place where they felt they belonged. When I try to understand others I also learn about myself.

The bad news is, there will always be a struggle. The good news is, the struggle is where the story is. When I look back to those who had stunned me, who stood up for themselves, who worked with the cards they were dealt, I see heroes. I may have become a writer despite the path I was on, but without it I would never have had the ideas for the stories that I write. I wouldn't have ever known that those ideas even existed.

When you are a trial-and-error species, you shouldn't go knocking the errors. You should be celebrating them.

FREEZING FAUX PAS

In 1905, 11-year-old Frank Epperson mixed up a drink made from soda powder. The next morning, after leaving the drink outside in exceedingly frigid weather, he discovered a stick of frozen soda water. In 1923, Epperson began producing Epsicles in fruit flavors. The name Epsicle was later changed to Popsicle® and summer would never be the same.

Dr. Peter Doherty

"If I had gone into something to which I was more suited, I would have never won the Nobel Prize."

Dr. Peter Doherty is professor of biomedical research and chair of the Immunology Department at St. Jude Children's Research Hospital in Tennessee. He is distinguished for his study of major antigens' role in immune recognition, particularly in virus-infected cells. He shared the 1996 Nobel Prize for Physiology or Medicine with Rolf Zinkernagel and was named Australian of the Year in 1997. But none of this might have happened if Peter Doherty had not made what, at the time, seemed like a devastatingly poor career decision.

As a kid, I always felt I was a failure.

I grew up in the north of Australia where it was really hot. Very high ultraviolet intensity. There was no such thing as sun block and I have fair, Irish skin, so I didn't fit into the bronze, surf-god culture that existed around there. 'Course you go back there now and all those people over the age of 40 look like rhinoceroses. Along with my stark pallor, I was surrounded by the Northern Australian sports frenzy and I was a klutz. Couldn't throw or catch a ball. Not very coordinated. I just didn't fit in. To make it worse, I was socially inept. My entire family was a bit odd. So, I spent all my time reading and back then you weren't supposed to do that. We had sort of the moronic American high school culture that's portrayed in all those bad teen movies. Absolutely devoid of any intellectual product whatsoever. We're talking about Australia in the '50s and early '60s, which was a lot like America. Kind of a complacent, boring place. Somebody

> *If you don't learn from your mistakes, there's no sense making them.*
> *—Anonymous*

described Australia as Kansas with beaches. Incredible tedium. Today it's much more interesting and varied. And here I was, interested in things that people in Australia aren't very interested in. Like individual liberty.

No wonder I always felt like an outsider and any kids I got along with were also on the outside and perhaps a bit odd. A bit more introspective. It drove me to look at things unemotionally. If you crash a few times, the last thing you want to do is react emotionally. I felt it would destroy me, so I came to look at situations analytically. And with that, I came to expect a fair amount of failure and found negativity in almost everything.

Failure is, in a sense, the highway to success, inasmuch as every discovery of what is false leads us to seek earnestly after what is true, and every fresh experience points out some form of error which we shall afterward carefully avoid.
—John Keats

At 17, I went directly from high school into veterinary medicine. Clearly too young to make that sort of decision. At the time, with Australia dominated by the rural agricultural industries, I became very enthused with the idea that people didn't have enough food in the world. I was going to do research on food-producing animals, which I now see as a very adolescent view of the world.

There were three years of basic science that was rigorous and intellectually satisfying, unfortunately you also had to deal with dogs and cats and worse than that, you had to deal with the people who owned those dogs and cats. It was appalling. I had no facility for that at all. I wasn't all that interested if dogs or cats died. It was a rather moot point. If you needed another dog you just went out and got a new one. So I got very depressed about the whole thing and bought a lot of cars and drank too much beer, which was a fairly common student thing to do. I was lucky to graduate. It was a mistake to have gone into veterinary medicine. If I had gone into something where I would have been more well suited, it would have been literature or language.

But veterinary school, as bad a career decision as it seemed at the time, placed me in a field where I could move into research. Amazingly, if I had originally gone into something where I was more suited, I would have never won the Nobel Prize.

Once I was in the research field, there were the usual disasters in experiments. You take something to a point where you can't take it any further. Usually that's because the technology doesn't exist to take it further or the method hasn't been invented yet. That's just the limits of the game. Or it can be an oversight. I remember looking down a microscope and missing something that turned out to be very important. You may be looking for one thing and fail to find it, but because of that research, you discover something you may never have found if you hadn't headed down that path. The reason we won the Nobel Prize was that we set up an experiment to look at one thing, and in doing that, we found something else. When we recognized that it was something else, we followed up on that.

The most exciting phrase to hear in science, the one that heralds new discoveries, is not 'Eureka!' (I found it!) but 'That's funny...'
—Isaac Asimov

Originally, we were looking into something where the techniques we had never would have given us a satisfactory answer. But the result we received was totally unexpected. We followed up on that for a couple of years. And that became the Nobel-winning work.

There were a number of frustrations over those years. We had made an important discovery which resulted in publishing some observations. At first, everyone found great difficulty in understanding them. When they finally did understand and followed up, they found that our observations were right. It caused an entire shift in that field of immunology. Everybody changed their viewpoints.

We then proposed an entire theory around it. It took a long time to show that theory to be true because, at that time, the technique didn't exist. Fact is, most of the work to prove our theory had to be done by other people who did different sorts of science.

In doing experimental research, a lot of what you do is fail. It's the nature of the beast. If you're trying to do new things, something that hasn't been done before, much of the experiments you do and the avenues you go down don't work out. Therefore, anyone who is involved with research and does this all the time has to be fairly resilient. Often it can be a technical failure or something wrong in the system. Or it can be that the results turn out to be what you originally set out to do but they're not nearly as interesting as you had hoped. All scientists deal with this, so it becomes part of the scientific personality. Successful scientists are generally rebuffed people. They're used to crashing. More so than most people in society. Most of the things people do tend to deal with things along very predictable lines. Scientists don't work on predictable lines, and if we do, we're not very imaginative scientists.

I failed over and over in my life...that is why I succeed.
—Michael Jordan

While the Nobel Prize was a wonderful recognition of my work, I don't consider it to be my greatest success. It was my experiments themselves that took me to my discovery. The Nobel Prize was only the acknowledgment of that success. It is always the journey that leads to the breakthrough that is the real success.

TENACIOUS & TIRELESS

Game company founder, Milton Bradley, who had wanted to be a lithographer, completed his first big project for the Republican National Convention in 1860. He produced photographs of their candidate, Abraham Lincoln, but by the time Lincoln won the election, he had grown a beard and no longer resembled the photographs. With the photographs and no other business to be had, Bradley was about to go out of business when a board game that he had been working on was sold. "The Checkered Game of Life," which later became "The Game of Life," sold 45,000 copies and Milton Bradley was on his way to a new and lifelong career.

Chuck Lorre

"When I'm beaten into submission and I become teachable, then it seems I make choices that turn out to be stunningly good ones."

Writer-producer Chuck Lorre enjoys one of the television industry's most successful track records. Creating such hit shows like *Grace Under Fire, Cybill* and *Dharma & Greg*, Lorre has his reputation built on a career of terrific characters, big laughs and great ratings. Chuck Lorre's whole life has also been built on many failures that gave birth to many successes.

Prior to the draft that became the *Grace Under Fire* pilot, I fought and argued and screamed over what the show should be.

Prior to *Dharma & Greg*, I had what I thought were great ideas, and no one was going to get in my way. I was very determined, very rigid and not very open-minded. I was going to execute these bright ideas. And I failed and I failed and I failed. I got my brains beaten out. It was humiliating and it was suffocating, it was exhausting and I was filled with despair. I didn't have the facility to open myself up to being teachable earlier in the process. If I did, I would have saved myself a lot of suffering and these corporations a hell of a lot of money because failure in the television production business is very expensive. I take it personally. When I waste money on a TV show that doesn't work, I feel it could have been spent on computers for a school or for inoculating children against diseases as opposed to blowing it on a failed sitcom.

In the late '80s, I developed *Cybill* [Cybill Shepherd's TV series] out of a failed screenplay I wrote, *The Road to Beirut*, that I couldn't give away. It was about two upper-middle-class divorcées from the valley who are both very angry about their lot in life and the bizarre turn of events that lead them to Beirut. Beirut in the '80s, what a wonderful place for a romantic comedy. The screenplay became very functional as a doorstop. But the relationship I created between those two women was still very good. When I was approached to develop a show for Cybill Shepherd, Tom Werner [Carsey-Werner Productions] asked me to consider using the relationship from my screenplay. Their friendship became the heart of the series. From that failed screenplay came the pilot for *Cybill.* It was the fertilizer, the compost, for the series.

When Christine Baranski read for the part of Maryann, I hadn't written the pilot yet, so she and Cybill read a part from the screenplay and it was magical. They were fantastic together. There was a great chemistry between the two of them.

> *The greatest failure is a person who never admits that he can be a failure.*
> —Gerald N. Weiskott

We then had trouble finding the right person for Cybill's younger daughter. It seemed like an uncastable part. Then this remarkable actress, Alicia Witt, came to read. She was nothing like the character I envisioned, yet she was perfect. We got her because of patience, because we didn't make a panic choice. From that point on, everything fell into place, and it was so much fun.

The writing process was delightful. I was starting to exert a bit more power in my career, taking fewer notes [from the network], and I had the support of Cybill Shepherd to follow my heart. The show was a breakout hit from the day it debuted. Then we came back for the second season and everything changed.

Cybill was no longer happy with the process or with her role in the show. She didn't like the character anymore. She didn't like the fact that Christine's character not only had a fan base but she had won an Emmy after just 13 episodes. Cybill was nominated but she didn't win.

I always thought the way to make her and her character succeed was to make her vulnerable. To make her flawed. She's a beautiful woman and she was playing a successful-enough actress to live in a beautiful home, wear nice clothes, drive a cool car and eat in fabulous restaurants. I thought that the only way to make that kind of woman accessible was to see that she's hurting, that she's wounded, that she's confused, frightened and that, regardless of her trappings, she's as bewildered as anyone else.

Cybill was deeply unhappy with the first scripts of the new season. They were really just a continuation of what we were doing the first season. She was making demands and I was intransigent. Cybill wanted jokes taken away from Baranski and given to her even though they were inappropriate for her. She was in story lines that were wonderful. I wrote a *Cybill* script with Alan Ball [Academy Award-winning writer of *American Beauty*]. We never shot it. It was hilarious. One of the funniest things I've ever been involved in and we never got to shoot it because Cybill decided that the story was hateful and homophobic. I wrote it with Alan who was about as *out* as you can get. We had to trash the whole script that we were deeply in love with. It was becoming a real nightmare doing the show, week in and week out.

They wanted me to fire a writer that Cybill didn't like and I wouldn't do it. She couldn't make me fire a writer. I didn't fire anyone who worked for her and she couldn't fire anyone who worked for me. The writer was a very productive and good writer and very important to the show. On the most holy day of the Jewish year, Yom Kippur, after shooting four or five episodes in the second season, I got a call from some underling at the Carsey-Werner company telling me not to come into work. This was four weeks into the second season and Cybill had fired me. I think she fundamentally felt that I was hurting the show and her career.

I was blindsided. That first season was so successful. It was such a love fest. I didn't see this coming, but by that point I was so beaten and exhausted, though surprised, I was also relieved. It had become such a mean and hateful environment. Having been on *Roseanne* for two years where there was a lot of discomfort and then *Grace Under Fire* for a year, I just couldn't tolerate it anymore. I didn't

> *Sometimes a noble failure serves the world as faithfully as a distinguished success.*
> —Edward Dowden

have the skin to protect me. I have some suspicions that I had a nervous breakdown. I became incapable of working for a while or doing much of anything. I went through remorse, regret, shame, embarrassment, humiliation, grief, apathy, anger, rage.

Thought is born of failure.
—Lancelot Law Whyte

I ran into [CBS President] Les Moonves who said, "Hey Chuck, what is it with you and these broads?" Perhaps there is a phenomenon in this world where you're supposed to learn a lesson and if you don't, it just keeps coming back until you get it. Still, there was an understanding in the industry, apparently, that the women I was working with were part of the reason things didn't work out. It wasn't like I was having difficulty working with Mother Teresa. I certainly haven't been the easiest person in the world to work with, but it takes two for one to get stabbed in the heart.

The result of the *Cybill* firing was that when I got to Fox [Television] I was determined to do a show from a male perspective. I thought I had found the perfect actor for that...Jim Belushi. The show failed. But out of that failure came the seeds of *Dharma & Greg*.

There was a scene in the Belushi pilot I had written that was never shot. In it, Jim meets up with an unbelievable woman who changes his life dramatically. He is literally swept away by her incandescence. When I was approached to develop something for Jenna Elfman, I sent that scene to her and from that scene, from that busted pilot, came *Dharma & Greg*.

Every element came together. You only see that in hindsight, but when you're on the right track it almost seems like, as Dharma would say, you're getting something from the universe. If you're doing what you're supposed to be doing, the sea parts. When I'm beaten into submission and I become teachable, then it seems I make choices that turn out to be stunningly good ones. The parts of the puzzle come together beautifully.

How many lightbulbs did Edison make before he found one that worked? I've made a lot of crappy lightbulbs. Prior to my reaching any success, I have to have some person, some institution or some variation of some outside force knock me senseless before I'm willing to surrender, throw my hands up in despair and say, "Okay, I give up." The remarkable result is that I become open to something appropriate, doable and absolutely wonderful.

HORRENDOUS HYPOTHESES

"Who the hell wants to hear actors talk?"

–Harry Warner, Warner Brothers, 1927,

in response to the advent of talking pictures.

Problems are to the mind what exercise

is to the muscles, they toughen and make strong.

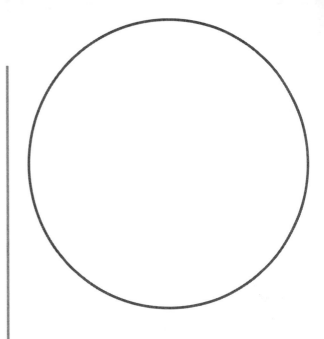

—Norman Vincent Peale

Bill Walton

"It wasn't until I lost the ability to play that I was able to understand."

One of the greatest basketball players of all time, college and pro, William Theodore Walton, III lead UCLA to two NCAA titles, including an all-time record 88 straight game-winning streak. He was a three-time recipient of the NCAA Player of the Year Award, a three-time All-American College Player and winner of the Sullivan Award as Best Amateur Athlete of 1973. As a scholar/athlete, he earned Academic All-American honors three years in a row. As a pro, he led the Portland Trailblazers to an NBA title, garnering Most Valuable Player honors in 1978. In 1997, he was named one of the 50 Greatest Players of All Time. Today Walton is one of television's most respected sports commentators.

It's difficult to imagine someone at this level of success having any type of problem, let alone self-doubt. But Walton's on-the-court accomplishments were often plagued by innumerable injuries and fear. In the end, a glorious career was cut much too short by those injuries. Even more stunning to discover was that this award-winning broadcaster was a severe stutterer until the age of 28. It is not too surprising to find that Walton used basketball to insulate himself from much of his pain. Without that pain, Walton may not have become the success he is today.

"Life is easy when you're hot. . .when you're in the zone. . .when all your jumpers are going down. But what happens when the ball bounces the other way? What happens when you're faced with January 19, 1974 at Notre Dame with a 12-point lead with minutes to go [71-70 loss ending the 88-game winning streak]? How do you handle March 23, 1974 at Greensboro with an 11-point lead in the second half [double over-time loss to North Carolina State in the NCAA semi-final]?"

I was once laughed out of speech class at UCLA. I had to give a speech and I couldn't. I couldn't speak at all until I was 28. When you're a stutterer, your whole life is affected by it. You can't communicate, you don't feel comfortable. You can't express yourself. You can't be you. You're so self-conscious about it and you're so reluctant to ever get involved with anything. You know you can't speak and it's just a harrowing nightmare existence.

I had always used basketball as a sanctuary; a protective shield. It was my religion. The gym was my church. It was also a convenient way to avoid my responsibilities, to keep from developing my human relation skills. I was good enough in basketball to never address the weaknesses I had. All I wanted to do was be a basketball player. That's what I lived for. That's what I loved.

It was only then, when basketball was no longer an option and there was absolutely no way I could ever play again, that I realized it wasn't basketball that I really loved. It was the effort to win, the competition, the effort to do a good job. It was the failures and adversities in my life that made me a better and happier person. While I didn't appreciate or understand it at the time, that was everything [UCLA basketball] Coach [John] Wooden was telling us virtually each and every day. We thought he was nuts, a lunatic, a walking antique...the stuff he would tell us. We thought we were great. All-Americans. We were winning 88 games in a row. It wasn't until our senior year that things fell apart for us. It wasn't until we left Wooden at UCLA that we realized he wasn't just teaching us about basketball, he was teaching us about life; teaching us about the problems that would invariably be there and what to do when the ball bounces the other way. I always wanted him to talk about strategy and basketball, but all he wanted to talk about was people and the great emotions that drive the human spirit. While I wanted something else from him, what

> *Well, well, what's that?*
> *Come up with a smiling face,*
> *It's nothing against you to fall down flat*
> *But to lie there—that's a disgrace.*
> *—Edmund Vance Cooke,*
> How Did You Die?

he was doing was teaching me how to become a man, a teacher; some-one who could do something else other than play; someone who could use his mind, make a contribution and not just score a basket.

When I joined the Portland Trailblazers, things like trust, con-fidence and loyalty, friendship and cooperation, all the elements that went into making a great team, were shattered. For the first time in my life, I was on a team that wasn't a team. It was now about selfishness, creepiness, individualism and who was making how much money. It was an absolute nightmare. I couldn't believe my whole life was falling apart. It made me angry and I didn't know how to deal with it.

The team problems were rectified when new coach Jack Ramsey was hired. But it was only golden for about a year and a half before my chronic foot problem returned, and with it, the other problems of dis-trust and accusations of me being a malingerer. All the elements that made it so great being on the team, after being so perfect, just totally disappeared again.

The injuries I endured during my playing career were devastat-ing. They ruined everything. At the time I didn't know what was hap-pening, and what was happening seemed totally out of my control. The doctors at that time said there was nothing really wrong with me. They told me this was all mental. I was sent me to a hypnotist. Later, I was sent to a faith healer. Still, I couldn't walk or run. That was because my injuries weren't in my mind. They were real stress injuries from playing too much basketball. I was given a big shot of Xylocaine and told that everything would be fine. I went out there and played with an undiagnosed stress fracture and then...the bone split in half.

I am always doing what I cannot do in order that I may learn how to do it.
—Pablo Picasso

When I went to the [San Diego] Clippers, I really couldn't play. Every time I tried, my foot would break. I'd stop playing and it would get better. Then I'd go out again and try to play...and it would break.

Later I would join the Boston Celtics where the legendary Red Auerbach and Larry Bird gave me back my career and my life. Still, up until that point, I defined everything in terms of basketball. I was always singularly focused on being the best basketball player I could be. Then, on March 15, 1990, they fused my ankle and I knew I would never play again.

I knew I would never run up and down that court yelling and screaming. I would never feel that wind blowing through my hair and feel that sweat just pouring down my body. Never get a well-placed elbow in somebody's rib cage and run back into the game. I knew it was all over. I was terrified, scared to death that I would never find anything. As I look back, I understand that was really the beginning.

> *To succeed means that you may have to step out of line and march to the sound of your own drummer.*
> *–Keith DeGreen*

I was 28 when a chance encounter at a social event with Hall of Fame broadcaster Marty Glickman completely changed my life in so many ways that things have never been the same since, nor have they ever been better. That day, in a very brief, private conversation (one way, mind you, since I literally could not speak at the time), Marty explained, patiently and concisely, that talking and communicating was a skill, not a gift or a birthright and that like any skill, whether it be sports, music, business or whatever, needed to be developed over a lifetime of hard work, discipline, organization and practice.

Marty gave me some simple tips that day and then encouraged me to take those keys and apply them to methods of learning that I had received from the special teachers that I had come across in my life, particularly the six Hall of Fame basketball coaches who I had played for throughout my career. The beginning of my whole new life was as simple as that.

There were no gimmicks, tricks or shortcuts. Just the realization that with some help, guidance and a lot of hard work I, too, could do what seemed so easy, simple and natural to everyone else, yet appeared impossibly out of my reach and comprehension.

Marty taught me how to learn, which has changed my life and given me a whole new life. I have gone from a person who literally could not say thank you, to someone who makes his living as a television commentator and public speaker. I have also become a spokesperson for the National Stuttering Foundation.

I was told to become a teacher to anyone, anywhere, on any subject. Start with young kids with a topic that you know. They won't care about your limitations. All they care about is that you are willing to spend time with them and are trying to give them the gift of knowledge. Move forward and don't be afraid to fail. Confidence will come out of repetition. If I can do it, why can't you? When you stumble, stop, then start again. Find your pace, your rhythm, your game. Everyone makes mistakes. It's what you do after those mistakes that will determine your ultimate success and happiness. Turnovers [mistakes] that come from taking action mean you're a player. As we say in basketball, "Never up, never in."

Adversity is another way to measure the greatness of individuals. I never had a crisis that didn't make me stronger.
—Lou Holtz

I have now found that everything that existed on the team existed in the rest of the world, too. All the elements of the team, the preparation, the visualization; all those things that made being a basketball player great exist in every walk of life. They were the lessons that Coach Wooden was trying to teach me. Today, my relationship with Coach Wooden is better than it's ever been. And it has held me in good stead with other problems and other ventures in my life.

And as my mom has said, who would have ever thought that little Billy Walton, with his red hair, freckles and speech problem, would now be sitting next to people like Dick Enberg, Bob Costas, Greg Gumbel and Marv Albert on national TV!

I'm a better and happier person today than I ever would have been had I never gotten hurt; had I never had this nightmarish speech problem. But it wasn't until I lost the ability to play that I could truly understand that.

PERSEVERING PROSPECT

A shoulder injury while playing minor league baseball seemed to end Jim Morris' dream of becoming a big-league pitcher. It wasn't until 12 years later, at the age of 35, when most professional athletes have already retired, that the high school players Morris coached made a deal with him: if they won the district championship, Morris would again try out for the Major Leagues. They did, he did, and with a fast-ball some ten-miles-an-hour faster than before his injury, he ended up being selected by and pitching the 1999 and 2000 seasons for the major league Tampa Bay Devil Rays.

Garry Marshall

"I learned that you can't really die of embarrassment. It only feels that way."

Garry Marshall has established himself as one of Hollywood's most respected writers, producers and directors of television, film and theater. Marshall has created and executive-produced some of the longest-running and most celebrated sitcoms in American television history, including *Happy Days*, *Laverne & Shirley*, *The Odd Couple* and *Mork and Mindy*. He has directed such successful films as *Pretty Woman*, *Nothing in Common*, *Beaches* and *The Princess Diaries*. His numerous acting stints include a regular role on TV's *Murphy Brown* and his memorable turn as a casino owner in Albert Brooks' *Lost in America*. Marshall has received the American Comedy Award's Lifetime Achievement Award and, in 1997, Marshall was inducted into the Academy of Television Arts and Sciences' Television Academy Hall of Fame. But it was his inability to go out and play with the other kids that first drove Garry Marshall over to the funny side. In college, it was failing to get the facts right that made Marshall realize that he was much better at making them up.

Some people look at a glass and see it half empty while others see it half full. I always figured that no matter what was in the glass, I was probably allergic to it.

As a little boy, I was sick all the time. I mean, coughing, wheezing, burning with a fever. Sick because of allergies. Not small allergic reactions to rare things, but major reactions to an awesome number of common things that most people take for granted. One doctor diagnosed my allergic reaction to 128 foods and pollens. Growing up, I wasted a lot of time being afraid over the smallest things and thinking I was near death from my allergies and ailments.

We had no TV back then, so to pass the time when I was sick in bed, I would cut out cartoons from comic books and newspapers and rate them. When I ran out of jokes to read from the books, I started writing them myself. I learned what jokes worked best, and that a sense of humor could help me survive.

By the time I was ready for college, I had no idea what I wanted to be. Even though my dad rarely encouraged me or helped me with my homework because he was usually out entertaining clients from his advertising firm, I asked him for his advice.

"Garry, you're probably going to be sick the rest of your life. You'd better pick a job you could do with a toothache, stomachache, headache or whateverache."

I decided that writing might be a job I could do if I was in bed with a fever and that maybe my daydreaming would be an asset. So I applied to colleges with journalism programs and ended up at Chicago's Northwestern University.

During my freshman year I learned a valuable lesson. There was no way I was going to be a journalist. In classes I was constantly getting into trouble because I couldn't get the facts straight. The first story assigned was to write a living person's obituary. I got sidetracked by a girl and ended up not doing the project. I knew I had to hand in something so I wrote, "Danny Kaye, who was reported dead earlier today, didn't die at all. It was a false alarm. He was sick, but he recovered."

> *Look at every obstacle as an opportunity.*
> *—Dr. Wayne Dyer*

My teacher said, "What is this?

"You made up he was dead, so I made up he was alive."

The teacher gave me a "D." I should have taken this as an early sign that journalism wasn't for me. Even though I continued butchering the traditional rules of journalism, I learned that you can't really die of embarrassment. It only feels that way.

Cultivating confidence and learning not to be afraid of failure is very easy to talk about, but not so easy to do. I began to believe that if you are not totally afraid of failure, if fear doesn't paralyze you, if you can work under pressure, then you've got a shot.

I have failed with dozens of other pilots and shows, including the unfortunate *Me and the Chimp* and a showgirl sitcom called *Blansky's Beauties*, which I tried to make five different ways and failed with each one. The important thing was that though I didn't enjoy failure, I got up the next day and tried to think of another show. I subscribe to the words of Samuel Beckett. "Try. I fail. Fail better."

> *Little minds are tamed and subdued by misfortunes; but great minds rise above them.*
> *—Washington Irving*

But a director can't become obsessed with reviews, because with critics you simply can't win with any consistency. I've gotten good reviews (*"Pretty Woman* is the most satisfying romantic comedy in years"—Vincent Canby, and about *Nothing in Common,* "Uncommonly splendid. Director Garry Marshall mixes comedy and drama with admirable ease"—Guy Flatley, *Cosmopolitan*) and bad (about a Chrysler Theatre TV special called *Think Pretty:* "Even Fred Astaire's dazzling feet could not lift Marshall and Belson's script above mediocre"—*The Hollywood Reporter,* and about *Frankie and Johnny,* "Primetime cuteness permeates the movie like air freshener. People don't speak. They quip. This is *Happy Days* with an apron on"—*The Washington Post*).

Whenever you go into show business you will get all kinds of criticism. A director, obviously, has little control over the reviews, but I hoped they would never say that I did a quirky job or that I sloughed it. No matter what, I always try to give the audience and my employer their money's worth. I've learned not to take a look at reviews until at least six months after a project is out. In the case of *Exit to Eden,* I waited nine months. Usually the studio or sometimes a mean friend tells me if they were generally good or bad.

Most people make the mistake of trying to beat down their flaws or deny them altogether. Don't use your flaws as an excuse to quit. I've always found it best to say, "Here are my flaws. Now, what tools do I have that will make me stand out?" And when I find that, I figure that out, I find what I'm good at.

I have a small statue of Sisyphus. The statue depicts a man in Hades who was forced to repeatedly push a large boulder up a hill. Each time he reaches the top of the hill, the rock falls back down to the bottom, and he has to go down the hill and push it up again. The myth is probably the source of my positive attitude toward show business. When the guy is walking down the hill to get the boulder again, he has a choice. He can say, "I'm sweaty and hot and I've got to push that damn boulder up again," or he can say, "Here's a nice break. I don't have to push that rock again until I get to the bottom. I can walk down the hill, whistling and pushing nothing." I've always tried to make great use of my *walking down the hill* time because often that's the happiest it gets.

> *Each is given*
> *a bag of tools,*
> *A shapeless mass,*
> *a book of rules;*
> *And each must make,*
> *ere life is flown,*
> *A stumbling-block or*
> *a steppingstone.*
> *—R. L. Sharpe,*
> A Bag of
> Tools

(Portions excerpted from the book, Wake Me When It's Funny, *by permission of Garry Marshall.)*

TERRIBLE TIP

"Try any other profession."

–John Murray Anderson,

Anderson School of Drama instructor to the young Lucille Ball.

Ann Richards

"Alcoholism and my additional treatment ended up becoming the most wonderful, most instructive, most important experience I've had in my life."

Ann Richards, former governor of Texas and role model extraordinaire, served on President Carter's Advisory Committee for Women. In 1988, she delivered a rousing keynote address at the Democratic National Convention and followed up by chairing the convention in 1992. As state treasurer, she became Texas's first woman to be elected to state office in 50 years. But with the great public challenges she faced on the state and national stage, it was her battle with personal flaws that delivered Ann Richards her finest triumph.

I always had such high expectations of myself. Whatever it was, I was going to be the best—the best mother, the best wife, the best entertainer, the best nurse. Of course, I could never live up to those expectations. So I drank. When I drank it repressed all my feelings of inadequacy. It made me feel cuter, funnier and smarter. Some people can have a couple of drinks and stop. With me there was no stopping. As years went on, I needed to have more and more alcohol just to feel what a little alcohol used to do for me.

> *Do not look where you fell,*
> *but where you slipped.*
> *—African Proverb*

It was while I was working very hard as county commissioner that I realized my marriage was falling apart. My drinking became worse, not because of the marriage, but because it lessened the pain of living.

I knew something was wrong. One day I told my doctor that I thought I drank too much. He asked me how much I drank. Now, if you're an addict, you're a liar. I told him I might have, two, three, maybe four martinis before dinner. He said he drank that much himself. So much for medical help.

In January of 1980, a friend tricked me into coming over to her father's house where I was surprised by a group of my friends and family. There were so many there it looked like the Last Supper. They had planned an intervention in which each person took turns telling me what I had done to embarrass them when I drank. It was frightening. I was on an airplane that afternoon to St. Mary's in Minneapolis. I haven't had a drink since. That was over 20 years ago.

> *Be not ashamed of mistakes and thus make them crimes.*
> —*Confucius*

My alcoholism and my subsequent treatment ended up becoming the most wonderful, most instructive, most important experience I've had in my life. There is never a time in your life when you are granted 30 days to spend looking at yourself, scrutinizing the way you live your life and coming to some conclusions about how you want to lead your life in the future. Even if you were offered those 30 days, you probably wouldn't take them. Certainly you wouldn't spend them the way I was forced to. I had to totally stop what I was doing and look at myself. I looked at the people I loved and the manner in which I was leading my life. It was such a gift. I think I was there about a week and a half before I got over my anger at my friends and family for confronting me with my alcoholism and my behavior. Once my anger decreased, I was able to understand just how much I was loved by those people to do what they did. I'm not an easy person to confront. It must have been agonizingly difficult.

The result was that I learned a lot about myself and the addiction of alcoholism. I became part the wonderful support group of Alcoholics Anonymous. It's a place where I can be drawn out of my isolation, where I can let go of my resentments, where my "poor me" thoughts are lifted and I'm set right again. So it really was a life-altering experience, for the better.

I think failure, by definition, gets a bad rap. The assumption that it is an irretrievable error is simply not true. I am no different from most people. If something turned out well, I thought I got lucky, that there was some serendipitous collision of the stars that took place to make something good happen. But if I fail, if something goes awry, then I'm pretty sure it's all my fault. As a consequence, I will sit and examine what I did wrong or how it went wrong. In that reexamination, I learned a lot. I learned how not to do that again. I learned what the impetus was within me that produced that failure.

Affliction comes to us, not to make us sad but sober; not to make us sorry but wise.
—Henry Ward Beecher

I have always thought that failure was the greatest learning experience one could have. I'm naturally not a Pollyanna optimist, but I've learned that you have only one life and this is it. You might as well make the very best of it.

When I lost the governor's seat to George W. Bush, I was immediately saddened by it—for about five seconds. I did feel badly for the people who worked so hard for me, but I learned that no matter how good you feel about your record, and no matter how positively people feel about it, it will not get you reelected. I learned that you run on what you are going to do and not on what you've done in the past.

I knew that the important thing for me was to move on. One of the positive things you can do when you fail is to set a new course. I had to change my mind and keep my feet moving. I realized that I probably had 20 years left in which I'd have all my faculties, so I made a list of what I wanted in those next 20 years. Realizing the new opportunities made a dramatic change for me.

When I was a practicing alcoholic, I didn't have full control over using and changing my mind. Sobriety has freed me to deal with failure and never give up.

The one thing you can count on in life is change, and the only thing to worry about is how you're going to adapt to that change. Change your mind and you can set yourself on an entirely new, wonderful and adventurous course.

I am never a failure
until I begin blaming others.
—Anonymous

MOLDY MISTAKES

In 1928, scientist Alexander Fleming left some bacteria samples he was working on by an open window. When he returned later, he found that mold spores had contaminated one of the samples. Fleming noticed the mold was dissolving the bacteria. Today, Fleming's botched experiment became the remedy for many an infection—penicillin.

Al Franken
(with special guest, Stuart Smalley)

"The fact is, there's no logical reason why someone should be able to create anything."

Any fan of NBC's *Saturday Night Live* remembers the phrase, "...but how will this all affect me, Al Franken?" It was repeated many times by him, Al Franken. Since 1975, Franken, with his partner, Tom Davis, became an important part of making *Saturday Night Live* a weekly success and viewing ritual in millions of homes. In front of the camera, Franken's *Daily Affirmations with Stuart Smalley* became a frequent sketch on *SNL* and led to the feature film, *Stuart Saves His Family*. A noted political commentator and satirist, Franken also produced and starred in the NBC sitcom *Lateline*.

My father didn't graduate from high school. Before my older brother, no one in our family had gone to college. My brother entered M.I.T. and received a degree in physics. He ended up becoming a photographer. I went to Harvard, met Tom Davis, and became a comedian. You'd think my parents would freak out, but instead they were both behind us.

I like collaborating. When you're with someone else and you run up against a problem, you're both in the same boat. It gets you going. If you make an appointment to show up, you gotta show up.

As Franken and Davis, Tom and I performed at the Comedy Store and Improvisation in Los Angeles. We were together when we got hired on our first big gig, *Saturday Night Live*. Most of the years at *SNL* we wrote and worked together. We always thought the show would be a success because we were on it. There was a lot of that thinking going on around the show. There is much to say for humility, but not on *SNL* back then. I thought the only thing that would stop me were the idiots who didn't know what I was doing. Back then, it was the arrogance of youth that kept me going. We were extremely successful and I found it very difficult to learn through success.

After 20 years, my partnership with Tom ended. That was very painful and scary. Tom was hilarious and I felt he had tools that I didn't have. I'm always fearful at the beginning of any new project, in fact, now more than when I was younger. Without Tom as my partner, I would be continuing my career, for the first time in many years, alone.

With only myself to look to, I went to my strengths. I have pretty good taste in material, a good instinct for what works and what doesn't work and I work hard. I continued to do those same things and found I was able to work alone quite well.

The problem I had with my failed television show, *Lateline*, was not the NBC creative people. They never messed with the material. It was with the NBC programming people who never really got behind the show, in promotion or scheduling. It went a long way in souring me on sitcoms. We shot 19 shows. It was all consuming. It is one thing to have it all pay off, and it's another thing to have it…kind of fade out. The hardest part of doing a TV show happens in the first year. I did an awful lot of work, acting, writing and producing.

> *I thank God for my handicaps for, through them, I have found myself, my work and my God.*
> —*Helen Keller*

I learned from *Lateline's* failure. I learned that I do not want to be a writer, producer and actor on the same sitcom again. That's not to say I wouldn't try it again without all the time-consuming responsibility. Even so, it's always a risk.

It was a risk to write my book about Rush [Limbaugh]. It was a risk in the sense that I had never written a book in my own voice. I had usually written with a character in mind or I wrote sketches. When I wrote *I'm Good Enough, I'm Smart Enough, and Doggone It, People Like Me!*, that was in Stuart Smalley's voice. My editor practically begged me to do something political because she saw me speak at the White House correspondents' dinner. I was scared, but they kept offering more money.

Finally, I said okay. I decided to write a book from my point of view. But it wasn't until I came up with the title that everything became clear: *Rush Limbaugh is a Big Fat Idiot.* From that point on everything fell into place. It was a best-seller from the first week it came out. I was shocked. It was unbelievable. But if I didn't get past the fear of failure, I would have never finished it.

I was always very political, but the success of the *Rush* book gave me the opportunity to say what I really wanted to say. I sent him a copy of the book with a note from my editor that said, "Dear Rush, Al thinks it would help sales if you would mention the book on your show." We never got an answer.

Even in success there's room for failure. My Stuart Smalley book was fairly successful, selling around 100,000 copies, but while I thought the movie worked creatively it did not make money. And again I learned. I don't know if you ever noticed, but I don't exactly have movie star looks.

> *Problems are only opportunities in work clothes.*
> —Henry J. Kaiser

Fear doesn't stop me, but it certainly doesn't help. It makes it more painful to do the work. But as Garrison Keillor said, "It's more painful putting it off than actually doing it." Still, I will procrastinate because of fear. How do you offset the fear? Faith. Writing is having faith that you'll think of something. To me the arts are all about faith. Why else would someone sit down and say, "I'm going to write something now and I know it's going to be worth doing." The fact is, there's no logical reason why someone should be able to create anything. It takes faith.

We don't always get to do what we want to do in life so we should do what we're able to do. That applies to writing, too. When we write, we always want to write the best thing that's ever been written. You might want to, but it's not going to happen. Because of this a lot of people end up not writing at all. So if you really want to be a writer, it's important to sit your ass in a chair, know that what you write doesn't have to be the best thing ever written, and just write what you're capable of. If you do that, you are a writer. If you keep doing that, there's a better chance than not that you may even become a pretty good one.

Daily Affirmations by Stuart Smalley
Only the Mediocre are Always at Their Best

(Oct. 16. Stuart tapes his shows) I did the 10 shows in the two hours, which mathematically breaks down to one five-minute show every 12 minutes, which isn't so bad, except that it took them about an hour to light the set, after which I was just freaking out. So, just before I went on, Carl, Andrea, Steve, Julia and I held hands and said the Serenity Prayer. The first show, "Today I Will Own My Own Panic," went very well and helped calm me down. Carl thought it would make a good first one, because it would be very much "in the now," since I probably would be panicking. The second show, "Today I Will Take My Time," was ironically a little rushed, so I had about 30 seconds at the end with nothing to say, so I did a silent meditation, and I don't think anyone could tell that I was covering up a mistake. And it's okay, because we all make mistakes. That's what makes us human, which was the title of the third show, "We All Make Mistakes, That's What Makes Us Human," which was Steve's idea for a show. I'd say my best show was "Today I Will Show Up," which, if I do say so myself, was magic. Andrea cried. My worst show by far was my last one called, "I Don't Have to Prepare," which was kind of an experiment any- way. You see, I had only settled on nine good topics before I got to the studio, so I just got the idea of winging one of the shows. Really do the show "in the now," having nothing prepared. And I just blanked. It was five minutes of me blanking, every once in a while saying something like, "I am blanking now. That's

If at first you do succeed, try to hide your astonishment.
—Harry F. Banks

> *I honestly think it is better to be a failure at something you love than to be a success at something you hate.*
> —George Burns

what's going on in the now, right now. Nothing." After a while I slipped into some of the material from "Today I Will Own My Own Panic," so it wasn't all dead air. After it was over, Julia tried to get them to let me do it again, but the studio was booked for a show on boudoir photography, so it was over. That's when Andrea said, "Only the mediocre are always at their best."

And you know what? I think she was right. I think I was better than mediocre!!

(Excerpts of I'm Good Enough, I'm Smart Enough, and Doggone It, People Like Me! Daily Affirmations By Stuart Smalley, *Dell Publishing, used by permission of Al Franken.)*

SILLY SUPPOSITIONS

"When the Paris Exhibition closes, electric light will close with it and no more be heard of."

–Erasmus Wilson,1878, professor, Oxford University.

Amy Hill

"I had always worried about being perfect. I found that only in imperfection could I be my best."

Whether on TV, film or stage, it is actress Amy Hill who steals the scene. She has appeared in a multitude of TV and movie roles and when she was in her mid-30s, Amy Hill starred as a 70-year-old grandmother on TV's *All-American Girl*. But it took losing the role she coveted to put her in the position to get what became her big break.

As a child, I had few visible Asian-American role models. We had nothin'. My mom is Japanese and my dad is Finnish. Mixed, I felt like an outsider. I wasn't perfect, not 100 percent anything. I felt I didn't fit in anywhere and that people would reject me just for the hell of it, because I wasn't one of them. I was damaged goods.

One year there was an exchange program where one student would get to spend a year in Japan. Speaking Japanese was essential. Though my mom was Japanese, she didn't speak it at home so I learned it in school. I ended up speaking Japanese better than anyone in my high school. I never wanted anything so bad as getting into that exchange program, and never worked so hard to get it. Both my teacher and I thought I would get it. I didn't. Another girl whose Japanese wasn't very good got it. How did that happen? I felt so rejected, again. I had put myself on the line. When you're a kid that isn't easy. I did every tiny thing I could and during the interview process I was totally open and vulnerable. I let them know how much I wanted it. It felt like a personal rejection, like there was something wrong with me. I thought I wasn't selected because of my mixed heritage. I felt that if I was pure Japanese or pure white I might have gotten it.

A year later, I was at a party and one of the parents told me why I hadn't been chosen. He said, "Amy, you tried too hard." Huh? What was I supposed to learn from that? The less I try the more I get? It enraged me. Over the years, people have told me that I overpower other actors, that I was actually too good. What was that supposed to mean? Were they telling me that I was supposed to be less than I am? That didn't connect in my brain.

I thought that if I failed in acting, I would try fine art. I worked hard to get it right. Eventually, I went to Japan on my own to study Japanese calligraphy. When I came back, I went to the University of Washington. One day, a teacher looked at my work and said in a very condescending manner, "This is so good, you could sell it. But it isn't art." I was devastated. Later, I realized that what he was saying was that I could make a perfect picture, but the good work lies in coming from a true and honest place that allows the imperfection. Because there is no perfect.

> *As long as a man stands in his own way, everything seems to be in his way.*
> *—Ralph Waldo Emerson*

My solo show, *Tokyo Bound*, helped shift my identity and make me comfortable in my own skin. I kept working on my show to get it just right. The writing, the acting, working with the director. Then, moments before the curtain rose for my very first show, I thought, "What am I doing?! Do I want to kill myself? I'm going to be judged on my writing, my acting and my life, all at once." I literally felt death standing next to me on stage. I was terrified and now it was too late to stop. The sound cue struck, lights came up. This was the real thing! I ended up *thinking* my way through the show. Bad thing to do when you're acting. From that moment on, I realized that if I was just honest, everything would be okay. I had always worried about being perfect. I found that only in imperfection could I be my best. When I asked myself what was I doing here, I had found myself. Perhaps for the first time I realized that I couldn't be perfect. That was terrifying. But it was also an epiphany. I couldn't be perfect, but I could be honest. And when I told my own story honestly, I was telling everyone's story. The elderly Jewish woman, the African-American guy, the

Russian immigrant. I did the show in places where, even though there were no Asians in the audience, so many people came up to me after the show to tell me this was their story, too. I had finally learned the lesson that had been before me for years. The performance is in the honesty.

When I did a show about my mother, there were a lot of things that I wasn't sure she'd want me to talk about. It occurred to me that some of the things that I was going to say may be upsetting to her. I didn't depict my mother as a perfect person. She told me that if it's true, I'd have to tell it. After she saw the show, her only criticism was, "Show is too short. You can't tell my story in just one hour." Again, telling the truth worked.

Around 1993, Margaret Cho and I had been performing on the same bill. She did her stand-up and I just jammed on doing my mother. If you asked me what I actually did that night, I wouldn't have a clue, but I can tell you, everything worked. Margaret said that she thought that my mother was exactly like her mother. A couple months later, I got a call to audition as Margaret Cho's mom in her new show, *All-American Girl.* When I got the script, I saw that the grandma part was the better role, but being only 10 or 15 years older than Margaret, I felt I could play her mother, but not the grandmother. Because I didn't even look old enough to play the mother, they had me wear a gray wig. I had to audition with an actor who I didn't get along with. He ragged on my wig and the entire time I auditioned, I'm thinking, "Why am I wearing this stupid wig." Needless to say, the audition went horribly. I felt I had let Margaret down. The only Asian-American sitcom on the air and I wasn't going to be on it. I was devastated.

Don't polish your performance so much that you end up rubbing away all the appeal.
—Harold Praw

I got a call from the producers who said they wanted me to come in and read for the part of the grandmother, but I shouldn't wear the wig. At that moment, I thought that I had no idea how I could possibly get this part. My goal now was to reclaim myself as an actor.

153

I didn't care anymore whether I got the part or not. I wanted to do my job and walk away with my head held high.

When I went in for the audition, I found a bunch of old ladies in the waiting area. Old ladies and me. I went in not caring if I got the role, and I got it, though one Asian-American network guy didn't think I was Asian enough. So, while I was hired for the pilot, that didn't mean I would end up on the show. I took the same attitude into the pilot. I would do my job, and whether I continued or not, at least I did the character the way I wanted to, honestly and instinctively, not trying to please anyone. I ended up testing as the highest-rated character on *all* the ABC shows that season. I was the most popular character on the show. All I did was try to be the best actor I could be. I realized that if I had had the same opportunity earlier in my career, when I had wanted it, I would never have been as ready as I was when it actually came. I now try not to worry about being perfect as much as I allow myself to be all I can be.

> *The moment avoiding failure becomes your motivation, you're down the path of inactivity. You stumble only if you're moving.*
> —Roberto Goizueta

ACCIDENTAL ACHIEVEMENTS

Charles Goodyear accidentally dropped a piece of rubber mixed with sulphur and white lead on a hot stove. The soft, flexible material became vulcanized rubber and the process of 'vulcanization' was born.

Michael *Medved*

"You can choose to feel sorry for yourself and remain isolated, or you can realize that there is an opportunity to invent yourself all over again, to create yourself as a new person."

Film critic, best-selling author and nationally syndicated radio talk show host Michael Medved reaches more than two million listeners in more than 130 markets, coast to coast. He co-hosted *Sneak Previews*, **the nationally televised weekly movie review show on PBS-TV. As a successful author, Medved has written numerous books, including the national best-seller** *What Really Happened to the Class of '65* **[the basis for a popular TV series on NBC], and collaborated with his wife, Dr. Diane Medved, on the book** *Saving Childhood: Protecting Our Children from the National Assault on Innocence*. **His columns on media and society appear regularly in** *USA Today*, **where he serves as a member of the Board of Contributors. Medved's success and popularity may have had its beginnings in a place where he tasted disappointment and no one knew who he was.**

It was the summer of 1963. I was 14 and living in Point Loma, California, a lower-middle-class area of San Diego where my family and I had lived since I was 6. I lived in the same house and had gone from first grade through 10th in the same neighborhood. I had all my friends there and was very comfortable. If you live in a place for that long, you know every detail about it. In high school, I was something of a big fish in a small pond. I had done very well academically and placed a couple of pieces in the citywide literary magazine. I was looking forward to a very successful high

The problem is not that there are problems. The problem is expecting otherwise and thinking that having problems is a problem.
—Theodore Rubin

school career with people who had known me since first grade. And then we moved.

It was emotionally difficult for me. I talked about boarding with my best friend and his mother in order to finish high school in Point Loma. My parents weren't too keen on this as I was the old-est of four boys and I was going to go away to college the follow-ing year anyway, so that was nixed. I was going to this large high school in Los Angeles where I didn't know anybody. It felt like such a wrenching experience.

My dad, who was a physicist, had gotten a teaching position at UCLA and we were able to rent a house for only $350, but it still placed us in the very expensive school district of Palisades High School. The entire money thing was never an issue in San Diego. It was a very mixed high school of all types of people. On the other hand, Palisades was a privileged high school with a lot of very rich kids. To make things worse, people there were very car conscience and we owned a beat-up old Rambler. I felt very left out.

Up to that point, I had received all "A"s in high school. In my first semester at the new school, I received a "D" in trigonometry. Considering the fact that I had been programmed from birth to become a candidate for an Ivy League school, and since my father was a physicist and mother a biochemist, getting a "D" in trigono-metry was unacceptable. It was the only time in my life I was suici-dal. To me, at the time, it was a nightmare of truly staggering pro-portions and unbelievable intensity. Everything about that semester seemed horrible. Kennedy was assassinated at the begin-ning of that semester, I didn't have any friends, and I thought the kids at Palisades were very creepy, very Hollywood. In San Diego, there was certainly a sense of looking down on L.A., which was considered an ugly, crass and unpleasant city. I've often said that if I went on some Oprah-type show whose theme was abused children, I'd have to talk about my

> *Bear small losses, reap large rewards.*
> *—Donna Castellano*

parents moving me to Los Angeles.

Things got worse and worse. I would make it more painful by visiting friends in San Diego whenever I could. The only girl I was interested in was in San Diego. The whole thing was nuts and depressing.

With no one knowing who I was and partly because of my desperate bid for attention, I advanced a very public campaign to abolish football at the school. The damp and marshy football field had irrigation problems, so I suggested that we turn the football field into a rice paddy to encourage the virtues of productivity, cultivation and agriculture to show solidarity with our allies in South Vietnam. It received a great deal of publicity and made me something of a celebrity in the class...but not in a good way. I learned the power of publicity. As controversial as that was and as widely discussed and condemned by everyone, particularly the football team, it did succeed in breaking the shell of anonymity, which can be crippling when you're an adolescent. It did wonders for my self-esteem.

Being defeated is often a temporary condition. Giving up is what makes it permanent.
—Marilyn vos Savant

I continued my resurrection by participating in the *Quiz Bowl League* television show, an academic high school competition based on the *College Bowl* television series. It was televised on CBS in L.A., so it was a big deal. I was the only junior member of the team. We won the league title, got on the TV show and went undefeated as we won the championship over a Beverly Hills High team that included Richard Dreyfus. I was a wiz at the important skill of pressing a button microseconds before anyone else did. I was able to go from controversial geek to high school hero because I could answer questions on TV and in competition. Is this a great country or what?!

I also got through trigonometry and no longer had to do math, thank God. The punch line of all of this was that, being an outsider at Palisades High School, which struck me at the time as being cruel and unusual punishment in itself, provided the basis for my first published book, which became a national best-seller. It also became a TV series on NBC. Because it had enough Hollywood glitz, it was chosen by *Time* Magazine as the focus of their cover story, *American Youth on the Fringe of a Golden Era.* There's no way the book would have been published if it were about my high school class in San Diego, or if I hadn't had the perspective of an outsider coming in and meeting all these strangers.

> *If you get up the same amount of times that you fall, you will make it through.*
> —*Unknown*

One of my favorite stories of all time was about Albert Einstein. He didn't say a word until he was 5 years old. The very first thing he said came on a day when he was eating soup. He said, "too hot." His parents, who assumed their child to be retarded, asked him why he hadn't said anything before now? Einstein replied, "Before now, everything was fine." In San Diego, I goofed off a lot. I didn't work hard. I didn't have to. Everything was fine up till then. The Palisades experience was a much more realistic parallel to what I've found in the business world. In the business world, you're thrown into a situation where nobody knows who you are and you have to attract attention and impress people with some energy, intelligence and actual performance.

At Palisades, I was a stranger. I was forced to try different things, making bids for publicity. It's followed me into my career. I expend a lot of energy and throw a lot of balls into the air all at once. Had I made the decision to stay in San Diego with my friend and his family and to finish at Point Loma High, my whole life would have been different and wouldn't have been nearly as interesting. Certainly, I would never have written a best-selling book from my high school experience. The interest I developed in movies was partially because of Palisades High School and dealing with so many kids whose parents were in the business.

At one time or another, we are all thrown into a world where nobody knows who we are. You can choose to feel sorry for yourself and remain isolated or you can realize that there is an opportunity to invent yourself all over again, to create yourself as a new person. The decision is up to you.

OBTUSE OBSERVATIONS
"The wireless music box has no imaginable commercial value. Who would pay for a message sent to nobody in particular?"
–David Sarnoff's associates in response to his urgings for investment in the radio in the 1920s.

Failure is a detour, not a dead-end street.

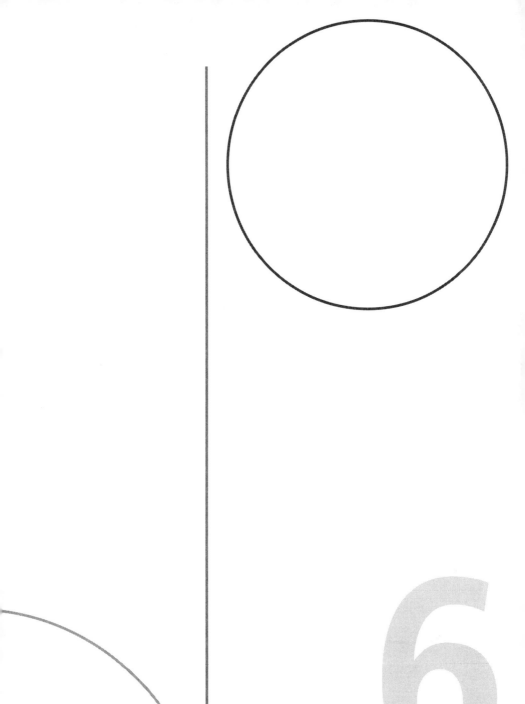

–Zig Ziglar

6

Steve Allen

"When bad luck does strike, which it occasionally will despite all our precautions and prayers, we can emerge from such experiences not only wiser but often with material benefits."

Steve Allen's list of credits may be the longest in the history of show business. Besides creating and hosting The *Tonight Show*, he authored 54 books, penned over 8,500 songs, starred in motion pictures, wrote for Broadway, and in addition to his more than 60 record albums, created, wrote and hosted the Emmy Award-winning PBS-TV series *Meeting of Minds*. Whew! And believe me, there's plenty more. Yet, with all those heady accomplishments, it was the failures that sent him jettisoning toward some of his greatest successes.

Through a combination of luck and good timing, I found myself, at age 25, with a daily coast-to-coast comedy show on the Mutual Radio Network, working with my then-partner Wendell Noble. After two years, however, the program was dropped, for reasons never specified, and there were no immediate prospects of a better alternative. In fact, the only offer I received was not from another network but a local station and they, at least at that time, had no interest in my abilities as a comic, such as they were. They wanted me, in fact, to simply introduce recordings for 30 minutes every night at half past eleven, a fate I viewed as not quite worse than death but almost as bad, professionally speaking. I nevertheless had to accept the offer since I was, at the time, the sole support of a wife and child. The step from local radio or TV to full network exposure is a very big one and somehow it seemed even more precipitous when it was made in reverse. So there I was, at age 27, heading swiftly in the wrong direction.

When you're ready to succeed, you will…
or not.
—F. Cooper

In the mid-'40s, a clever comedian named Abe Burrows, refer-
ring to his own professional progress, mentioned an earlier cancellation
as demonstrating that he was moving from obscurity to oblivion. At
about the same time, the great radio comedian Fred
Allen described the broadcasting medium as a
"treadmill to oblivion." At 27, I knew what
he meant. But the story had a happy ending. After a few months, I began to tinker
with the too-limiting format which had
been imposed on me, and within two years
had turned it into a nightly 60-minute comedy and talk show that became a roaring success and easily provided a launching pad for all the
television work I would subsequently do.

*Experience is that
marvelous thing that enables
you to recognize a mistake when
you make it. . .again.*
—F. P. Jones

Another fortunate failure presented itself when, after a happy
six-year relationship, CBS-TV could no longer find an assignment for
me and therefore released me from my contract. The prospect of once
again being out of work was far from good news. Yet, without that setback there would never have been a *Tonight Show*. For it was shortly
thereafter that Ted Cott, the manager of NBC's New York station,
called out of the blue and offered me a late-night, five-a-week slot during which, he assured me, I could do any sort of show I wanted.

What I put together was actually much like what I had been
doing for CBS, but somehow, at 11:00 at night, it seemed more exciting, looser, more fun. Because we had no real competition, the program
quickly dominated its time slot. So much so in fact that Pat Weaver,
who was then programming head of the NBC network and had
already launched the still-successful *Today* show, was looking for a late-
night equivalent for which he already had decided on the title *Tonight*.
He asked me if I would mind changing the name of our program from
The Steve Allen Show to *Tonight* and when I did not object, he added our
nightly party to the full network schedule.

The success of *Tonight* led to an even more important assignment a few years later. The network had for years been troubled by its

> The biggest job we have is to teach a newly hired employee how to fail intelligently. We have to train him to experiment over and over and to keep on trying and failing until he learns what will work.
> —Charles K. Kettering

inability to offer strong ratings competition to *The Ed Sullivan Show*, which aired at 8:00 Sunday evenings. Ed's program had quickly become an institution, and the best that NBC could oppose it with was a series of comedy specials featuring such formidable stars as Jimmy Durante, Dean Martin and Jerry Lewis. No matter how good one-shot shows are, they cannot, by their very nature, build up a viewer loyalty habit. In any event, the NBC programmers thought I might be the solution to their Sunday-night problems, and for the next four years I had a delightful time putting on an early evening comedy party, with the able assistance of our great comedy gang—Louis Nye, Pat Harrington, Don Knotts, Bill Dana, Dayton Allen, Gabriel Dell and Tom Poston.

Again, the point is that if I had not been cast adrift by CBS, none of the exciting years at NBC could have come to pass. When bad luck does strike, which it occasionally will despite all our precautions and prayers, we can emerge from such experiences not only wiser but often with material benefits.

The cliché phrase to describe such phenomena is a *blessing in disguise*. The point is that we must learn to roll with the punches and derive such benefits as we can from life's unhappier experiences. There's a great possibility they'll end up leading to a much better state of affairs than the one we have left behind.

[Widely praised as television's Renaissance Man, Steve Allen died October 30, 2000.]

FOOLISH FINDINGS

"Everything that can be invented, has been invented."

–Charles H. Duell, commissioner, U. S. Office of Patents, 1899.

Johnny Unitas

"You can't worry about missing a pass or a ball getting knocked down. If you worried about stuff like that, you'd never do anything."

In many people's minds, Johnny Unitas, Number 19, is the greatest quarterback of all time. He led the Baltimore Colts to the 1958 and 1959 National Football League championships. He was Player of Year three times and voted Most Valuable Player three times in ten Pro Bowls. He completed 2,830 passes for 40,239 yards and 290 touchdowns. Yet Hall of Famer Johnny Unitas had to be cut from his first professional team before he would ever find his place in sports history.

In 1955, I was drafted number nine out of the University of Louisville by the Pittsburgh Steelers. I did well in the training camp, but as a rookie and fourth-string quarterback, my performance wasn't important to them. They acted as if I wasn't there. I was pretty upset. They really had no idea if I could actually play or not. I was cut before the season started without having the opportunity to play in any of the five preseason games. If I had been given the opportunity and screwed up bad, then I would have understood why I was released. But I wasn't given the chance and I told Coach Walter Keisling just that.

Paul Brown, who was head coach at Cleveland, had interest in me while I was in college. So when I was cut by Pittsburgh, I called Brown and asked if I could come to Cleveland. He said if I could wait until the following year, I could come to camp.

The man who tries to do something and fails is infinitely better than he who tries to do nothing and succeeds.
—Lloyd Jones

I considered going into teaching. I had graduated from Louisville with a B.S. in physical education and economics. Someone suggested that I play for a semipro team that year. I was unsure since I was married with a child and another on the way. I didn't want to get busted up to where I wouldn't be able to work. I finally decided to give it one year so that I'd be in shape if Paul Brown brought me to camp. For the rest of 1955, I played semipro sandlot ball for $6 a game, fully expecting to sign with Cleveland in '56. Sandlot ball got me ready for the NFL.

The following year, the Baltimore Colts called me in February of 1956, looking for a back-up quarterback. They asked if I was still interested in playing football. When I saw that Baltimore had only one quarterback on its roster, I signed with the Colts. Starting quarterback George Shaw came down with pneumonia, leaving me the only quarterback in camp. Our first game in preseason was against the Pittsburgh Steelers. I started the game for the Colts. The first pass I threw went for 40 yards and a touchdown. We beat Pittsburgh that night.

The good things which belong to prosperity are to be wished, but the good things that belong to adversity are to be admired.
—Francis Bacon

The next day, my wife and I were driving to my brother's house. I pull up to a red light, and who pulls up next to me but the owner of the Pittsburgh Steelers, Art Rooney. In the car with him were his son and Coach Walter Keisling, the one who cut me, who was in the backseat. I waved a hello to Mr. Rooney and went to the next light. The Rooneys pulled up next to me and Mr. Rooney rolled down his window and said, "Unitees [sic], great game last night. I hope you go on to become the best quarterback ever." With that, Keisling fell off the backseat. In my rookie year with the Colts, I completed a record 66.7 percent of my passes and I ended up playing and starting for the Colts for 16 years. Looking back, being cut by Pittsburgh turned out to be my big break.

I never felt that mistakes in life or in sports were a big deal. They happen. In football, when you're under center, ready to get the ball, you've got 11 players on your side and 11 on the other side of the ball, and they're getting paid to do the same damn thing you are. You can't worry about missing a pass or a ball getting knocked down. If you worried about stuff like that, you'd never do anything. It's part of the game just like mistakes are a part of life. I felt the same if [Hall of Fame receiver] Ray Berry dropped a pass. I knew that no one could catch everything.

You can't really figure out what's going to happen, no matter what the situation. At the end of my career, I was playing with San Diego and Coach Tommy Prothro didn't want me there. He told me that if I wanted to watch the games I could do it from the stands. The only thing he would talk to me about was his bridge game, and I only wanted to play football. The team asked me to retire. You would think this wasn't a very good thing, but within a week, CBS-TV contacted me to become a color commentator. When I signed the contract with CBS, the Chargers stopped paying me what they owed me. They told me that I had all this preplanned, which was baloney. I even crossed the players' picket line that year because I felt I had an obligation to the contract. CBS finally made up the difference and I not only ended up making my money but doing it in a whole new career.

Great works are performed not by strength, but perseverance.
—Samuel Johnson

You have to find out what you really want to do, whatever it is. You search out the people who have *been there* and know how to do it. Then, with that guidance and information, you put your nose to the grindstone and keep learning all you can. Whether you're a writer, actor, athlete or you dig ditches, the more you do it the better you get. You've gotta be willing to work, sacrifice and put a lot of time into whatever you do. Work to the best of your ability and don't let anyone or anything stand in your way.

RED-LETTER REJECTS
Beatrix Potter's first book, *The Tail of Peter Rabbit*, was rejected by at least six publishers before becoming a children's classic.

Julia Sweeney

"Sometimes you need to first discover what you can't do before you're able to discover what you can."

Comedienne and actress Julia Sweeney starred in NBC's *Saturday Night Live* and her own movie, *It's Pat*; she is also the author and playwright of *God Said, 'Ha'*, a chronicle of her and her brother's battles with cancer. As much as she is a success in many areas of comedy, it took a humiliating failure at one comedy venue to start her in the right direction in another.

Failure has been a large contributor to my success.

I never thought of myself as a stand-up-type comic. I didn't think I could think up jokes so, thinking I could learn, I took a stand-up class. They told me I needed to have a persona. I thought of my character Mea Culpa, and thought, "What would Mea talk about?" Well, I'm really into hagiography, which is the study of saints' lives, and some of these saints are hilarious. I decided I would go on stage as Mea, as if she were doing a book report in school, with posters of saints that I had made.

There is the greatest practical benefit in making a few failures early in life.
—Thomas H. Huxley

I went to the Comedy Store on Open-Mike Night. I went up on stage...and it was a disaster. People were yelling at me. No laughing. They just did not get it. I was dressed as Mea...and the audience didn't understand that this was not me, that I was in this getup. They thought this was how I really looked, and I looked like a real loser. But, unfortunately I didn't look enough like a loser so that they would know that this was only a character.

It was painful. I had horribly failed. Just fail-ail-ailed. People were just screaming, "Get off the stage." Which I did.

I tried to keep myself together, then this other girl from the class, who I had driven there with and who had performed earlier said, "Hey, guess what. Mitzi [Shore, the club's owner] wants me to come back." Mitzi hadn't even looked at me or acknowledged my presence. I wanted to go home, but no-o-o, this girl wanted to hang out. She needed to stay and bathe in her success. Hang out with her new friends. But I was dressed as Mea and I had these huge posters of saints with me, so it was incredibly awkward to just hang out. She asked me if Mitzi asked me back. I told her no. "I bet she will," she said. "You just have to go up and ask her." I told her that the audience didn't get me, and she said, "So what. Mitzi's a genius. She can see right through that. You've got to be aggressive in this business. Find her and ask."

> *All honour to
> him who shall win
> the prize,
> The world has cried for a
> thousand years;
> But to him who tries and
> fails and dies,
> I give great honor and
> glory and tears.*
> —Joaquin Miller

So I put down my posters and headed down the hall to see Mitzi walking in a door. I follow her and we're in a bathroom. She's already in a stall and I'm waiting for her, thinking that this isn't right. But I have to report back to this girl. I mean, I'm 24 and I'm an accountant. I didn't know. Mitzi finally comes out of the stall, and I say, "Hi. I just performed and I was just wondering…" I don't think I got it all out and she says… "You were terrible! You were terrible." I was so taken aback by her. I was so shocked, I felt like I was going to cry. It was such a vulnerable situation. She said, "Didn't you hear that no one was laughing?" And I said, "Yeah, yeah." And she said, "If you're asking to come back, you can't come back." Tears well up and I say, "Okay…thank you." I walked the 100 miles back to my friend. I'm sure it was more like 20 feet, but it felt like 100 miles. All the comedians were standing there. I was wearing polyester pants, my hair was parted in the middle, and I can't believe I didn't bring a change of clothes. I had to just *exist* until my friend, who was basking in her glory and flirting with other comedians, was ready to go. Dennis Miller was there and I remember thinking how he was looking at me thinking what a big loser I was. I'm sure now that he wasn't, but at the time I was thinking that everyone was looking at me that way.

Most of the important things in the world have been accomplished by people who have kept on trying when there seemed to be no hope at all.
—Dale Carnegie

Toward the end of that evening I had the wherewithal to think that this had been so horrible, I almost couldn't feel bad about it. I went home and thought that I guess I'm just not funny in *that* way. But I still didn't know in what way I could be funny. Still, there was part of me that said if you can get through that type of experience, you can get through anything. Nothing's ever going to be that bad.

I didn't know then, but I learned that the Comedy Store was not my thing. I refused to come up with the type of material that the Comedy Store audience would want to hear. That environment was not the type of environment for me.

I didn't do any comedy for a year. Did accounting. Got a promotion. Then I read a review of the Groundlings [improvisational company], and thought maybe that's what I should be doing. It wasn't stand-up comedy, but I still could be funny. At the end of the review, it mentioned class auditions for nonprofessional actors, and that was me. After two classes, I knew that this was my future.

We must accept finite disappointment, But never lose infinite hope.
—Dr. Martin Luther King, Jr.

It's a lot like environment. How we evolve. We try this, we try this, we try this, and finally we find the environment that we thrive in. But I didn't even know what environment I could thrive in.

See, when I first went to the Comedy Store, I didn't realize there were a thousand different ways of being funny. That there were other audiences that would enjoy my type of comedy. If I didn't fail that night, I might not have found that out. Found out there were other ways I could be funny; other ways that I could do what I did best. I discovered that sometimes you need to first discover what you can't do before you can discover what you can.

TERRIBLE TURNDOWNS

"So we went to Atari and said, 'Hey, we've got this amazing thing, even built with some of your parts, and what do you think about funding us? Or we'll give it to you. We just want to do it. Pay our salary, we'll come work for you.' And they said, 'No.' So then we went to Hewlett-Packard, and they said, 'Hey, we don't need you. You haven't got through college yet.'"

–Apple Computer Inc. founder Steve Jobs on attempts to get Atari and HP interested in his and Steve Wozniak's personal computer.

Dr. Arnold Fox

"Internal messages of failure sap our confidence, energy and creative juices."

Dr. Arnold Fox has been a specialist in cardiology and internal medicine for more than 30 years. A former commissioner for the Medical Board of California, Dr. Fox has served as adjunct professor of graduate studies of pain management at the University of the Pacific, president of the board of directors of the American Academy of Pain Management and is the director of the National Anti-Aging Institute in Los Angeles. Dr. Fox is also a best-selling author of several highly acclaimed publications, including *Beverly Hills Medical Diet, Wake Up! You're Alive, Beyond Positive Thinking: Putting Your Thoughts Into Action* and *Alternative Healing*.

When I was a Little League coach, I put a kid on the team who had cerebral palsy. People were upset with me, but I put him in right field hoping no one would hit the ball to him. The last game of the year was for the championship, and I was told to bench him. I refused. When it was late in the tight game, he was up to bat and we expected him to strike out, because he always did. Even though he had been struck out every other time he came to bat, he didn't stop trying. While kids on the other team were making fun of him, he held his bat out like he always did and by some accident the ball hit the bat. With the fielders playing deep, not expecting him to hit the ball, it rolled down the third base line. He lumbered and lumbered toward first base. He got to first safely and we scored the winning run. Over the years I've run into his parents who've told me how that opportunity—keep in mind, it was one in which everyone thought he

> *Even a mistake may turn out to be the one thing necessary to a worthwhile achievement.*
> —Henry Ford

would fail—changed that kid's life.

For better or worse, every thought in our head, positive or negative, affects our internal biochemistry. Fear, worry, self-doubt and other emotional "downers" do much of their behind-the-scenes damage by stepping up the secretion of adrenaline and other hormones called catecholamines. Catecholamines can trigger a skipped or rapid heartbeat, which has been linked to increased levels of cholesterol, higher blood pressure and sudden death. The result is increased risk of heart attack and stroke.

If you want to increase your success rate, double your failure rate.
—Thomas Watson, Sr.

Our fear of failure can keep cholesterol at peak levels for long periods of time. Chronic worry also wreaks havoc on the immune system, reducing the effectiveness of our protective T-cells. Anxiety can also stimulate the adrenal glands to secrete more cortisone, setting the stage for peptic ulcers.

It's amazing how many people say they have no faith. But they do. Unfortunately, their faith is a faith in the negative. They believe that they know the future, how things will turn out. Sometimes you feel what you do doesn't serve any good purpose, that it's a waste of time so you might as well not attempt it at all. But a thought like that could be fatal.

Once I was giving a talk in Atlanta. It was right after lunch which seemed like the worst time of day to speak. My biggest job would be to wake them up. Even though I was just supposed to speak about nutrition, which tends to be boring, I mixed in a little motivational information. The next week I get a letter from a woman in Atlanta. She had planned to commit suicide the same afternoon I was speaking. Her friend interrupted her as she was literally placing her head in the oven. She had invited her to come hear me speak. She said the funny thing about suicide is that if you don't do it at noon you could always do it at midnight. So she had put her suicide on hold and came to my talk. She said that it was like I spoke directly to her and she would never contemplate suicide again. Certainly I didn't approach that talk intending to save someone's life. I didn't know she would be there any more than I know who reads my books. That's why you have to give 100 percent effort all the time.

The key to counteract the deadly fear of failure is to realize that failure is an unavoidable fact of life. Certainly, stumbling from time to time doesn't make us failures. People who view themselves as failures are simply stuck in their negative scenes. A vicious cycle ensues, as the belief that they are failures and the constant fear of failing again discourage them from trying new experiences or persevering tasks that can lead to more positive results. That holds true for their health, their careers and their relationships.

Internal messages of failure sap our confidence, energy and creative juices. When our mental eye is fixed only on images of weakness and embarrassment, we block out positive, encouraging images.

Concern of how we look to others robs us of our initiative and of the freedom to take control of our lives. It programs us to behave according to others' expectations, setting us up for chronic anxiety.

Over every mountain there is a path although it may not be seen from the valley.
—James Rogers

Fear of failure can lead to smoking, alcohol and drug abuse, overeating and other potentially deadly habits.

The word "worry" comes from the Old English "wrygan," meaning "to strangle." When we worry, we strangle our ability to think and perform effectively, along with our strength, flexibility, enthusiasm and belief in ourselves.

Concern, an awareness of problems and a desire to overcome them spurs us on and helps us find solutions to our problems. By contrast, worry keeps us from taking any action at all.

How do you go from negative to positive thinking? First, you must recognize there is a problem. Second, you must take action. If you don't feel enthusiastic, act like you feel that way. Every morning wake up and greet the world enthusiastically. It's okay to feel like a phony. You put on an act until it becomes you. It's what we do with children. We practice the right way to behave. Remind yourself that everyone makes mistakes. Divide your journeys into small, manageable trips. Don't sweat the little things. Look for the humor. Smile even if you don't feel like it. Act as if and soon you won't be acting.

> *Perfection is the ideal prescription for failure.*
> —S. Young

Help someone else. Take the focus off your fear, your failure and yourself. Even if that only means offering companionship or support to someone else. Focus only on the things you can control, and most important, remember, you don't have to go at it alone. If you need it, always ask for help.

ACCIDENTAL ACHIEVEMENTS

In 1894, Will Kellogg assisted his brother, John, a hospital chief physician, in trying to improve the diet of the patients, especially in the research of a digestible wheat bread substitute. He accidentally allowed a pot of wheat to boil for too long and when they placed the wheat through the standard rolling process, the grains of wheat came out as flakes. This became the favorite of the patients and in short time was to become the basis for Kellogg's Corn Flakes®.

Scott Ellis

"I don't believe there's any right or wrong road. I believe you make your choice and whatever choice you make, if you're open, you learn from it."

Tony-nominated Scott Ellis is known as one of Broadway's most successful directors. Ellis's resumé includes directorial runs with *1776, Company, A Thousand Clowns, A Little Night Music* and *She Loves Me,* for which he garnered London's prestigious Olivier Award as Best Director. Success has surrounded Ellis's career, but it was a disastrous performance where he found that failure doesn't have to mean the end of a career.

I was just about to graduate from the Goodwin School of Drama in Chicago when the national tour of *Grease* hit town. They had an open call so I auditioned. Though I wasn't cast, I was called back a couple of times. That in itself was quite an accomplishment.

Without further thought, I finished school and went off to work in summer stock. I soon received a job offer to work with the Alliance Theater and accepted it. While I was getting ready to start with Alliance, I received a call from New York asking me to come in and audition again for *Grease*.

I drove from Colorado to New York for the audition and was offered an understudy role. At this point, I had to make a decision. I had already accepted the position at Alliance, but *Grease* would be my first professional acting job. After some serious consideration and feeling *Grease* was a better career move, I contacted Alliance and turned down their job offer. Soon after, I received a letter from Alliance saying that they understood my decision, but they added that once a person accepts a job, taking another one is just not right. I basically got my wrist slapped with love and I would soon learn how insightful they were.

But how could I not go with *Grease*? I would get my Equity card. I was 21 and I would be making my debut on Broadway. To add to all that, I was getting paid $375 a week, which was the most money I had ever seen in my life.

I became understudy for four different roles, only one of which was truly right for me. But still, I was on Broadway and you do the best job you can.

> *You may not realize it when it happens, but a kick in the teeth may be the best thing in the world for you.*
> —*Walt Disney*

It wasn't long before I had to fill in for one of the cast. Unfortunately, it would be the one role I was most uncomfortable with. Coincidentally, it just so happened that the producer of the show was in the audience that night. I guess he was less than dazzled by my performance. The next day, I was called into his office and fired.

It was devastating. On top of that, immediately after the firing, I had to go back to the theater. Once I got there, I didn't know what to do. Everyone knew I had been let go. I had never been so self-conscious. I headed down to the theater's basement and found a small room that I don't think anyone knew existed. I just sat in a corner and cried.

After a while I remember thinking that I had a choice. Either I could stay in the business or get out. And if I was getting out, this would be a real good time to do it. I was being fired, but to make things worse, they gave me one week's notice. That meant I had to stick around the theater for seven more days with everyone knowing that I had been fired. Not only that, but I had told everyone I had ever known that I was in the show. It had to have been the longest week of my life.

I had given up a wonderful opportunity at the Alliance Theater and moved everything I owned to New York. I had no savings, so once I was fired, I had no money coming in. I was pretty sure that coming to New York had been the wrong choice.

During that final week, Peter Gallagher, who was in the show at the time, tried to reassure me.

A success-ful tool is one that was used to do something undreamed of by its author.
—S. C. Johnson

"I know this is very painful for you but it will pass," he said. "It'll be okay."

The way I felt at the time, it was difficult to believe. But this small bit of encouragement was enough for me to give show business a little more time.

Within the next couple of weeks, I got myself up enough to audition for a two-person play. I got the role. It was a small theater and I wasn't getting paid anything, but it was an incredible role. It was everything I always thought theater could be: extraordinary, a great experience and I got to work with a terrific actress. It reminded me why I loved acting. It made me realize how funny life works.

If I had somehow done well that night in *Grease*, or if the producer hadn't been in the audience, my life would have turned out so differently. I certainly wouldn't have been able to do that wonderful two-person show. I wouldn't have found the agent I got from the show. I wouldn't have developed the relationship I did with the woman in the show. What I learned in that show added to my repertoire of tools I would take with me as a director.

I don't believe there's any right or wrong road. I believe you make your choice and whatever choice you make, if you're open, you learn from it. I try not to think of where a different choice might have taken me. Who knows how that would have turned out?

That first New York experience made me stronger. It taught me how to handle the good news as well as the bad. Especially the bad reviews. Today, I don't even read the reviews. I have a sense of what they are. Reviews are just personal opinions. They shouldn't change my opinion of how I feel about the project I'm working on.

I listen to the audience for guidance. After all, you don't actually know how good a show is until you put it up in front of an audience.

The more successful you get the tougher it becomes. There are more people watching you. There are more people after you. The more people expect of you. And you never see it coming.

When my show, *Steel Pier*, was canceled, it was completely unexpected. I worked on it for some five years. It's a project I loved and believed in. I still believe in it. But you go on. It is about survival. Maybe *Steel Pier* was a failure in the critics' eyes, but not in mine. There's not one show that I've done, whether it was a success or not, that I did not learn from.

When I auditioned for the Goodwin School of Drama, the dean said, "If you are happier doing anything else, you should leave right now and do whatever that might be." The point is, this business is so hard you have to love it as much as anything else to sustain you through the rough times. Everyone is good at something, though it may take some longer than others to find out what it is that they are good at. I was lucky to find my passion at such a young age. If you don't know, you must keep searching. If you are willing, you will find it. My greatest successes, in business or in life, have come from taking a chance and growing from it.

It is said that show business is called show business for a reason. It's half show and half business, but you have to be willing to commit to both. It doesn't matter if they have the most talent. The reality is that only a small percentage of those who want to be in this business will be in it 10 years down the road. These are the people who choose to stick with it and say, "This is what I have to do."

> *When defeat comes, accept it as a signal that your plans are not sound, rebuild those plans, and set sail once more toward your coveted goal.*
> —Napoleon Hill

THIRST-QUENCHING SURPRISES

In 1886, pharmacist John Pemberton attempted to create a general "fixin'-what-ails-ya" syrup. His assistant accidentally mixed carbonated water into the brew. The resulting brew didn't fix anyone, but it sure quenched thirst and Coca-Cola was born.

D

Don't cry when the sun is gone, because the tears

won't let you see the stars.

—Violeta Parra

Ann Bancroft & Liv Arnesen

"Look for what makes your heart beat; what makes your blood run. When you find it you will find what is important to you."

Ann Bancroft made the first American woman's expedition across the Greenland Ice Cap, climbed Mt. McKinley and was the first woman to ski to both the North and South Poles. Liv Arnesen became the first woman to solo to the South Pole and has climbed Mt. Everest. In 2001, with classrooms all over the world following their trek over the Internet, explorers Ann Bancroft and Liv Arnesen became the first women to cross Antarctica on a 1,717-mile, 94-day expedition. Both women found that it was previous failures that led to their teaming up and their ultimate success.

ANN BANCROFT: I had been trying to get across Antarctica for 11 years. My first trip was in 1993, when I attempted to lead three other women to the South Pole. The trip was meant to be a traverse and we were forced to stop at the South Pole. It was one of the hardest decisions of my life to not continue on from the South Pole to attempt the traverse.

I was devastated. It was a horrible decision, yet it was the right one to make. Typically when an expedition fails it's because they've run out of food, or they've run out of the time limit that Mother Nature imposes, or someone has been injured or the team isn't working out in one respect or another. We had run out of funds.

In 1993, I was in the best shape of my life. The food was in place. I had the team members. There was enough time left in the season to support the trip. I felt like it was an achievable goal given all the typical sources and elements of a project like ours. To be forced to stop due to a lack of funds was crushing, primarily because people at that time didn't believe that women could accomplish such a thing.

We had gotten as far as we did because of a grassroots movement of thousands of people who believed in us. It became clear to me that it would have been irresponsible of me to continue on a quagmire that would drive our supporters into a legacy of deep debt for what really was, ultimately, my personal goal.

In retrospect, I don't think stopping at the South Pole was actually a mistake. What I didn't know at the time was that it would lead to me finding Liv and doing the traverse with my dream partner. The Antarctica traverse and my relationship with Liv would have never happened if I hadn't had the earlier setbacks. It also created a dream project with 12 other people that I always wanted to do but was unable to pull it together until then.

The first failure gave me a deep understanding of the bigger picture—the concept of *legacy*. Our decisions and goals in life are not made in a vacuum. They have repercussions for others, even those we may not personally know or ever have contact with. Perhaps this was because we were making history as an all-women's group and were eliciting outside help to fund the expedition, which made it their trip as well. I really became acutely aware, in a rather schmaltzy way, how I fit into the universe, that my actions do have an effect on others as others' actions have an effect on me. It was an invaluable lesson built on great hardship from years of attempting to mount that expedition, a lesson that will stay with me for the rest of my life. I couldn't have learned it without the struggle.

I always joke that I have to go to the far-reaching ends of the globe to learn life's simple lessons, but they became profoundly clear there. I'll never have to relearn that lesson.

LIV ARNESEN: I had dreamed of the South Pole since I was a kid. In the early '80s, I remember a 58-year-old sailor who skied across Greenland. I thought that if a man that age could do it, so could I. I tried to join a team of men that was going to cross the Greenland Ice Cap, but they would never allow a woman to join them. They thought I couldn't make it. Three other male teams turned me down for the same reason. I was a woman. I think they felt that if a woman was on the team, it would not be as dramatic and that, in their eyes, it would diminish the heroic story.

He only is exempt from failures who makes no efforts.
—Richard Whately

For five years, I searched for other women who would cross with me. In 1999, I put a team of four women together. I had a gut feeling that one of the women should not go, but I didn't listen to my intuition. The first difficulty we faced required us to drag her along. We had a terrible trip and had to turn back before we completed out expedition. I learned that I would never ignore my own intuition again. I eventually joined one of the women on that team and actually completed the expedition across the Ice Cap.

LA: (Re: The Antarctica Expedition) We had terrible time pressure on us from the very beginning. The weather was not on our side. We had expected better conditions.

AB: Every day you are constantly adjusting, trying to figure out how to solve problems that are totally out of your control: weather and time. We had incredible pressure. We always knew that it would be an important part of the journey. It's the nature of any outdoor endeavor. I don't think we thought it would be as constant as it was. The triumph of that 94-day struggle was that it didn't impede our relationship. It just continued to grow. We probably laughed every day so it didn't diminish the fun. It never diminished the privilege of being there and enjoying where we were going. It took a lot of teamwork to remind ourselves that we were in this remarkable place and we needed to focus on it while we were waiting for the wind to return or whatever the obstacle was at the time. All outdoor trips are fraught with obstacles, but when you get home they become the very elements that make your perseverance and survival worth it. Whether it's a two-week canoe trip with the bugs eating you alive or the time pressure in Antarctica, it becomes the fabric of great learning.

The greatest failure of our expedition, and I'm still struggling with this, was that we didn't arrive at exactly where we wanted. This was very similar to my 1993 trip. Sometimes I feel like I'm on a series of *successful failures*. When you have such a big goal, you have lots of objectives to meet. Liv and I didn't meet all of our personal goals, but we did meet many other objectives that we were able to share with others. Our story is replete with small failures that accumulated to bring us through the larger struggle. These became far more important in the scheme of things. Most important, we understood the bigger picture and that in itself allowed us to come home holding our heads up high.

I had hoped Liv and I would come out of this expedition as friends, but I never dreamed our bond would be as strong as it is. When I look at future goals and dreams—I think of doing it with Liv. In all my other relationships on long trips, I've come away with good friendships but never as enduring as with Liv. Dealing with the obstacles together had so much to do with that.

AB: With a learning disorder, I was a kid who couldn't quite hit the mark academically. Since first grade I had to be tutored. This led to a lot of self-doubt. I felt like I was the only one who was experiencing that pain and anguish. I wanted so much to be like the other kids; I felt different and separate. I had dreams that my peers felt weren't very cool. How do you keep your heart beating with hope when all the messages are telling you it shouldn't? Much of that struggle is painful and lonely. You can't do it alone. There is always somebody out there who can help you keep your dream alive. Whether a teacher, coach, parent or peer, you have to find that someone who can help find that "glint."

I really needed to find people to believe in me. Someone who would see that something special in me, who could tell me that I had value and could contribute, which ultimately,

> *They who lack talent expect things to happen without effort. They ascribe failure to a lack of inspiration or ability, or to misfortune, rather than to insufficient application. At the core of every true talent there is an awareness of the difficulties inherent in any achievement, and the confidence that by persistence and patience something worthwhile will be realized. Thus talent is a species of vigor.*
>
> *—Eric Hoffer*

Surrender does not mean defeat.
—Unknown

every kid wants to do. There was one teacher who saw what I call "a glint in my eye." She knew I had something unique. To have a teacher take such an interest in me had a profound effect. She recognized a leadership ability in me, gave me a sense of purpose and the energy to stay with the struggles that were so painful that I just wanted to give up. When she found out that I went on expeditions to the North and South Poles, it was no surprise to her.

LA: I did quite well in school but I was bored. I didn't have the traditional interests that other kids had. I wanted to go to the South Pole. I wanted to find a man like Thor Heyerdahl and take a trip around the world. Others would tell me that it was impossible. It made me feel like an outsider. But through it all I found what was most vital—I had to be true to myself. That was what made my blood run, what made my heart beat. When you find that in yourself, you must stick with that, no matter what your parents or your friends say.

TENACIOUS & TIRELESS

As a miner in Alaska in 1910, Jacob Schick weathered temperatures of 40° F below zero. Finding shaving in cold water to be extremely uncomfortable, he conceived the idea for a dry shaver that could shave without water or lather. While he couldn't interest anyone at the time, Schick felt so strongly that his design would replace the "wet shave" method that he never forgot about it, and in 1927, he started a corporation to manufacture and sell Schick® electric razors.

Dr. Anthony James

"Since there's a good probability we will live a long time, we should do something we actually like."

In all of history, no creature has delivered more death to more human beings than the mosquito. The annual human mortality rate from malaria transmitted by just one species, *anopheles gambiae*, exceeds two million. Dr. Anthony James, professor of the department of molecular biology & biochemistry at the University of California at Irvine, led the team that developed mosquitoes that are unable to transmit disease. A Burroughs-Wellcome Award winner in molecular parasitology, a Fellow of the Royal Entomological Society and the American Association for the Advancement of Science, Dr. James found that years of so-called failure in his research would actually be necessary to bring about his final and successful objective.

I was the result of a mixed marriage. My father was African-American and my mother was Irish. While each side of the family was very kind to us, I always felt a sense of nonbelonging, of being different.

Name the greatest of all inventors: Accident.
—Mark Twain

This would become even more evident in school. When you're in high school, conformity and fitting in tend to be goals. Racism was going to keep that from happening. Things like that can have either a crushing or stimulating effect on a person. Faced with many failure scenarios, I decided on pursuing less-risky pursuits. In school, these pursuits tended to be intellectual.

My father was a mathematician and while he didn't push me into that field, I was around it all the time. Since I believed you go to college to become an intellectual, and I didn't want to be a philosopher, I thought that mathematics would be interesting.

I entered university as a math major and soon found that it was a big mistake. For all the time I put into mathematics, I would have liked to have been better at it. I just didn't have the discipline. I wasn't prepared for it. I felt broadsided. I didn't enjoy it and my grades reflected it. I felt like a failure. I had friends who were doing well. Why wasn't I?

Success is 99 percent failure.
—Soichiro Honda

It was around 1970, a time of cultural upheaval on college campuses, a time that provided many distractions like the shootings at Kent State in Ohio. It wasn't the best of years for college kids. I was politically active, there was so much confusion, and I was doing miserably in my major.

At the time, we had a first-year teaching assistant who, in his attempt to humanize math, would tell us stories about mathematicians. It seemed that all the mathematicians he spoke of were always sad. After a few weeks of these stories of sad mathematicians, I realized that I, too, was unhappy, and I certainly didn't want to be another unhappy mathematician. I figured that I was going to graduate in two years and perhaps it might be a good idea to try and do something I liked. I remembered that I really liked biology in high school. I liked seeing things through microscopes and going out into nature. Perhaps failing to become a mathematician was just what I needed to do to find out I belonged in biology.

At the end of my sophomore year, I changed my major to biology and took a summer job as a "dishwasher" for the department. Basically, I cleaned equipment. I washed beakers one day while students were busy with research. During lunch I asked them what they were doing. They explained the genetics experiments they were doing on fruit flies. It was my epiphany. This was what I wanted to do. The next day they had me pull up a bench and I was where I was meant to be. Some people tell me that I was lucky to be there at that moment. The fact is, I took an action. I certainly didn't know that by washing beakers I would find my life's work. Sometimes being lucky means doing the work that's necessary so that you'll be prepared for the moment when it comes along. I turned to biology. I sought out work in the field. It was that work that put me there when the opportunity came along.

Today, there are two things that I always tell my students: First, science can create its own reality and this reality is rooted in the real world. Second, since there's a good probability we will live a long time, we should do something we actually like.

When we do our work we never anticipate failure in the sense that we don't start something expecting it's going to fail. That turns out to be an extremely self-defeating approach to any kind of work at all. It doesn't make any sense. So whenever you undertake some endeavor there's an expectation that it will succeed. That's why you do it in the first place. The question is, what happens when you have a failure on your hands?

I found that failure is useful if I examine it in a number of different ways. First, I have to recognize what I was striving to do that *didn't* happen. I have to acknowledge the fact that there's been a failure. Then I have to ask myself if I can learn anything from the process of failure. Did it teach me some-

If there was nothing wrong in the world there wouldn't be anything for us to do.
—*George Bernard Shaw*

thing that I didn't anticipate, or is there an aspect of the failure that will contribute to the next set of experiments. And again, when I undertake the next work, I must do so with the expectation that it will succeed. Now I've incorporated what I've learned from the previous failure and it becomes a repetitive and successful process.

We worked on transgenesis, which is the ability to put genes into mosquitoes, for over seven years. This type of effort either works or it doesn't work. You don't get any points for all the failures. You go to a meeting and people want to know if it works. If it does, they want to hear about it. If it doesn't, they don't. In our work, the success in reaching the goal is ultimately a study in retrospect, so the failed efforts along the way must be understood in the context of a learning process.

While I might have been despondent about particular negative data, I wasn't going to quit because I knew that the only sure way to fail was if we quit. Eventually we were going to figure out how this would work.

Of course, you have to consider that there may be a point in any effort in which you have to ask yourself, "Why isn't this working?" How many failures in a row can you take before you figure out there must be some basic flaw in the design? The consequence of that is knowing when to quit. We used to have a situation in the lab where we had to figure out at what point we trust our negative data. If we're confident an experiment doesn't work, and there's a good reason why it doesn't, the negative aspect is actually meaningful.

There could be a million reasons why things go wrong. But for those reasons to have real value you have to troubleshoot them, then you've found the value in that failure.

> *I am not discouraged, because every wrong attempt discarded is another step forward.*
> *—Thomas A. Edison*

The classical example is man's development of flight. When people first started looking at birds, they saw the flapping of their wings. They focused on the supposition that somehow the flapping motion was going to lead to flight. There were a lot of designs and devices that were based on the concept of developing a flying machine that must somehow mimic this flapping motion. It never worked. It was eventually supplanted by a model that tried to understand what actually caused lift.

Their initial concept was wrong. While the flapping motion was important for maintaining forward motion, the actual lift was provided by the shape and lift of the wings. Once people figured that out, the problem was broken down into something approachable.

We had techniques that basically worked for certain parts of the experiments, but we were lacking a key piece. When that key piece was plugged in, we could almost guarantee that it was going to work because everything else necessary for success had been developed.

We had workshops where a bunch of us transformers would get together. There wasn't one story of success among us. Yet we would give each other suggestions. Within a short time, hundreds of ideas popped out that wouldn't have worked alone.

> *An inventor fails 999 times, and if he succeeds once, he's in. He treats his failures simply as practice shots.*
> —*Charles F. Kettering*

Another thing that maintained us through the failure periods was the enthusiasm for our work. When things go well it creates euphoria. When something exciting happens, it's a thrill. For example, we had been working on finding how a particular gene in the salivary gland of the mosquito would be secreted. When you get a mosquito bite, they actually salivate this into your skin and it prevents platelets from forming. It's one of the reasons for the reaction you receive from a mosquito bite. Platelets normally counteract the mosquito's ability to feed. When we found that gene, for just a second I felt like I was looking back 120 million years. That's pretty wild. For that moment I accomplished something I never expected. I saw something I never expected to see. It was absolutely wonderful. And now, when things aren't so wonderful, it's the possibilities of those very moments that keep me motivated.

PERSEVERANCE IN PRINT
Author John Creasey received only 730 rejection slips before he sold his first book in 1930. He went on to publish over 560 more.

Victoria Williams

"My stumbling blocks became my steppingstones."

While Victoria Williams' gifts as a singer and songwriter have been vividly documented on her albums and live appearances, ironically, the work that served as her initial introduction to many listeners barely featured the Louisiana-born artist at all. *Sweet Relief: A Benefit For Victoria Williams* **was a career summation any artist would deeply envy. Performing many of Williams' finest songs were more than a dozen of rock's most respected performers, including Pearl Jam, Lou Reed, Matthew Sweet, Lucinda Williams and the Jayhawks. What those artists knew—and what an expanding audience soon discovered—is that Victoria Williams is a writer of craft and talent, an artist who, with vivid words and melodies, can paint unforgettable pictures. That album and much of Williams' success was born out of a devastating diagnosis no one could be ready for.**

It was the early '90s. I was having a lot of problems and doing some heavy drinking. I figured the drinking had a lot to do with my problems and that I had become an alcoholic. So I stopped drinking and joined Alcoholics Anonymous.

Still, I had mega-discomfort. I was in New York recording my first album and I called my husband to play harmonica on it, and he said, "Come to New York? I don't even know if I want to be married to you." I was devastated. I wanted to go into every bar I saw. I talked to my record label and told them I wanted to quit recording the album. They said I couldn't, that there was way too much money invested in it. I had to finish. I was under a lot of stress and I had a manager who wasn't there for me.

The record went out on the Geffen label and it got excellent reviews, but they didn't put it out on compact disc. I met someone from the company who was distributing my records and she said, "I feel so bad…we have a whole room filled with your records because we never shipped them." I left Geffen and made a record for the Rough Trade label and they went bankrupt. The record never really got out there. My husband and I divorced, leaving me very depressed.

Out of the blue, I got a call from a woman who booked Neil Young and she wanted to know if I would open up for Neil on his solo tour. Here I was, without a record out and nobody really knows who I am. Who wouldn't do it? I love Neil. He was my favorite. It was a dream come true.

The tour was pretty grueling and with audiences really there for Neil, sometimes they weren't all that thrilled when I walked out on the stage. That, and the schedule, was pretty hard on my nerves. By the 26th show of the tour, it became obvious that something was physically wrong with me. I couldn't walk very fast and couldn't move my hands. I had no idea what was wrong. Here I was, no money, no medical insurance, no record label, no husband and something was going on in my body no one could figure out. It took visits to three different hospitals before a doctor finally told me what was wrong. I had multiple sclerosis.

The doctors said they didn't exactly understand the disease and there was no cure for it. It was very scary. Even though I had friends visiting me in the hospital, I felt very alone.

Character cannot be developed in ease and quiet. Only through experience of trial and suffering can the soul be strengthened, vision cleared, ambition inspired, and success achieved.
—Helen Keller

But a wonderful thing happened the day I got out of the hospital. There was an incredible benefit at the Whisky in Los Angeles to pay for my medical bills. Musicians in New York heard about the benefit in L.A. and held a benefit for me there. Many people I didn't even know reached out to me. Even Frank Sinatra sent me a thousand dollars. He didn't know me at all. I wondered how many times he had helped people that we never even heard about.

Turn your wounds into wisdom.
—*Oprah Winfrey*

This disease would force me to face many trials. At one point I was struck blind. It was terrifying. The doctor said that it was neuropathy and that it could last two weeks, two months or two years. No one seems to know with this disease. It was hardly reassuring. It only lasted two weeks, but that terror led me to writing some self-pitying songs.

There were times when I couldn't even walk and my husband, Mark, whom I had married in 1994, had to carry me like a sack of potatoes and put me on the toilet. I couldn't even feel if I was going to the bathroom. I could only listen. I was pretty scared not knowing whether the MS would get worse.

When I started playing the guitar again, my hands would get numb and I wasn't able to move my hands like I used to. It was pretty depressing, but I still had my strong faith in God, a strong faith that I learned from my mom, who was a cancer survivor. I wasn't about to let the pain or the MS rule my life. Instead of shying away from using my hands, I pushed to do more. I went out into my yard, dug with my hands and planted a garden. As a guitar player, I learned how to play differently. I discovered all different kinds of tuning so I could play *open strings*. I play that way a lot now. I love the new chords and discoveries I've made along the way. It's amazing what being *limited* brings out. You're forced to find out so many other things you can do and ways to do it. My limitations actually provided me with opportunities. My stumbling blocks became my steppingstones.

Sometimes I get spasms while playing guitar. My hands seem to go off on their own. I used to be tight and try so hard to control what I did, playing a song the way I *thought* it should be played rather than letting it come to me. I used to be so hard on myself, but now I've learned to laugh at myself, even on stage. I started to learn about the freedom that was available to me. I had a choice. I could get really depressed about what was happening, which is a no-win situation, or I could do like the Carter family and *stay on the sunny side*.

My hands are always numb. My feet are always numb. And they hurt. They cramp up when I play, especially when I play the piano. It really bugs me. But many others have it worse. I see people with severe arthritis and I think how devastating that is, too. Most people wouldn't trade their disease for someone else's. I know that even though I have a disease, I'm still the same person with the same spirit I had before I got MS.

There were times when I thought to myself that I didn't want to live with this disease. I didn't want to be a burden to other people. I felt suicidal. About the same time, I learned that my husband's father, who I felt had chickened out on his family by committing suicide, had done so because he had MS. He couldn't live with it. I felt very bad about how I had judged Mark's father. All of a sudden, I was walking in his shoes.

We were still having money problems, so Megan Ochs [legendary folk singer Phil Ochs' daughter] and Sylvia Reed [Lou Reed's wife] put together a benefit album with many great musicians and singers who recorded my songs. There was Pearl Jam, the Jayhawks, Soul Asylum, Lucinda Williams, Lou Reed, Michelle Shocked and many others. I thought about how fortunate I was that all these musicians were so kind to donate their time and talent to help another musician. This was so special that I decided to take a percentage of what came in from that album and used it to create *Sweet Relief*, a fund to help other musicians who may not have the insurance to cover their medical problems. Today, through donations and benefits, *Sweet Relief* continues to help many needy musicians in many ways.

Effort only fully releases its reward after a person refuses to quit.
—Napoleon Hill

I've never said that it was a good thing that I got MS, but I have said that it taught me many things that I might not ordinarily have learned. It made me more aware of my body. I've changed the way I eat.

No fried food. No bread…hardly. I used to go until I dropped. I know now when to slow down. If I hadn't been sick, my career might have never taken off. Most people I meet tell me that they first heard of me from the *Sweet Relief* record.

The things which hurt, instruct.
—Benjamin Franklin

My MS has been a great teacher. I've learned to appreciate each day. I know what all of us can do when we work together to help each other. Sometimes we need to go through a storm before we can see the sun. Sometimes we need that hurricane to bring people together.

SURGICAL SLIPS

While working on an apparatus to record irregular heartbeats, researcher Wilson Greatbatch accidentally used a wrong resistor. The resulting pulsing rhythm acted similarly to a human heart and Greatbatch had developed the mechanism for the first pacemaker, small enough to be implanted. Soon after, he came up with a corrosion-free lithium battery to run the pacemaker.

Sonny Hill

"It's not so much the adversity you face, but how you deal with it that counts."

Ask anyone in Philadelphia who Mr. Basketball is and the most likely answer will be Sonny Hill. He was a legend in the old professional Eastern Basketball League, co-founder of the world famous Baker League, and one of the first African-American announcers for the National Basketball Association. Presently an executive consultant for the Philadelphia 76ers and the CoreStates Spectrum, Hill has spent years in the forefront of community service, creating large numbers of community programs and recently receiving the Commission on Human Relations 50th Anniversary Clarence Farmer Award for his outstanding contributions to the promotion of intergroup harmony and cooperation. With all the lessons he learned on the court, Sonny Hill found that adversity and racism would be some of his greatest teachers.

I was raised by my grandmother. She always saw something special in me and allowed me to be myself. My grandmother knew how far to let me go and when to pull me back in. This became my foundation on which I live my life. When I came up against obstacles in my life, I would challenge them because I knew I would be successful if I worked hard, persevered and made an honest effort to be the best I could be. The challenges started early.

When I was growing up, racism was commonplace. In my neighborhood, baseball was king. In 1949, I became one of four black teenagers to break the color line in American Legion baseball. We were the only team in the American Legion with black players. While I was the pride of the neighborhood, I still felt threatened and was insulted by the fact that people dealt with us solely from a racial point of view.

We would play other teams in other towns where there were no other black players, and we were met with negative behavior. Although it was hurtful, I found that this gave me tools to deal with life. I learned something positive from those bad times by *evaluating* what was really happening. Of course, I thought some of those people were just idiots. Our white coach, who took the initiative to select us for the team, went through even more grief than the players. Fact was, many whites opened doors so that blacks could walk through.

In high school, where black players were just starting to have opportunities to play varsity, I became captain of both the basketball and baseball teams. Again, we faced teams and places with no black players. There were those who weren't happy with us playing. I found this seeming hardship gave me the opportunity to open doors for those who would follow me.

I went on to get a grant in aid from Central State College in Ohio, stayed a year and a half, then went into the professional Eastern Basketball League [EBL]. I was 5 feet 9¹/₂ inches tall and all of 143 pounds. I was not only one of the shortest, but I was the lightest player in a physical contact league. I could play *above the rim* in an Allen Iverson-style of play and refused to be denied. If they were going to get physical with me, then I had to show them they couldn't stop me from making my $25 a game. I'd play two games a weekend, that was $50, which was big money in 1958. There weren't many people making that a week. I picked up another $15 barnstorming with the Harlem Comedy Kids. For the era, I was doing pretty good.

I am not judged by the number of times I fail, but by the number of times I succeed; and the number of times I succeed is in direct proportion to the number of times I can fail and keep on trying.
—Tom Hopkins

I originally played for the Allentown Jets. At the time, there were eight teams in the NBA and eight more in the EBL, so I was playing big-time ball. We had great players, many of whom should have been playing in the NBA, but couldn't because they had been caught in a national scandal from betting fixes. Others weren't playing because of continuing color bias. It was 1958 and many of the NBA teams still didn't have a single black player. Hal Lear, who was the first player to average 40 points a game in the EBL, wasn't even given a shot. So for many of us, playing NBA ball was out of the question.

If you are doing your best, you will not have to worry about failure.
—Robert S. Hillyer

I played 10 years in the EBL making $125 a game during my best year. We played many games against teams in upstate Pennsylvania: Allentown, Wilkes-Barre, Scranton, Williamsport. Many places that were unfriendly, to say the least. During my greatest season in the EBL, when I was averaging 26 points a game, the coach replaced me with a white player, not because he was better, but because he was white.

I remember going into Baltimore to play the Bullets. A bunch of us, including some white friends, tried to get served in a restaurant. We were met with, "We don't serve niggers in here." Certainly we weren't happy, but we simply left. We dealt with it because we knew the terrain. The white players left with us, which showed me that we weren't just teammates on the court. Knowing that turned that experience into a positive one for me.

There were times when I was *backed into a corner* and actually threatened by some people. Many times I wanted to strike back but found that there were other ways to handle the situations. One that had better results. In one basketball tournament, I was the only black player. My defender was pushing me around and taunting me. Instead of lashing out like I wanted to do, I told him that every time he fouled me I would make that shot. I ended up setting a tournament record with 55 points and was named Most Valuable Player. When the crowd saw how I handled the situation, their reaction was nothing but positive.

In 1960, the best players of the era didn't have an organized league to play in during the summer. I went to my peers, including

[Temple University coach] John Chaney and [Detroit Pistons] Ray Scott and we formed the Charles Baker Memorial League, the first-ever professional summer league. Even though I played in the EBL, worked for the Teamsters and played with the Harlem Comedy Kids, I did the nuts-and-bolts footwork for the Baker League, from getting the players' shirts to paying the referees. I also played and coached. It became a regular showcase for the best players like Wilt Chamberlain, Guy Rodgers, Woody Salisbury, white players as well as black. Many of the players who were named as the NBA's 50 Greatest Players of All Time played Baker League ball.

Even with my successes, there was adversity. But it's not so much the adversity you face, but how you deal with it that counts.

More men fail through lack of purpose than lack of talent.
—Billy Sunday

My people are from the South; I should have had a southern drawl. That in itself would seem to be enough to have kept me from doing well in many careers, but when I was young, I worked on self-expression. I worked on my speech until I not only developed strong pronunciation and articulation skills, but when I retired from playing ball, I was hired to do commentary on NBA games for CBS-TV.

Although I never got to play in the NBA, my knowledge of the game and my relationship with the players was outstanding. If I walked into a team's locker room with a Brent Musburger, the players would yell out to me. They had no idea who Brent was at the time. When I would want to speak with Bill Bradley, Rick Barry, Earl Monroe or Wilt Chamberlain for an interview, they would come to me.

After four years, I was dropped by CBS with no explanation. I was only told how terrific I was. It seemed like they wanted me to play the "proper negro." If I had, I'd probably still be there today, but I had an obligation to be myself. I was let go, but even that opened up more doors that led to more personal and career growth.

You have to have pride in who you are. You can overcome everything as long as you're willing to persevere and let anyone who opposes you know that you will weather the challenge by outworking them. Given the opportunity, you can always do a good job and then some.

There's no mystery about being successful, but people look for a magic formula. There is none. Just like basketball, life is about fundamentals. Know how to say "please." Know how to say "thank you," "good morning" and "good night." You have to work hard, do what you have to do today and take care of tomorrow when tomorrow comes. Look adversity in the face and rise above it. Be a person who only deals in success, even when that success might first appear to be failure.

KELVIN'S KRAZY KONCEPTS

"Heavier-than-air flying machines are impossible."

–Lord Kelvin, president, Royal Society of London, 1895.

Betty White

"I felt I had my big shot and I blew it."

Television Hall of Famer Betty White started her career in radio at the age of 16 and has since garnered four Emmys, enjoyed myriad stints as a game show panelist and host and has been a favorite on the talk show circuit. While White has starred in a number of television series, she is probably known best as the man-chasing Happy Homemaker, Sue Ann Nivens, on the *The Mary Tyler Moore Show* and as the lovable Rose Nylund on *The Golden Girls*. But when her first network show was canceled, Betty White thought she'd never work again.

The Betty White Show, which was actually my second *Betty White Show*, was my very first network production. I had done television before, in 1954, but this was the first one that would be broadcast nationally. It was done live on kinescope on the West Coast. There were other changes from the first show.

Besides a new NBC studio and a dressing room with a shower, I no longer had to do my own hair. I even had a wardrobe lady. *The Betty White Show* had my name in the title, but it was basically variety with a cast of many talented people.

When you fall, don't get up empty-handed.
—Unknown

Twelve noon, five days a week on national TV. We were having a ball and as a bonus we were receiving some very good ratings. And then someone at NBC stepped in. Our audience had been used to watching us at lunchtime, but in an attempt to strengthen ratings later in the afternoon, they decided to rearrange the schedule and we were moved to 4:30.

Well, we didn't improve NBC's afternoon and by the time they realized and moved us back to the noon hour, 12:30 to be exact, our audience was completely confused. And when the audience is confused, it isn't long before there's no longer a show to be confused about. By the end of the year, *The Betty White Show* was replaced by *The Tennessee Ernie Ford Show*. To make it all harder to swallow, our canceled show was later nominated for an Emmy.

I was devastated. I felt it was the end of the world. I thought I would never work again. I sat on the floor and thought, "It's over." Of course, that attitude didn't do me very much good.

We all carry on these horrendous conversations in our head. You just have to try and still those voices for a little while. They're not on your side and they have a tendency to spin you downward. The minute you replow the same tired field and go back over what happened, you're not only not progressing, you're regressing. You have to shut those voices out.

After I was able to cry the cancellation out, I got as quiet as possible. I decided to follow this with getting as busy as possible. When the game show *Password* was canceled the first time, Allen [Luden, Betty's beloved, late husband who was the show's host] didn't dwell on it. He would always have seven projects going at the same time. He just buckled down and kept very busy. He never depended on just one thing.

I have always felt that although someone may defeat me, and I strike out in a ball game, the pitcher on the particular day was the best player. But I know when I see him again, I'm going to be ready for his curve ball. Failure is a part of success. There is no such thing as a bed of roses all your life. But failure will never stand in the way of success if you learn from it.
—Hank Aaron

Of course, if you're ranting and raving, something good could come by and you would end up missing it. Shortly after my show's cancellation, the phone rang with an opportunity presented to me that was even better than the one I had just lost. I was going to star in my first sitcom. It is difficult to grasp when you're in the middle of the pain, but it took the cancellation to make me available for something that has become such an important part of my career.

Failure? I never encountered it. All I ever met were temporary setbacks.
—Dottie Walters

You can also use your friends to get you out of your funk. When you're down it's difficult to give yourself a pep talk. Other people can. When another *Betty White Show* was canceled, I think it was around the fourth, I was crushed. I was really sick for about a month because again, I thought I'd never get another series. I felt I had my big shot and I blew it.

About a month after the cancellation, I went out to dinner with Dick Martin and Bob Newhart. It was hysterical. Once you get your sense of humor back, once you can laugh at something, everything begins to shrink down to its proper perspective again.

I was always brought up to be an optimist. My parents gave me a great support system. It was in my genes. That doesn't mean that failure doesn't hurt. But you do learn that failure in one field might lead to an opportunity in another.

When I was young, I wanted to be an opera singer. I started studying at 14 and I just knew that it would be my life. There was one minor problem. I didn't have an operatic voice. So the door closed on opera and I had to start doing other things. It would have been altogether different had I continued with the operatic studies. Most of the wonderful things that had transpired in my life might have never entered the mix. Of course, that's only proven in retrospect. You just never know it at the time. Maybe that's what makes life so interesting.

PREPOSTEROUS PROCLAMATIONS

"Stocks have reached what looks like a permanently high plateau."

–Irving Fisher, professor of economics, Yale University, 1929.

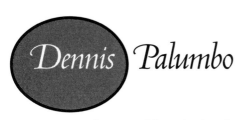

Dennis Palumbo

"I stopped acting like I had to know everything."

Dennis Palumbo burst on to the Hollywood scene by co-writing the classic film, *My Favorite Year*, starring Peter O'Toole. His widely praised column, *The Writer's Life*, appears monthly in the Writers Guild of America journal, *Written By*. At the age of 40, and after much success in show business, he made a career jump into the world of psychotherapy where he now specializes in helping new and established screenwriters, directors, and novelists address creative issues, as well as those involving midlife and career transition. He has continued this work with his bestselling book, *Writing From the Inside Out*. It was his transition into psychotherapy where Palumbo found himself totally unprepared for the trials he would face.

I'm the first of nine grandchildren to go to college. It was laid out for me when I was a kid that I would be an engineer. I left engineering school after the first year to become a writer. It was very difficult for my family. Now that I'm a father I have empathy for how panicked my parents were. I was 18. I didn't know any writers. Everyone told me how horrible the odds were, as if I didn't already know. There's not a single fear or concern that someone mentions to you about an artistic career that you haven't already been thinking about all night long when you can't sleep. We're ready to self-invalidate so fast it's not even funny.

I first went to Louisville, Kentucky, and wrote radio and television ad copy for two years. I then quit my job and moved to L.A. where I starved for two years. I sold jokes to comics, which may be the lowest rung job a writer could have. I couldn't get anyone to read my material. In desperation, I went to The Comedy Store and auditioned so that someone in the business might notice me. After about eight or nine months, the owner, Mitzi Shore, told me I wasn't going to make it as a comic, and if Mitzi didn't like you, you weren't going to get any good time slots on stage. That hit hard. However, she had also told comic Gabe Kaplan to come see my act, not for my performance but for my writing ability. He read some of my material and months later, when I was about ready to pack it in, Gabe called and hired me to go on the road with him. A year later I was writing on his hit series, *Welcome Back, Kotter*. Talk about irony, if Mitzi had felt that I was a good comic, I may never have met Gabe. Then, with my success of *My Favorite Year*, I began what was to become a fairly successful career in show business, one in which I felt very lucky.

For a year and a half I traveled the world working on a film for Robert Redford about mountain climbers. I climbed mountains, lived in the Himalayas and hit a midlife crisis. I started to see there was a larger world than the world of show business. I began to toy with the idea of another career, even though I was doing quite well. Well, more than toy, I went to graduate school at Pepperdine University for the next three and a half years.

After getting my marriage and family degree, I took a job working as an intern in a psychiatric facility dealing with psychotic people. To tell you the truth, I thought I was the one making them crazy. It was very painful. I thought I'd be the one who ended up jumping out the window.

I took a couple classes, one of which was with a teacher who was working with schizophrenics doing psychodrama in a psychiatric hospital. He invited me to co-lead the group. You cannot imagine what this was like. These were thoroughly psychotic people in intense pain, but we had an opportunity to be incredibly creative with these people whom society had labeled "crazy."

Failure—
The man who can tell others what to do and how to do it, but never does it himself.
—Unknown

My life was changing. I would be in a very expensive restaurant discussing a movie deal with a producer and find myself constantly checking my watch because I couldn't wait to get back to the psychiatric facility. During my first couple of months there, I had no idea what I was doing and was so afraid of saying or doing the wrong thing. I thought I could set these people off at any time. I hadn't realized that my experience in show business was very good training for working with schizophrenics. My psychotic clients weren't that much different from the stars and producers I had worked with.

If there is no wind...row.
—Old Proverb

In one group, I remember speaking with a very frightened client who was seeing demons coming out of his television screen. I was trying to get him to enact some of his hallucinations. He declined and I kept pushing. The entire room became quiet. I noticed that everyone was staring at me. One of the other clients said, "Christ, this guy is crazier than we are." It was like I was telling a bunch of people what I thought was a great joke and nobody was laughing. I thought I lost any chance to have credibility with the group. I was told by my instructor, "Don't try so hard. Just be with them."

The next client I worked with had been diagnosed as a paranoid schizophrenic. I told him he wasn't. That he was a human being, just like everyone else. After an hour of trying to get him to buy my approach, he freaked out. To him, I was taking away from him the only thing he could grasp—that he was a paranoid schizophrenic. What I saw as a negative and restrictive label, he experienced as an anchor and something he could hold on to. Once again my approach failed. Not only that, but in order for the insurance companies to pay for treatment, they needed a particular diagnosis. There I was arguing against this client having one at all. The two guys who were running the psychiatric facility sat me down and said that perhaps this wasn't what I should be doing. I felt that I might not belong there. Maybe I should forget the whole thing. I thought, "Suddenly I'm going to help these people? I couldn't even help myself."

I was raised to be a perfectionist. I thought I was supposed to hit the ball out of the park the first time I came to bat. Here I was making huge mistakes that were having a big impact on my self-esteem as well as the clients. I was being told that I was wrong for this business and I was beginning to believe it. At the same time, I had to question myself. Did I belong someplace else? Someplace where I won't make mistakes?

Those are cultural messages. I didn't realize then that if I have the desire, it doesn't matter how long it takes. It took Harvey Keitel seven years to make it into New York's Actors Studio. He had the desire and felt that he belonged. He kept coming back until he made it. You have to love the doing, not only the end result. I decided to stick it out a little longer.

A couple weeks later, I worked with a client who was hearing voices. I finally said, "Look, could you stop being crazy for five minutes so we could talk?" And he said, "Okay." It was the first time I felt comfortable being myself. I had just had a breakthrough.

Those mistakes were all necessary to my education. I needed to learn that I had to make mistakes before I would be able to do a good job. I had been so suspicious of my right to become a therapist that if I failed at anything along the way, I felt that I should just give up.

There was so much shame attached to failure that I couldn't see anything as a learning experience. I had a lot of luck as a writer and was used to success. I had no idea how fragile that idea of myself as a successful person was. I started to realize that not only were my clients on a learning curve, but so was I.

I wanted to help people, but first I had to give up the idea that just by believing in myself, working my hardest and never giving up, I would succeed. It had stood me in very good stead, but it was a two-edged sword. It might have gotten me where I wanted, but when things aren't going so well, there's not much left for self-love. When you're not performing well, your view of yourself is very fragile.

In show business, you can stay in perpetual adolescence and fool a lot of people. But this was the real world, with people in real pain and diagnosable conditions. I was dealing with their doctors, the drugs they were taking and making recommendations for their best treatment.

Who the hell was I? A guy who could barely hold his life together, whose marriage had ended and was now floundering. As an intern I saw how conditional my self-acceptance was. Sooner or later everyone bumps up against a wall. Samuel Johnson said, "Adversity introduces a man to himself." That was what happened to me. I thought all my big lessons were done because I was successful in my 20s. But when you're sitting in a psyche hospital with a bunch of schizophrenics who are yelling at you because they think you're the one who's nuts, you can't help but think, "Who the hell am I?"

You shouldn't be surprised about running up against obstacles in your life; there's a good chance you're living that life for the first time.
—S. Young

It was a very low point. I was turning down writing jobs left and right so my agent dumped me. I couldn't get another agent. I couldn't get a job. And I was afraid to go back to the hospital. I felt like everything I did was a tremendous mistake. Why had I changed careers? Now show business was doing fine without me. That ship had sailed and no one was weeping my departure. That was the lowest point of my life. I felt like I had nothing left.

But the fact is, those missteps ended up being what I needed. I had been trying too hard, giving up me to empathize with the client. When I said, "Will you just stop being crazy for five minutes," we connected at a human level. This was not a decision on my part. This was a desperate action of a person who had hit bottom. It was a momentous bit of clarity. Despite his mental illness, this client actually had a moment of empathy for me. He understood how frustrating it was for me to be with him. He actually touched my arm. I realized that I might have made contact with someone there for the first time in six months. It was a beginning for me. I didn't have any ideas or methods. I just showed up. I stopped acting like I had to know everything.

Now, whenever I'm working with therapists in training, I'm always aware of those who are willing to wait for the moment to emerge compared to the ones who start therapizing right away. Then, while you're busy being the therapist, the patient disappears.

While failing might seem like the easiest time to get down on yourself, it's important to remember that all the successful people in the world didn't start out that way. They all started out struggling. Every successful writer was once an unsuccessful writer. Every successful banker was an unsuccessful banker. This is what you are doing to lay the groundwork for the person you are going to become, and that person succeeds. So your job is to learn. In the Warrior's Code it is said, "Risk, fail and risk again."

I think our schools underestimate the value of failing, which I believe to be another way of saying "risking." By not risking, you're not going to grow. In watching actors in acting class, you can tell the ones who would only do things as safely as they could so the teacher and the other actors would like it. The good acting teacher would remind actors to "be willing to make a fool of yourself" because that's when you learn. Jon Voight said, "You wait for the mistakes. That's where you get the good ideas." As a writer and a therapist, I've found that when things don't turn out the way I thought they would, that's when I truly learn my craft.

Our education system mirrors our culture, including the idea of individual competitiveness. A system that rewards students for getting the highest grades does not create an atmosphere that encourages students to take risks. We should be limiting some of the competitiveness, especially in the earlier years. Allow students to draw outside the lines, allow a lot more freedom to explore, to risk and to fail. This way they get to see it won't kill them psychologically. We have to give kids the feeling that they're on a journey. We have to help them find what excites them. Structure needs to be porous enough to let the spontaneity move through it.

We work best when there is a benign relationship with our own process, as opposed to feeling good only when someone buys the end result. It's the process that is important.

Ask yourself, "Am I learning? Am I getting better? Am I in touch with my authentic self?" Nothing can be determined by an external idea of success or failure. Eleanor Roosevelt said, "No one can make you feel bad about yourself without your permission."

The first thing a student should do is forget about the outside world, that part of him collaborating with the enemy. It's never about saying, "I'm a great person and it doesn't matter what other people think." If those kinds of morning affirmations make it to lunch it's a miracle, because it does matter what others think. We're human beings, after all. This is about looking at the critical voice inside of you. Invariably, it'll be the voice of one or both of your parents. It's a shaming message that's been hammered into you. When the outside world validates that shaming message, you think it's right because this is the real world. So you have to go back to when you first felt that

In great attempts, it is glorious even to fail.
—*Vince Lombardi*

way and be willing to risk the discomfort of feeling differently; in other words, what makes you anxious about believing you're okay. The big paradox of therapy is that most people come into therapy to get rid of a trait that they cling to like a life raft. Most people are so dependent on another person's opinion of them that they would feel lost and confused if they were liberated from that dependency.

My whole view has changed over the past 10-plus years. Until then, I was only a believer in success. Failure was unacceptable. It took some time, but today I know that failure is the only way to learn how to do anything.

ACCIDENTAL ACHIEVEMENTS

While walking in the woods, Swiss engineer Georges de Mestral noticed burrs sticking to his clothing. Using the burr as a blueprint, Mestral designed two pieces of fabric that clung when placed together and could be easily pulled apart...and Velcro® was created.

J

Just because something doesn't do what you

planned it to do doesn't mean it's useless.

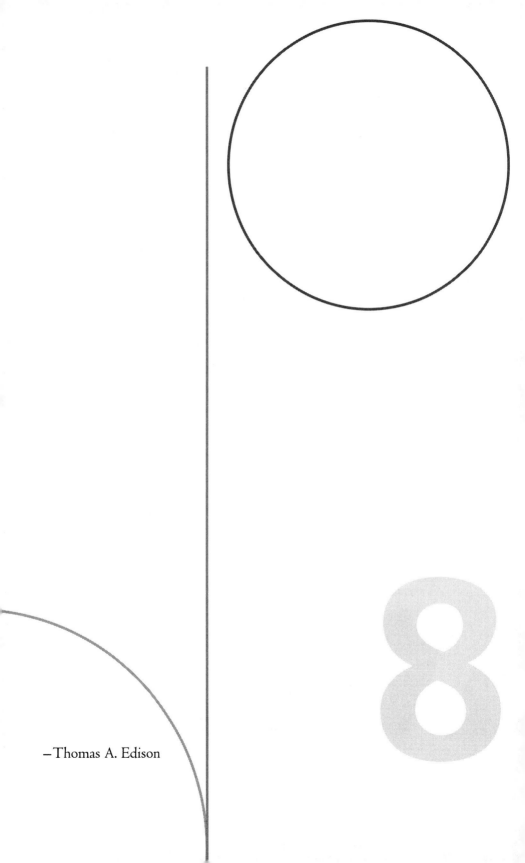

–Thomas A. Edison

8

Guy Gabaldon

"What appeared to be a personal disaster was a blessing in disguise."

On July 7, 1944, the World War II battle to secure the Japanese-occupied island of Saipan peaked in one of the largest banzai charges of the Pacific War. The next morning, a lone American Marine [Navy Cross] Medal of Honor selectee, Private Guy Gabaldon, ordered 800 Japanese soldiers and civilians to surrender. Already known for capturing hundreds of die-hard enemy troops using a brisk combination of fluent "street" Japanese and point-blank carbine fire, his solo raids into Japanese lines became legend. His heroics were captured in the film *Hell to Eternity*, but it was Guy Gabaldon's childhood loss of his original family that started him on a path to saving many lives—both ours and the enemy's.

I was a 10-year-old Chicano living as a waif in the ghettos of Los Angeles, shining shoes on Skid Row, eating at the missions where I was the only kid among the homeless winos and other dregs of society. Skid Row in the '30s was a place where you could get a fast education in life. A 10-year-old kid can acquire a lot of chutzpah and moxie around the boxers, B-girls and hustlers. I'd run errands for the "girls" and they'd slip me a nickel now and then. To get around, I would hop trucks and ride "cow-catchers."

Though the cops would pick me up once in a while, I learned how to survive. The years I spent on the street provided an education that could not be bought. Street smarts meant survival. By the time I was 13, I was in my East L.A. barrio, fighting and raising hell. At the rate I was going, I wasn't going to last past the age of 20. It was then that I began spending a lot of time with Japanese families in Little Tokyo.

I liked everything Japanese—the food, the traditional samurai stories, the pretty Japanese girls, the proud yet not haughty demeanor of the Japanese people and the determination to succeed in all they undertook. Eventually, I moved in with the Nikano family. What I learned from my adopted people helped keep me alive in near-impossible battle situations.

I helped my brothers deliver the Japanese daily newspaper. I helped my adopted mom at her florist shop. I even attended a Japanese school where I learned kana (Japanese alphabet), a few kanji (ideograms) and some phrases. My brother Lyle would spend hours teaching me how to write the kata-kana. It was a feeling of great accomplishment to speak Japanese, although broken and limited.

I was especially fascinated by the samurai traditions of the Japanese, but years later I would end up killing many of the "Superior Race Samurai" in battle. One little East L.A. Chicano knocking off Hirohito's best.

I wanted to fight for our country in the worst way, but obstacles were great. At 17, I tried to enlist in the Navy. I weighed 126 pounds, was 5 feet 3 inches and had a perforated eardrum. They turned me down.

It was the biggest disappointment of my young life. What I didn't know then was that Divine Providence was leading me to a greater purpose than just serving on a submarine. What appeared to be a personal disaster was actually a blessing in disguise.

I remembered reading that the Marine Corps needed Japanese interpreters. I knew my Japanese was limited, but it was enough to bullshit a Marine recruiter. If they needed interpreters that badly, they'd surely overlook a broken eardrum. This time, they did overlook my bad ear. I became a Marine.

Unfortunately, it wasn't long before I was thrown out of the Marine's language school for fighting and was reassigned to an 81mm mortar squad. At least I was still in the Corps and I was soon to be trained as a scout and observer. I ended up as part of the 1944 Saipan Island invasion in the Marianas.

Once on Saipan, I decided to go out and look around on my own. I came upon three Japanese soldiers. This would be the first time

Misfortune is the test
of a person's merit.
—Seneca

I would try to speak Japanese to the enemy. "Te o gaete" (Raise your hands), I demanded. One of them spun around with his rifle so I blasted him. The others dropped their rifles and I convinced them that they would not get hurt if they did as I said. They were my first captures and I thought I had done a good job until I was confronted by my very angry captain. I was told never to go out alone again and I agreed. The next day, I went out and brought in 12 more. This time, my captain reacted much differently. We had gotten important information out of the two prisoners I brought in the day before. These 12 provided even more. Now they were happy with my disobedience. This would begin the start of my *freelance operation* on Saipan. Soon the "impossible" would take place.

It was the morning of July 8, 1944, when I took two prisoners on top of the Banzai Cliffs. I talked with them at length, trying to convince them that to continue fighting would amount to sure death for both of them. I told them that if they continued fighting, our flamethrowers would roast them alive. I pointed to the many ships we had lying offshore waiting to blast them in their caves. "Why die when you have a chance to surrender under honorable conditions? You are taking civilians to their death, which is not part of your Bushido military code."

The big job was going to be convincing them that we would not torture and kill them—that they would be well treated and be returned to Japan after the war. I understood that their Bushido Code called for death before surrender, and that to surrender was to be considered a coward. This was going to be a tough nut to crack. And if I wasn't able to convince them that I was a good guy, I would be a dead marine within a few minutes. I knew that there were hundreds of the die-hard enemy still about and if they rushed me I would probably only be able to kill two or three before they ate me alive. Would I be able to pull this off? I had beaten the odds so far, but the odds of getting these suicidal Japanese to surrender seemed insurmountable. I finally talked one of my two prisoners into going to the cliffs below and attempting to persuade his fellow Gyokusai Banzai survivors that they would be treated with dignity if they surrendered.

I kept the other one with me, not as a hostage, but because he said that if he went to the caves with my message and they didn't buy it, "off with the head." I couldn't help but agree with him. The one that descended the cliff either had lots of guts, or he was going to double-cross me and come back with his troops firing away.

The other Japanese soldier finally returned with 12 military personnel, each with a rifle. This was it! This time I couldn't tell them to drop their weapons. I couldn't tell them they were surrounded. I would now be a prisoner of the fanatical Manchurian campaign veterans.

They didn't say a word. They just stood there in front of me waiting for the next move. If I fired they would have the drop on me. They'd chop me down before I had a chance to fire a round. I had to keep my cool or my head would roll.

"Dozo o suwari nasai!" (Please sit down!) I must make them feel that I have everything under control. This is the first time I thought I might be too young to demonstrate authority. But what else could I do? I offered them cigarettes, trying to build up my own courage. "Heitai-san!" (Fellow soldiers!) "I am here to bring you a message from General Holland 'Mad' Smith, the shogun in charge of the Marianas Operation. General Smith admires your valor and has ordered our troops to offer a safe haven to all the survivors of your intrepid Gyokusai attack yesterday. Such a glorious and courageous military action will go down in history. The general assures you that you will be taken to Hawaii where you will be kept together in comfortable quarters until the end of the war. The General's word is honorable. It is his desire that there be no more useless bloodshed."

These Japanese didn't know General Smith from General Pancho Villa, but they

When the student is ready, the teacher will appear.
—Old Chinese Proverb

respected the word "shogun." I told them that the American Navy, with its firepower, could kill all of them. I pointed to the hundreds of ships sitting offshore. They began to mumble among themselves, but the very fact that they came to talk with me showed a breakthrough. They could have easily shot me from behind the rocks on the edge of the cliffs. This scam had to work or it was "Adios, mother."

The one in charge was a chuii (first lieutenant). He reached over and accepted a cigarette. A break. They were starting to come around. I tried the Japanese adage I learned in East L.A., "Warera Nihonjin toshite hazukashii koto o shitara ikemasen" (Being Japanese we should not commit a shameful act). They smiled, probably at my poor pronunciation. They knew that I wasn't Japanese. I looked like a typical Chicano, but it was working.

The chuii asked me if we had a well-equipped hospital at our headquarters. Madre mia, they were going to buy my proposition. I said that we had fine, well-equipped doctors. The chuii gazed at the ships just a few hundred feet off the cliffs. He has to know that to resist is sure death for all, me included. I can see that this guy does not want to die or he would have done himself in the night before during the earlier attack. "So da yo! Horyo ni naru!" (So be it! I become your prisoner!). My thought was, "Guy, you short-ass bastard, you did it!"

The chuii left four men with me and took the rest of his troops over the cliffs. If I pulled this off, it would be the first time in World War II that a lone Marine private captured half a Japanese regiment by himself. We wait and wait. In the meantime, I carried on a conversation with "my prisoners." We talked of their families, where they were from, and so on. I told them about having lived with Japanese Americans in California and my love for my foster family. I told them my belief that we, the common soldiers, obeyed orders and in reality had nothing to do with starting wars. They agreed. They liked my American cigarettes as well as my K-rations.

In less than an hour, the chuii and over 50 men come up over the cliffs. My heart is in my throat. This is the first time in the campaign that I did not have the drop on the enemy. They all sat down in front of me. They did not look like defeated men. They were proud and serious, as if they hadn't really made up their minds. The best thing for me was to show a self-assured demeanor. The chuii tells me that there are many hundreds of people down below, some wounded, some civilians. He wanted medicine for the wounded. It looked like I wasn't out of the woods yet. I showed him my sulfa powder and told him that there was much more medicine at our Command Post. I told him to bring everyone up to the flat area and we would begin moving back to Garapan, then to Chalan Kanoa. He wanted water and medicine immediately for those in dire need. "Be patient," I said. "I give you my word that once you have all your people here, I will make contact with my troops."

They started coming up. The lines up the trails seemed endless. My God, how many are there? I might as well have thrown my carbine and sidearm away. If they rushed me, sayonara! But they seemed to know that they were surrendering. They all looked for someone in authority. Perhaps they thought that there would be hundreds of American troops here. I began giving orders, separating the civilians from the military and getting the wounded in one area. There were many wounded, some seriously, but they still had a lot of fight left in them. The majority wanted to give me a chance to come through with my promises, but some of the younger military wanted to continue fighting. The situation was shaky and the enemy was getting nervous. They wanted food and water and medical care. If it was not forthcoming, they would kill me and go back to their caves. I needed help right away or we'd have to fight this group, with hundreds ending up dead on each side.

People who take risks are the people you'll lose against.
—John Scully

A few marines on a hill saw us and seemed bewildered at what was happening. I had one of my "prisoners" wave a shirt on a stick. They saw it and I could see them getting into their Jeep. Other marines came running down the hill on foot. I was so damn busy trying to get some semblance of order, I don't know how long it took for help to arrive, but I remember hundreds of marines finally arriving on the scene. I got them to take the seriously wounded to sick bay and get me some more help.

I had single-handedly captured over 1,500 soldiers and civilians from the most fanatic army in the world!

People might wonder why I was so calloused to the harshness of battle while only an 18-year-old kid. I was Chicano, orphaned as a young boy, shining shoes on Skid Row, which could have easily had me going the wrong way. If it were not for the way my early life went, I would never have been raised by my Japanese-American family, nor would I have became fluent in Japanese. When you are raised in the ghetto, it can be a good thing or a bad thing. I made a decision to make it a good thing.

●

[Guy Gabaldon's commanders requested that he receive the Medal of Honor, but somehow a silver star arrived, which was only later elevated to a Navy Cross. Compared to Alvin York's 132 prisoners, Guy's 1,500 prisoners would seem to have assured the awarding of the Medal of Honor. Only recently have veterans become anxious to resolve this long-delayed case and pushed for Guy's Medal of Honor. More recently, the City of Los Angeles and district congressional representatives have petitioned the Navy to investigate this matter to help assure a fair resolution.]

(Portions excepted from the book, Saipan: Suicide Island, *by permission of Guy Gabaldon.)*

DUBIOUS DOUBTS

"Drill for oil? You mean drill into the ground to try and find oil? You're crazy."

–What prospectors said to Edwin L. Drake, the father of oil drilling, when he tried to enlist them in his oil-drilling project in 1859.

Dr. Joan Borysenko

"I refused to give in to despair. I told myself that if I could help even one other family avert such a tragedy, my father's death would have meaning."

A noted lecturer on health and spirituality, Joan Borysenko, Ph.D., is a former cancer cell biologist at Harvard Medical School. She is the author of *Minding the Body, Mending the Mind* and *A Woman's Book of Life*. Dr. Borysenko has found that divorce, a near-fatal car accident and the suicide of her father all played a part in her learning process.

Emotionally resilient people view crises as opportunities for problem solving, as challenges, not as threats to survival. I witnessed this phenomenon in my own life when my three children and I ran aground while boating in Scituate, Massachusetts.

I immediately began to imagine the worst, thinking, "We'll be stuck here all night." But my 14-year-old son, Justin, was thrilled. "I'll rescue us," he said.

> *To begin to think with purpose is to enter the ranks of those strong ones who only recognize failure as one of the pathways to attainment.*
> *—James Allen*

He had us step onto a sandbar, then began casting the anchor farther out in the river, pulling the boat along until we were afloat.

Justin's attitude was a wonderful example of emotional resilience. Mine was not.

Emotionally resilient people recognize that while they cannot control everything that happens to them, they can control their response to events. They also know when to stop struggling...and when to just let things be. They personify Reinhold Niebuhr's famous serenity prayer: *God grant me the serenity to accept the things I cannot change, the courage to change the things I can, and the wisdom to know the difference.*

> *Each difficult moment has the potential to open my eyes and open my heart.*
> *—Myla Kabat-Zinn*

Emotionally resilient people believe there is a higher purpose for even the most painful events. That doesn't mean they view problems as intrinsically good, but they recognize that some good often does come from even the most traumatic events.

When my dad killed himself in 1975, I felt not only grief but also terrible guilt. As a cancer biologist, I felt I should have done a better job of helping him endure the difficult treatment process he was undergoing.

I refused to give in to despair. I told myself that if I could help even one other family avert such a tragedy, my father's death would have meaning.

I quit my job at the lab and retrained as a behavioral medicine specialist. Then I founded a mind/body clinic at one of Harvard Medical School's teaching hospitals, beginning a new career helping patients and their families cope physically and spiritually with life-threatening illnesses.

A friend went through something similar when her son died in a car accident. To survive the wrenching pain, she forced herself to think about how her experience might help others. She now volunteers as a support group facilitator, helping other parents who have suffered the loss of a child.

The late psychiatrist and Holocaust survivor Viktor E. Frankl maintained that it is the meaning that we ascribe to negative events that allows us to endure suffering without giving into despair.

Emotional resilience doesn't always come naturally. It certainly didn't come naturally to me. But it can be developed.

Observe your usual response to emotional stress. Do you *catastrophize*? Believe nothing you do will make a difference? Blame yourself?

Simply noticing these responses is often a starting point for change.

Learn more productive ways to respond to problems. Whenever you feel worried or annoyed, ask yourself, "How does this situation challenge me? What can I learn from it?"

Take care of yourself. When we're under severe emotional stress, we tend to abandon our healthful habits. But that is precisely when we need them the most. No matter what else is going on in your life, always eat a balanced diet...exercise regularly...and get plenty of sleep.

Feed your soul. Each day, do something you find deeply pleasurable—whether it's walking in the park, listening to music or curling up with a book.

Find social support. Sharing your problems with friends and/or family members is the best buffer against stress. If you lack close relationships to call upon, join a support group. There's one for practically every crisis you may face.

Telling the future by looking at the past assumes that conditions remain constant. This is like driving a car by looking in the rearview mirror.
—Herb Brody

Practice gratitude. Spend a few minutes each morning and evening listing five things for which you are grateful. This will help you focus more on life's gifts instead of its burdens.

(Portions excerpted from The World's Greatest Treasury of Health Secrets, *by permission of Bottom Line Publications.)*

SAFEGUARD STUMBLES

In an attempt to make a synthetic rubber for airplane fuel lines, a 3M scientist spilled some of her creation on an assistant's canvas shoe. They couldn't remove the liquid, but they found that as time went on, the only part of the shoe that wasn't dulling was where the substance landed. A few years later, a solution that prevents dirt from staining fabric –Scotchgard™–was on the market.

Mark Victor Hansen

"No one buys short stories."

**Mark Victor Hansen and his partner, Jack Canfield, created what
Time magazine has called "the publishing phenomenon of the
decade" with the hugely successful and inspirational book series,
Chicken Soup for the Soul. A master motivator, Mark Victor
Hansen has helped people reshape their personal vision of
what's possible for themselves. But this man who breathes optimism with every breath and sits on top of a motivational empire
had to first lose everything before he found something more.**

It was 1974. I was 26 and building geodesic homes in New
York. Geodesic homes that required no load-bearing interior walls to
support the roof were developed by Bucky Fuller. I was doing
extremely well. Making very good money. Then the oil embargo hit.
At the time, we were using plastic materials to construct the homes. I
couldn't get any more supplies, went upside down in a day and lost
two million dollars.

I wanted to kill myself. I thought that self-esteem and net worth
were the same. I began sleeping 18 hours a day. I was escaping. I was
eating peanut butter until my tongue stuck to the roof of my mouth.
We were in a recession in America and so was I. I didn't feel anything
good was going to happen. Any day you read the newspaper, it would
show you all the aberrant behavior on the planet and confirm that
nothing, in fact, is going right.

I was taking in all negative ideas. When one's conscience input is
negative, then the output, or what we call results, will be negative. It's
very much like the classic archetypal story about the guy who gets his
leg broken and because of it, he's the only one who lives through a war.
Unfortunately, when the yogurt is hitting the fan, it's difficult to
understand that. When you get a higher, more cosmic point of view,

you begin to understand that if there's a recession going on at one level, there's a ton of other business going on at the other end that is doing blissfully well.

Luckily, I had received an audiotape entitled *Are You the Cause or Are You the Result?* by Cavett Robert. [Known as the dean of Public Speakers, Robert was the founder of the National Speakers Association.] I listened to this one tape 287 times. Cavett asked, "Are you the creature of circumstance or are you the creator?" I asked myself, "Holy cow, did I create this?" And I had. I created it so I could get to what I thought was my right place.

The mind at its most basal is a very simple system. Like Bill Gates says. It's binary. 1's and 0's. Cavett's tape explained that we should take the input and turn it into a positive. I had never heard a tape that had so strongly wound up people and it worked that way for me. Today I think, "How can I do it?" instead of "Why can't I?" In time, Cavett became my friend and mentor.

I learned everything from my business going under. Everyone can relate to failure, but very few can relate to success. When we ask ourselves if we're enough or not enough, most will say, "I'm not." It doesn't help that all of us are programmed by advertising to feel that we're never enough. So how do we overcome adversity? You change your thinking. You change your life at the most basic level. I also now know that when your self-esteem goes up, so does your net worth.

So, here I was, only 26 years old. I looked around and I thought, "What did I learn from Bucky Fuller and now what do I really want to do?" It was then I decided that I wanted to talk to people who care about making a life-changing difference.

> *It is often the failure who is the pioneer of new lands, new undertakings, and new forms of expression.*
> —*Eric Hoffer*

My soon-to-be partner, Jack Canfield, told me about a little book of positive short stories he was putting together, *Happy Little Stories*.

I told him that was the stupidest title I've ever heard. After filtering through different titles, we agreed to do the book together. We spent three years perfecting this art and I came up with the first *Chicken Soup* book. At the time, we were both about $140,000 in debt, but we were enthusiastic and knew we had something special. We knew it would sell.

Thirty-three publishers in New York turned us down and made it quite clear that "No one buys short stories." To add an exclamation, our agent fired us!

After spending a great deal of time on the road attempting to sell our book, we went to the American Book Expo. Sixty thousand people in the book business were there. The who's who of the book industry. Former presidents go there to sell their books. Along with the authors, there are publishers and 33,000 independent bookstore owners. It was an intellectual orgasm for me.

Jack and I carried backpacks of our spiral-ring notebook and another 130 people said, "Buzz off and get out of here."

Then, the publisher of Health Communications, a small publication that was going bankrupt at the time, said he would read it overnight and call us in the morning. The next day, the publisher said he had tears in his eyes reading our stories.

The rest is history. Though it was far from the greatest deal, it became an unimaginable success. We have sold over 75 million books and the number continues to climb.

Many people fear failure. Some of the top grief counselors agree that there are only two real tangible fears: the fear of loud

> *Not many people are willing to give failure a second opportunity. They fail once and it's all over. The bitter pill of failure is often more than most people can handle. If you're willing to accept failure and learn from it, if you're willing to consider failure as a blessing in disguise and bounce back, you've got the potential of harnessing one of the most powerful success forces.*
> —*Joseph Sugarman*

noises and the fear of falling. Everything else is a pseudo-fear. Fear is not so much real as much as it is something we buy into. It's actually your thinking that makes it so. If you were to look back just before you die and see an instant replay of your life, you'd find that all these other fears were really learning experiences at one level or another. Though yogurt may be hitting the fan, it's hitting it for your benefit. You just can't see it at the time.

> Intelligence is not to make no mistakes, but quickly to see how to make them good.
> —Bertolt Brecht

For me, the most important line in the Bible is found in Genesis.

"What you meant for my harm, God meant for my good."

UNBELIEVABLE UNDERSTATEMENTS
Where a calculator on the ENIAC is equipped with 19,000 vacuum tubes and weighs 30 tons, computers in the future may have only 1,000 vacuum tubes and perhaps weigh only 1.5 tons.
–Popular Mechanics, March 1949.

Robert Pinsky

"Proving those teachers wrong, at some point, became an attractive idea."

Robert Pinsky, poet laureate of America (1997-2000), had his *The Figured Wheel: New and Collected Poems 1965-1995* nominated for the Pulitzer Prize in poetry. He received the Lenore Marshall Award and the Ambassador Book Award of the English Speaking Union. His writing has also won awards from the Guggenheim Foundation, the National Endowment for the Arts, and the American Academy and Institute of Arts and Letters. A member of the American Academy of Arts and Sciences, Robert Pinsky found that academic failure provided him with motivation and something to prove.

The truth is, I was never a great student. In the seventh and eighth grades, I was in what was called unofficially, but with admirable frankness and concision, "The Bad Class." I was neither a good athlete nor a social success. I was very young and was already very aware of failure.

Even in English, the best I received were "C"s and "D"s. I could read well, except for what was assigned. I had a lot of trouble doing what people told me; consequently I was told by teachers that, "with your attitude, you're going to end up as a bum in the Bowery." I would study derelicts just to see how bad being a derelict would be. I'd see some wino in the doorway and actually think, "that's tolerable."

> *The greatest mistake you can make in life is to be continually fearing you will make one.*
> *—Elbert Hubbard*

My motivation came from how bad I could make my teachers look. Some teachers seemed good, but many seem sadistic or stupid. I believe that if kids don't seem able to grasp structure or grammar, it's not that they're stupid, it's that they're not being taught

228

properly. Proving those teachers wrong, at some point, would become an attractive idea.

The thing that saved me was music. At 13 or 14, I started playing the sax. I wasn't very good, but being in a band gave me confidence in myself. I was Mr. Sax Man. I believe it kept me from giving up altogether until my way of working and thinking became acceptable. It also brought me to poetry.

Like many poets, I received plenty of rejections, but my attitude was, "Good, other poets who aren't that serious would quit over this." I would be that little thrashing spermatozoa that keeps thrashing his tail as hard as he can. You see, I figure all the others will go into something more profitable.

I'm insane. I'm the madman who wouldn't give up. Any rational person would quit. I was already told I was going to be a bum, so just the fact that I was getting up in the morning to get those rejection slips was pretty good. I wasn't scared of failure. You see, failure armed me against frustration and risk. I had been there at a very young age and survived it. And I wasn't awed by the institution or by recognition. I was awed by my heroes...like Yeats or Williams.

I don't know why people need to talk about me only as a success. Failure gives me something to prove. It is a source of aspiration to excel. Just looking for approval and recognition can cause a person to become satisfied and complacent.

Creators court mistakes as part of their creative process. They learn that a drip of paint on their canvas, a wrong chip in the marble, even a mistake in an otherwise well-planned experiment can lead to a major breakthrough. When a mistake shows up, most people despair. But the creator seizes the mistake as a way to break out. Seizing upon the mistake, the mind suddenly bursts into the open and takes a new route toward vision. This approach is very different than the one taken by our education system which punishes mistakes and marks them wrong. This may well be one reason that creators as a group don't do well in school.
—John Briggs,
Fire in the
Crucible

I still fail today. Recently, I was approached by someone who was writing a book for adults who were learning to read. I thought it was a great idea. He wanted some work from me that was simple, with simple words. I tend to use technical terms when I write. For the life of me, I could not find anything that was appropriate. I failed. But I won't stop trying.

If you're not failing every now and again, it's a sign you're not doing anything very innovative.
—Woody Allen

If a kid feels he's no good at writing, I would have him use language in whatever context he felt comfortable. From there, you can begin to look for the eloquence.

When I think of my own personal failures as a teenager, failures that to this day can make me feel humiliation and shame, I'm grateful for the comforting idea that anything good I have accomplished is part of a dialectic between the sting of failure and a reflexive craving for what is supremely excellent. Not just pretty good, or good enough, but magnificent; the best, because the best can pull me up from awareness of my failures.

SAMURAI SONG
by Robert Pinsky

When I had no roof I made
Audacity my roof. When I had
No supper my eyes dined.

When I had no eyes I listened.
When I had no ears I thought.
When I had no thought I waited.

When I had no father I made
Care my father. When I had

No mother I embraced order.

When I had no friend I made
Quiet my friend. When I had no
Enemy I opposed my body.

When I had no temple I made
My voice my temple. I have
No priest, my tongue is my choir.

When I have no means fortune
Is my means. When I have
Nothing, death will be my fortune.
Need is my tactic, detachment
Is my strategy. When I had
No lover I courted my sleep.

(Samurai Song *from* Jersey Rain *by Robert Pinsky. Copyright* © *2000 by Robert Pinsky. Reprinted by permission of Farrer, Straus and Giroux, LLC.*)

ASININE ASSERTIONS

"The foolish idea of shooting at the moon is an example of the absurd length to which vicious specialization will carry scientists working in thought-tight compartments. "

–A. W. Bikerton, 1926, professor of physics and chemistry, Canterbury College, New Zealand.

Billy Idol

"If you don't believe in something, find something to believe in."

Billy Idol and his band Generation X were one of the main forces in England's punk rock music scene. When punk began to wane, Idol came to America where he eventually built a solo career that included hits like "Dancing with Myself," "White Wedding" and "Eyes Without a Face." With all his party style and popularity, it was the obstacles he faced that gave him his distinct attitude and drove him to the success he has become.

I was a lousy student in school. The only lessons that interested me were in history. I could remember dates and enjoyed reading about the wars. I loved biographies. But if they stuck chemistry in front of me, I was in hell. I hated chemistry: the tests, the litmus papers. But I didn't care. You didn't meet girls in a chemistry lab. A physics teacher told me that I wasn't stupid and I could do it if I tried, and I said, "I don't want to try."

When we moved to London, I was put in a class with kids who couldn't read. They never checked my report to see that while I may have been bad in math and chemistry, I was great in history, and I got stuck in this horrible class where the kids couldn't read. It was just another thing that turned me off to school. The only reason I ever went to university was to stay away from working.

At the time, I was told the safest thing for anyone to do was to work for your father. Either that or be a teacher. Just don't take any risks. Back then, even if you wanted to be a teacher, there weren't any teaching jobs, so the only thing you could do was work for your dad. My dad had a psychological way of scaring me to death, so it led me to do the minimum. I certainly didn't want to work for him. It would have been hell. I love my dad, but the way I could keep loving him was not to work for him.

I had grown up with a dream of being in a rock and roll band, though I kept it to myself. My dad wouldn't get me an electric guitar because he felt it was part of what was wrong with me...my long hair, my fashion thing, my friends, my love of rock music. And I went to a school full of kids who didn't like rock and roll. There were only two or three kids who liked what I liked, so we used to head over to another school about two miles down the road where all the kids seemed cool. David Bowie and Peter Frampton had gone there. It was my grandad who bought me a Ringo Starr snare drum when I was 7, and when I was 10, he bought me a guitar. That was enough to get me going.

There was enough alienated youth all around the major centers in England who were very much like me. The lack of jobs had a lot of kids coming out of school and going right on welfare. There was a general feeling of no future. There was only boredom and depression. Everywhere I looked there seemed to be an attitude of doom and gloom with no future. It became the banner cry of punk, "No future! We're bored!"

By 1974, I had finished my first year at university and I came home that summer. Long hair was out and I had cut mine and dyed it black. I was following David Bowie and the pop culture. My parents thought I'd gone normal. Then I told them I was quitting school and joining a punk rock group. My mother was shocked. My dad didn't see it coming. He thought his son had gone mad. He was sure I would fail and he'd say, "Then what are you gonna do? You have nothing to fall back on. After two years with a band, you'll never be able to get a real job because they'll be wondering what you've done for the past two years." And unfortunately he was right. Any employer who saw that I'd been in a band instead of working would react the same way. "Yeah, right. I think we'll go with that bloke over there who stayed in school or didn't have weird hair or didn't try something different." My dad didn't talk to me for the next two years.

I stuck to my guns though. I held on to my dreams and the belief in myself, even though everybody was telling me I couldn't do it. Still, all I could really expect from what I was doing was failure. I knew what to expect from looking at other people's careers. Sooner or later, it's over. Do you know how many former band members I've met who ended up driving taxis?

At that time I was playing early The Who. There's a saying, "Imitation is the sincerest form of flattery." There's a second part to that no one knows which is "Invention is the sincerest form of criticism." And that's what we were doing. We would watch David Bowie, but instead of imitating what he did, we turned it around on itself and became inventors.

Every Saturday night we would play dances. We took a lot of stuff from the '60s, like the Animals' "We Gotta Get Out Of This Place." It's how a lot of punk rock got started. Start with the simple stuff, then mix in strange, sexual stuff. We used a lot of the anger that had gone out of rock music.

> *Behold the turtle:*
> *He only makes progress when*
> *he sticks his head out.*
> *—James Bryant Conant*

We soon headed for London where there were a lot of outcasts: sexual outcasts, music outcasts or professional outcasts. At the time, The Sex Pistols were handled by Malcolm McLaren, who owned a clothing store. At that time, clothing stores would promote themselves by having a band. That way, kids would hang at the shop. Their particular competitor was another clothing store named Acme Attractions.

Acme wanted to form a band and I came in to audition. I looked different. I dressed different. There were two other guitarists waiting in the room with me. They were straight rock and roll, and I'm sittin' there looking like I'm from the other side of the moon. These guys had been in all kinds of bands. At this point, I had played one gig and hadn't even gotten paid. These guys were laughing at me. I was terrified. I went in to audition and just let it all go. I didn't have the playing ability yet, but they knew I had the attitude, the passion. Five minutes later, they told the two guys who had been waiting that they might as well go home. I had the gig. Man, that felt good. They'd been torturing me for the past hour and I got to send them packing with no job. They didn't see what the future would be. I mean, these guys were already 25.

But it was more than just playing in a group. It had to do with attacking society. Chelsea, then Generation X, was all about attacking what the establishment wanted you to do. It was assaulting people about their working at some depressing job where they'd end up with a two-week holiday and when they get to where they were going, it rains.

It wasn't easy, and to make things worse, The Sex Pistols started rippin' up places where they played. Soon all punk bands were being banned, so we started our own club in Soho. The club took off, putting 500 people in a 200-capacity space. The clubs that had banned us started taking notice. They realized that every time they tried to stop us, we would succeed some other way. Now everyone wanted to sign us up. And from that point on, punk rock exploded everywhere.

We didn't sign with anyone. We decided to make them wait. And when we did, the offers grew from £10,000 up to a million. We signed.

We sold records and had a fair amount of success. Around 1980, we had a falling out with our managers and we were forced to go out with another name, GENX. It didn't work out. We were basically washed up. We tried one more album, which had a song on it called "Dancing with Myself." It didn't sell and the band's days were over.

He conquers who endures.
—Persius

I came to New York in 1982, changing my name from Idle to Idol. At that point, no one in punk rock had been successful to the mainstream audience and it was now something called Dance Rock. The Ramones were struggling. Even Blondie had died by this time. Nothing was happening, including my career.

For about six months, I couldn't write songs. I couldn't find people to play with. I was finished. My dad and mom had been right. I was at the end of the plank and there were sharks waiting in the water. Someone in my manager's office showed me a Rick Springfield album cover and said that this is what I should be. I said, "I don't think so. I'm not going to become the David Cassidy of rock and roll for you."

One night, I'm hanging at this bar in New York. There were just a few people dancing. All of a sudden, I heard the long version of "Dancing with Myself." These kids from all over the club dived over furniture to get to the dance floor. They were going absolutely crazy. I was standing there watching in amazement and I finally realized what I had to do. I had to become my own Generation X. I had to follow this up. I had to keep what I was seeing on the dance floor alive.

I used to do this old Tommy James song called "Mony, Mony." I pitched it to my managers and everyone thought it was a great idea. In two weeks I was in L.A. recording it. We put an EP together with "Dancing with Myself" and "Mony, Mony." Soon after, I went to this New York club and asked the D.J. to play it. The dance floor had been empty, but when "Mony, Mony" went on, the kids filled up the floor.

Somehow there were enough people who believed in me so I could hang on long enough until I was able to believe in myself. We followed with "White Wedding" and here I was on MTV. It was never really a hit song, but it was a hit video. I was now being played on the radio. "Eyes without A Face" went to number four. Four years after I arrived in America, I had a top-ten album. And now I'm a mainstream act. Even my dad has come around.

Just don't give up trying to do what you really want to do. Where there is love and inspiration, I don't think you can go wrong.
—Ella Fitzgerald

I've discovered that everything in my life that seemed to crash was a part of what pushed me forward. Even though school had made me angry, the fact that I felt they screwed me gave me the attitude that carried into my music. By doing me wrong, they helped turn me into what I became. It was an unlucky, lucky break. If I didn't have the negatives, I would have never had the positives. If that London school had put me in a good history class, I may have not turned out the same.

It was my one-track mind keeping me from having any interest in most other matters that led me to music. I believed powerfully in the power of rock and roll. Myopia may shut a lot of doors, but it can also lead down a powerful road that can give you that great experience. If I hadn't stuck to my guns, I could still be sitting behind a desk working for my dad filling invoices. Instead, I chose to live in a world where I could dream.

If your world doesn't allow you to dream, move to one where you can. If you don't believe in something, find something to believe in.

RED-LETTER REJECTS
Eleven publishers turned down George Bernard Shaw's first novel, *Immaturity*. Perhaps that's why he was thought to have said, "You can be right when others are wrong."

Joseph Batory

"Going to school was a terrifying experience. I ended up crying alone in my room every night."

A nonacademic from the mean streets of Philadelphia, Joseph Batory rose to leadership status in one of Pennsylvania's largest school districts. During his 15-year tenure, he took an underachieving school system in the midst of labor and community turmoil and turned it into one of the most harmonious and effective school districts in the nation. His highly successful book *Yo! Joey!* has become a guidebook for educators across the country. His unique style was born not out of academia, but from what he learned on the streets. And it *weren't* always easy.

I grew up in the very Italian and very tough neighborhood of South Philadelphia. Unfortunately, many of my friends ended up either going to jail or getting into gambling operations and working in a sort of junior Mafia. If you weren't tough and able to speak up for yourself, you didn't survive. Unfortunately, my dad taught me not to rock the boat. No confrontations.

In high school, we were bussed from South Philly to a high school with 3,000 boys. That just spells trouble. Since I was small and quiet, I was bullied terribly. It was just awful. I experienced everything from having my books knocked out of my hands and my locker broken into to being smacked around on the school bus. Going to school was a terrifying experience for me. I ended up crying alone in my room every night. I was fearful all the time. I learned to run. When I saw a particular group of kids coming, I would try to go a different way. Sometimes that wasn't possible and I ended up walking into trouble. I dreaded going to school.

I was walking home from playing basketball one night when I was about 16. I heard moaning coming from the alley and found Sal, a teenage gang leader from the neighborhood. He had been beaten up pretty bad and was very bloody. He said, "Joey, get me out of here. These guys'll be coming back to finish me." I wanted to run. I was scared. But I hauled him back to the safety of our neighborhood. Sal's father was a *connected* guy, so I became a hero with the *wise-guy* community for saving the son of the Boss. His father was very grateful and told me that I would always be remembered and if I ever needed anything, he would be there for me. It was very *Godfather*. Since I was still being regularly beaten to a pulp in school, I told him there was something he could do. And boy did he. The next time the gang that was beating me up followed me into a vacant building ready to pulverize me, Sal and his friend, Rocco, were there waiting. Sal explained to the gang that I was under the protection of *a family* and that they were never to come near me again. Sal and Rocco also taught me how to fight so that I could stand up for myself. Sometime later, I ended up in a fight with the leader of the gang. I won that fight and it was the end of me being bullied. I was able to begin focusing on my studies. Being bullied taught me well how unacceptable that behavior was. As a result, when I became superintendent, I instituted a zero-tolerance policy on bullying.

Life in our community was pretty formulaic—getting through high school, if you could, then go off to work at the local General Electric plant. I almost went there to work with my father. College seemed irrelevant to me. There was a bookie in the neighborhood. I wanted to join up with him so that I could get the money, the cars and the women. But he kept telling me that I had potential, that I could make something of myself and that I should go to college.

I became the first one in the neighborhood to go to college. It was always a struggle for me. For kids from the street, education didn't seem to matter when they were just trying to survive. It all seemed very

> *Adversity has the effect of eliciting talents, which in prosperous circumstances would have lain dormant.*
>
> *—Horace*

We should not let our fears hold us back from pursuing our hopes.
—*John F. Kennedy*

surreal and difficult, but I managed to get through school. After graduation, I had no idea what to do next. The only career I could think of was teaching. The white suburban districts weren't interested in ethnics, and Batory read Italian. By default, I ended up going to Camden, New Jersey, a very tough urban city just across the bridge from Philadelphia. Ironically, while it had been my last chance, I ended up loving the place. The kids were much the way I used to be. They were feisty and energetic, many of them from poor, noncollege family backgrounds. I related to that. I basically spent six years of my life doing *missionary work*, just trying to save kids from drowning. I did everything from coaching basketball to taking kids to Europe, unheard of at an inner-city school system. I chased them off the streets into places where they could deal with their problems with drugs, parents or God knows what. It was a very exciting time. I was actually making a difference.

While I enjoyed my time there, by 1970 I had had it with teaching. I was tired and burned out. My alma mater, LaSalle College, needed a sports information director. I have no idea why, but they gave me the job. After a while I began to think that what I was doing was somewhat frivolous. At the time there were *attacks* and criticisms on the public school system and they needed help with their "image," so they looked to people with public relations experience. There was a job opportunity in Upper Darby, a suburban school district just outside of Philadelphia, for a communications and public relations administrator. It was their lowest-level administrator, and I took the job.

It was a horrible experience. I thought I would be able to communicate with the general public, helping them understand what the schools were doing. But there were other agendas going on. I found that the school board had actually hired me to help them defeat the teachers in a teachers' strike and to make the public accept school closings more readily. It was pretty ugly. Lots of community turmoil. It was truly a horrible environment and I couldn't wait to get out. I was ready to take a job as vice president of a corporation when suddenly and without warning, the school superintendent had a heart attack. That became a turning point. For me AND the school district. The newly appointed superintendent, Mike Maines, called me and asked me to stay on. He would match my VP salary and give me personnel responsibility. I would basically be assistant superintendent.

Mike was amazing. We began building bridges. Instead of shutting the parents out of the process, we involved the community. Instead of working against the teachers, we asked them for their help. There was a complete turnaround and I would have been happy just being the best assistant superintendent I could be. And then Mike Maines had a stroke. Surprisingly to me, I became his replacement.

On the very first day as superintendent, I received a call from the South Philly bookie who had prodded me to try for something better 25 years before. I was terrified. I had about 1,000 people in my employ and I was convinced he would want to put a gambling operation into the district. After three days of not returning his calls, my wife reminded me of my roots, and I returned the call. He had just wanted to tell me how proud of me he was, and he started to cry. Here I was, the prodigy of a bookie, becoming a school superintendent, and he wanted to tell me that he was proud. I had received an unlikely but supportive pat on the back from this guy and it had worked. Inspiration can come from almost anywhere.

My first public school board meeting was loud, with people very upset over school taxes and other assorted problems. They, of course, wanted to know what I was going to do about everything. It was awful. I dreaded the next monthly meeting, and when I got there I found something even more foreboding. At the back of the room

> *When we treat man as he is, we make him worse than he is; when we treat him as if he already were what he potentially could be, we make him what he should be.*
>
> —Johann Goethe

stood Rocco, one of Sal's *soldiers*. A kind of Steven Segal character. He was pacing back and forth. I hadn't seen this guy for over 20 years. He told me, "No one was gonna be takin' off on one of the guys from the neighborhood who's come this far." He told me that if anyone acted up that night, he would *straighten them out* in the parking lot after the meeting. I explained about America, democracy and how this is not the right way to do things. He told me to just do what I had to do and he would do what he had to. Luckily, this meeting was quiet, but I knew I had to take some action. I met with Sal. Here I was, a school superintendent meeting a gang leader and his bodyguards in the back of a Catholic church. I begged him not to "watch my back," that I had to sink or swim on my own. I had finally learned that I could do it on my own. He backed off. Later, when I explained to him how some kids don't have the financial wherewithal to take advantage of certain educational opportunities, Sal was there with the money to make those benefits possible. Soon after I became superintendent, I was sitting in a bar with an older superintendent and I asked him how to do the job. He told me to stay out of the limelight, not to go out on a limb, and to keep my door closed. It seemed so cynical and such a sad way to live. I remembered how negative all my early school experiences had been and how my family taught me not to speak out or take risks. I knew that if I didn't speak up for my teachers, students and myself, I would end up like the guy in the bar. From then on I became the most outspoken school superintendent in Philadelphia. I challenged authority wherever and whomever I had to in order to get what I needed. Governors, presidents, anyone. And it worked. You've got to take the risks if you want to get the rewards.

> *America was discovered accidentally by a great seaman who was looking for something else.*
> —The Oxford History of the American People

We became an extremely progressive school district with our schools growing rapidly, and I am proud to say that we became a refuge for people and immigrants escaping the city of Philadelphia who sought better schools and a better life. If a superintendent of schools lasts five or six years, they're doing pretty well. I lasted for 16 years in Upper Darby running one of the most diverse and successful school districts in the country. Not bad for a guy who hated school.

I have no magic formulas for saving turned-off kids. One thing's for sure, the older they get, the more difficult the challenge. But here are some basic ideas that I tried to foster among teachers and principals as a school superintendent:

> *It's Not Where You Start.*
> *It's Where You Finish.*
> *—Dorothy Fields & Cy Coleman,*
> *from the musical* Seesaw

1. There's too much *peculiar artificiality* in the academic curriculum for many of these kids. What they study in school has no relevance to their daily lives. No interest usually equals failure. These kids need to be somehow hooked! So it makes sense to try to build learning and attitude change by letting the student do something in a structured school environment that they like to do, e.g., work with hands, art, music, sports or whatever and try to spin off of that interest to other areas.

2. An adult who sincerely cares and believes in a *down and out* kid can make the difference. Problem is, these kids are experts at spotting phonies. Still, someone who's there for a youngster, no matter what, can build trust over time. This kind of involvement is very demanding for any adult, so the volunteers do not exactly line up at the door.

3. Success stories are not just measured through high test scores or college admittance alone. The educational and societal value system has to do a better job of encouraging and rewarding those adult professionals who devote their careers to changing behavior in problem students.

4. Positive reinforcement conquers all. Kids tend to become whatever

you tell them they are. When a kid gets the frequent message that he or she is a bum, they begin fulfilling the prophecy. Great teachers never look at a problem child for what he or she is, but rather for what he or she might become.

ACCIDENTAL ACHIEVEMENTS

In 1943, in an attempt to create an inexpensive yet durable synthetic rubber, General Electric's James Wright mixed silicone oil and boric acid. Not only wasn't it strong enough, but it also bounced.

GE found no use for the substance. In 1949, a down-on-his-luck ad man, Peter Hodgson, borrowed $147 and bought the production rights from GE. He placed the substance in plastic eggs and marketed it to children as Silly Putty®. When he died in 1964, Hodgson had accumulated an estate of $140 million.

Y

You don't drown by falling in the water,

You drown by staying there.

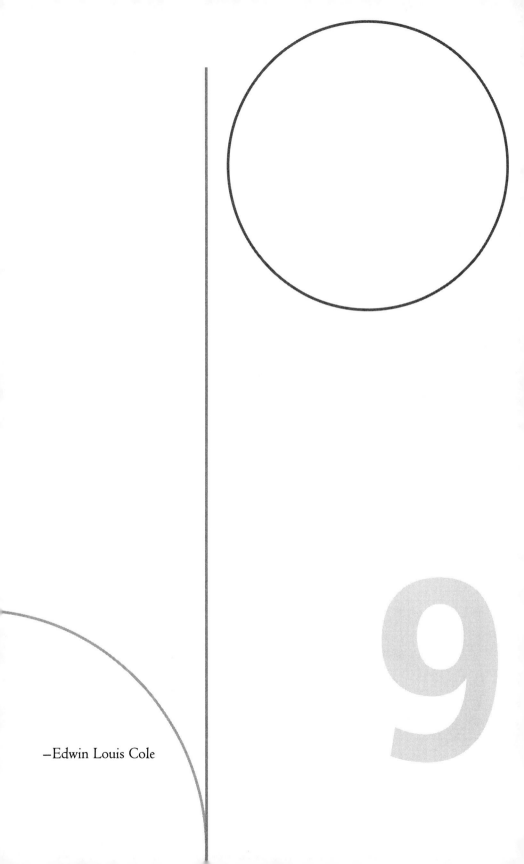

—Edwin Louis Cole

9

Robert Townsend

"I told my agent that I want to do more of that [black movies] and she told me that they only do one black movie a year, and I just did it."

Comedian, actor, producer and director Robert Townsend has appeared in such prestigious films as *A Soldier's Story*; directed Eddie Murphy's blockbuster concert film, *Raw*; and cowrote, directed and starred in feature films like *The Five Heartbeats* and *Meteor Man*. He has also starred in his own television series, *The Parent 'Hood* and directed the Showtime film *10,000 Black Men Named George*. While there's been much success, Townsend's early career was continually stymied by the stereotypical casting of African-American actors. It was this constant disappointment that led Townsend to make his most profound decision—and his first film, *Hollywood Shuffle*.

As a kid, my nickname was *"TV Guide."* I watched everything on TV. I would do impressions of Alfred Hitchcock, *The Wizard of Oz*, Walter Brennan and James Cagney. My father wasn't there so Andy Griffith became my father. Whatever he taught Opie, he taught me. I can still see Jimmy Stewart standing up for the little guy in *Mr. Smith Goes to Washington*.

We were really poor, on welfare, and because we would get behind in the rent we had to move around a lot. To make new friends, I would make people laugh. My mom saw this and took whatever little money we had and registered me for acting lessons.

If necessity is the mother of invention, then failure must be its father.
—Nora Wright

I can still remember how nervous I was when I first auditioned for a play. It was a typical audition. So dark you can't

248

see out to the seats and you don't know whether they liked you or not. So after I said my lines, I didn't exactly walk right off the stage.

"Excuse me...I can do things."

I'm not sure why I said that, but they ended up saying, "Okay, do things." I started doing a bunch of impressions and characters I had done for years and low and behold...

"You got the part."

And there I was. 15 years old, a 60-seat theater and I had only two lines. But when people started to drop out of the play, I ended up with 14 different characters to play...a drunk, a car salesman, a thief. I was still in high school and in our dressing room women were changing right in front of me. I thought, this theater is a good thing! I would get there two hours early to make sure I didn't miss anything.

History has demonstrated that the most notable winners encountered heartbreaking obstacles before they triumphed. They finally won by their defeats.
—B. C. Forbes

In college, I faced my first real failure and it really messed me up. I auditioned for the role of Hamlet in the school play. I had watched the Royal Shakespeare Company do *Othello* on PBS, so I knew I could do Shakespeare. The first thing they tell me is that I can't play Hamlet. They did say I could be a spear thrower or something along those lines. I ended up coaching the guy who got the role of Hamlet. Soon everyone was coming to me for help with their roles. I felt used and ended up refusing to do the play.

Every time I auditioned for a play, I was never considered for the lead. I decided to get together with some other students and created a black repertory theater where we could play the lead roles and not just second banana. I thought this would be a big turning point for me. But instead, when I asked my acting teacher about the possibilities of success in New York, she said, "You'll never make it in New York. It will eat you up and spit you out."

I thought, "How does she know? How can she tell me what would happen?" I was defiant. I had to find out for myself.

I transferred to a school near New York City where they did the traditional plays like *Oklahoma!* and *The Rainmaker*. I wanted the Burt Lancaster part. They didn't seem to see it the same way I did. So again, I formed my own theater group. I had already worked on films like *Cooley High* and *Mahogany*, so I was able to create an original stage show, *On the Darker Side*.

When I did finally get to New York, I felt my life really began. I was still auditioning for pimps, drug dealers, slaves, all the stereotypical roles, but that's when I discovered stand-up comedy and found an outlet for all my characters. At first it was fun, but as an actor I found myself in a box and my spirit began to be eaten away. The roles available to me were getting more negative and I began to think about the funny stuff. Funny stuff like white directors telling me how to be black.

> *Sometimes fate nudges you. Sometimes it kicks you in the butt.*
> *—Unknown*

Then, I was shooting an educational show in Kentucky. We shot a breakfast scene and the set designer came in to throw crumbs and pieces of fruit on the table. She said this was how it's supposed to look in the ghetto. It really messed with my mind. I was thinking, "I can't sit here anymore. This is a joke." I told the director that I was from the ghetto and this is not how it is. The director was a good guy and had the table cleaned up. All of a sudden it became clear to me. This whole world is created by the director. I went back and looked at old movies and noticed how black people talked versus how white people did. Everything in my head was being turned upside down. I started to understand how it worked. I began to watch where the camera was and I made sure it saw me. Every time I went to the set, I would be like a heat-seeking missile seeing how I can get into the story. I learned that it's the odd stuff you do that gets noticed and the money you made depended on it. With the knowledge, I was able to get my performing scale upgraded from $60 to $200 a day.

With a new outlook, I drove to
L.A. with my friend and comic
Keenan Wayans. That's where my
agent told me that I'd be perfect
to play a wiry, young pimp.
I quickly got a new agent. But,
instead of a new start, I felt like
it was more of an end. Was this all
there was?

*It's a little like wrestling a gorilla.
You don't quit when you're tired, you quit
when the gorilla is tired.*
—Robert Strauss

It was then that I auditioned for Norman Jewison for *A Soldier's
Story*. I had seen the play and thought there was no part in there for me,
but I was actually cast. It was the first time I was in a film where I wasn't
the *black guy*. It changed my life because it wasn't about color. We were
just actors doing a gig. And now I'm in a film that's up for an Oscar. I
told my agent that I wanted to do more of that and she told me that
they only do one black movie a year, and I just did it. I auditioned for
The Color Purple, didn't get it and thought, I just missed this year's black
movie. I am in big trouble.

I figured, okay, since I missed my *black movie*, I'll make my own.
Directing didn't look all that difficult. Of course, it was Jewison who
made it look simple. Frankly, I thought I had to do that movie or I
would become a drug addict or do something crazy. As much as the
movie was driving me and I was driving it, it had to be born.

I called most of the actors I knew from auditioning and began
to make *Hollywood Shuffle*. Even though everybody thought
it was crazy, Keenan and I wrote it together based on
our own experiences. I used a lot of those characters I grew up with from *TV Guide*.

I didn't know much about making movies
but I knew what I didn't like. I didn't even know
how to talk to my cinematographer. I would just
say, "Light me like Billy Dee Williams."

*Creativity is
making mistakes. Art
is knowing
which ones to keep.*
—Scott Adams

I ended up blowing all my money. I had saved

up about $60,000 and went through it just like that. That's when the legendary story about the credit cards comes in.

I basically went on the road to do stand-up comedy to pay my bills, came back home and asked God to give me a sign; to show me what I'm supposed to do because, damn, this moviemaking feels good. That's when the mail arrived and there was a stack of applications for credit cards and I thought, "I could finish this movie on credit cards." I would charge everything: food, painting supplies, film stock, wardrobe. I signed up for every single credit card and so began the real journey.

The most important of my discoveries has been suggested to me by my failures.
—Sir Humphrey Davy

Although I was doing "making-a-black-movie" material in my stand-up act, *Hollywood Shuffle* wasn't just about the jokes. Even the serious stuff was all so funny: *The Black Acting School, Winky Dinky Dog* and *Zombie Pimps. Sneaking into the Movies* was my slap at the critics.

I would have died if I hadn't stopped doing the stereotypical roles. What saved me was *Hollywood Shuffle* and with it I also learned discipline. Now all my projects come in on time and under budget because I still move like that filmmaker who began with no permits, scouting his locations in a way so that the police wouldn't catch me. *Hollywood Shuffle* was shot in 12 nonconsecutive days.

Hollywood Shuffle become a catalyst for dialogue. It also opened doors for black actors and directors as well. In fact, Eddie Murphy came to a private screening of *Hollywood Shuffle* and after laughing through it, asked me to direct his concert film, *Raw.* We hadn't pulled any punches and Hollywood couldn't ignore the things that had to be addressed.

Some people hit one wall, get scared or hurt, quit and end up living in regret. I didn't like it when I failed to get those parts early in my career. But if I had to settle for those parts, I probably would have never made *Hollywood Shuffle.* It's been said, "to be known, you must go into the unknown." You hit obstacles for a reason. You just have to choose to learn from them and remember that a waterfall begins with a single drop.

Nolan Bushnell

"People are always looking for innovation until they find it."

In 1971, Nolan Bushnell—considered by many to be the father of computer games—built one of the first video games, *Computer Space*. Far too complicated, it flopped. Bushnell learned from his mistakes and created Pong, the first widely played computer game. Bushnell then founded the game giant, Atari, handing America joysticks and a new kind of home entertainment. He followed up by developing a child's favorite theme restaurant, Chuck E. Cheese. All this by the age of 34. Nolan Bushnell, known for his savvy business planning and ability to handle many successful balls in the air at one time, suddenly lost everything when he failed to anticipate betrayal and egos that were beyond his control.

I started a company called Atari, built it to a very significant size, sold it to Warner Communications and became much richer at 34 than I ever thought I would be. I realized very early on that you can make more money in an enterprise; you could make more money than selling your labor at dollars per hour. At 8 years old, I was selling strawberries door-to-door. When I was 10 or 11, I fixed TV sets in the neighborhood. Starting a company may look like a risk to a lot of people, but it's really not if you do your homework.

I continued to run Atari under Warner. While there, I started a Chuck E. Cheese. After the sale to Warner, they decided that they didn't want to be in the restaurant business, so I bought Chuck E. Cheese from them and it grew to 280 restaurants, an Initial Public Offering [IPO] and a great success. All of a sudden I was, at a very young age, responsible for two different companies, each worth hundreds of millions. I was perceived by all as one of the smartest businessmen around.

But it still wasn't enough for me. I started a business incubator process that clearly exceeded my grasp. I started working on various different projects including Etak, which had many of the most fundamental patents on automobile navigation and mapping technology; Bi-Video, which represented some of the very early information kiosks and merchandising systems; Magna Microwave, which created some of the core technology for the satellite communication systems; Compower, which had some of the fundamental patents on switching out power supplies on today's desktops, to name a few. But the darling of them all was a company called Androbot.

Androbot was the first anthropomorphic robotics company and it was going to be the equivalent of U.S. Robotics. The company was moving forward. I had hired management and we went to a trade show with a prototype that was probably six months from production. We sold $30 or $40 million worth at the show, and this for a product that was not even finished. I thought that not only was there a market, but the market was much bigger than we had figured. In general, at a trade show, you don't really write that many orders. Usually you get the orders in subsequent months. I did a quick calculation and figured there was a market for several hundred million of these robots that we had yet to build.

If you can force your heart and nerve and sinew, To serve your turn long after they are gone, And so hold on when there is nothing in you, Except the Will which says to them: 'Hold on!'
—*Rudyard Kipling,* If

At the time, I had a large line of credit at Merrill Lynch. They said that this was clearly a public offering. In the next couple months, we had written a contract, settled on a public offering, and everything looked like we were ready for a third major wonderful win. I was 35 years old. It couldn't be better. A huge win with Atari, a huge win with Chuck E. Cheese, and now I was going to add the Triple Crown with Androbot.

The prospectus was written, the success was happening. With the offering oversubscribed, I was getting calls asking if we could figure out a way to allocate some shares. Everything was wonderful. Then, three days before the offering, I got a telephone call from Merrill Lynch in which I'm coldly informed, "We're not going forward with the offering." It seems that someone at Merrill Lynch decided that they were not going to invest in development-stage companies. They had been involved in a couple of development-stage companies that had dipped below their initial offering value. They figured it was too risky and they weren't going to do any more.

I found myself with a *damaged* company. Everyone knew that we had been oversold, so they wondered why the deal had been pulled. Merrill Lynch wasn't going to admit that they had just decided, in the middle of the night, that they weren't going to do this type of business anymore. We had gone from an oversold situation to a canceled deal overnight, so therefore there was a taint. A taint without any substantiation. I found myself with a company that was burning cash like it was going out of style. I was into the company for over $15 million in debt and now I had a tainted IPO that I had expected would bail me out. I went from the top of the world to insolvency in a matter of three weeks.

I really didn't understand how badly the taint would affect us. I thought this was just a bump in the road. There were other fish in the sea. I knew the terms would not be as good, but surely I could raise the money privately. I didn't realize how formidable the taint was until I tried to get another underwriter. There would be no funding.

I had to begin laying off people. As a business, we went from soaring upward to a stall. We were running out of money rapidly. Our technology was still three or four months away from shipping in any kind of volume. Personally, financially, I was tapped.

> Failure does not count. If you accept this, you'll be successful. What causes most people to fail is that after one failure, they'll stop trying.
> —Frank Burford

I ended up selling the company at a fraction of what I had put into it. By that time I had about $18 million cash invested in the project. I sold it for $2 million.

I still had debt with Merrill Lynch and, though I had enough assets to pay it off, I was cash flow insolvent. And though the Merrill Lynch people said they would take some responsibility for the failed IPO, I ended up paying them about $28 million with interest on a deal *they* backed out on. I got screwed. But there were even more surprises to come.

People of character find a special attractiveness in difficulty, since it is only by coming to grips with difficulty that they can realize their potentialities.
—Charles de Gaulle

I was about to do another deal, an entertainment restaurant for adults totally removed from Androbot and fully funded. I had paid Merrill Lynch all but half a million, which we had agreed to let stand for tax purposes. To my thinking, we were totally settled, and then we get sued by Merrill Lynch.

At first I thought the suit was specious. Then, without a hearing, a jury trial or any fact-finding, a judge decided to give them a $7 million summary judgment against me. I had come from the self-concept of being a *wonderboy*, thinking we were finally clean and then had this thing come back to whack me on the head. My entire family was being attacked. All our assets were attached, I couldn't do business and we lost our house. I had hit bottom.

With everything lost, we *escaped* to London while our appeal was being heard. While I had a lot of fear about the things spiraling out of control, I felt that it was all fixable if I remained relentless. Anything that's just about money is fixable. Other issues can be much more pernicious. When you look at the absolute worst thing that can happen, it usually isn't so bad. Sometimes, the worst thing can result into unforeseen benefits. During the six months in London, I had a wonderful time getting reacquainted with my family. We came back invigorated, ready to go.

We settled with Merrill Lynch and ultimately came to Southern California with virtually only the clothes on our back. And now I'm having the time of my life.

I think my work and my family are much more integrated. I used to come home from work and we were like two separate camps. My wife, Nancy, would ask me what was happening at work and I would say, "Nothing." Much like a kid might say to his parents' questions about school. Now I'm loving the fact that my wife is working with me at Uwink.com. I never realized that it would be so much fun.

Only those who dare to fail greatly can ever achieve greatly.
—Robert F. Kennedy

My experience with Merrill Lynch left me with a level of healthy cynicism that I didn't have before. I'm much more aware of how I document and conduct my business. I cover my bases. I felt that people would operate in their own best interests and that there was always some way to commingle your interest with theirs. In most deals, there is value received for value given. But I learned that there are people, particularly in the bowels of corporate America, who are more driven by petty aspects of existence. It's an "I have power over somebody who has been very successful and I'm going to use it." In my case, none of the economics made any sense. Merrill Lynch was spending a lot of money on attorneys. The equities just didn't make sense. There were things going on that were fundamentally mindless, only bureaucratic motions. People are always looking for innovation until they find it.

A lot of people want things to be perfect before they act on anything. I call it the *paralysis of perfection*. Most services and products fall far short of what is ultimately envisioned. If you are unwilling to take a risk on something that you know is better than what's out there, but not as good as you think it could be, then you will fail because you are now paralyzed by your own requirements of perfection.

Young people shouldn't be so quick to judge themselves negatively. They should only worry about becoming the sum total of what they put into themselves: good food, good knowledge, good skills, good habits. Sooner or later they will find they are the sum total of these good ingredients and will have what it takes to bake a very nice cake.

> *True success is overcoming the fear of being unsuccessful.*
> *—Paul Sweeney*

IMPERCEPTIVE PERCEPTIONS

"I have traveled the length and breadth of this country and talked with the best people, and I can assure you that data processing is a fad that won't last out the year."

–Editor, business books, Prentice Hall, 1957.

Kathy Buckley

"The only thing I really ever failed was myself."

Successful comedienne and well-respected motivational speaker Kathy Buckley has appeared on the late-night talk shows, is considered by *People* magazine as being one of their most touching stories, and has been profiled in depth on the *Today* Show and *Good Morning America*. She received the American Hero Award from the City of Hope and the Toastmasters International Communication and Leadership Award. Kathy has also overcome public school system's ignorance; molestation and rape; being run over by a jeep while sunbathing; dying and receiving last rites five times; living on welfare and years of loneliness. When you meet her, it's obvious that Kathy Buckley is an attractive, six-foot-tall woman. What isn't obvious is she's hearing-impaired.

I had a severe hearing problem. My school had a severe problem dealing with it. Each year I was pulled out of my class, placed in a little room and analyzed by a bunch of adults. They show me these inkblots.

"So, Kathy, what do these inkblots look like?"

"They look like someone poured ink all over the paper."

The flower that blooms in adversity is the most rare and beautiful of all.
—From the Disney movie
Mulan

I didn't get it. Every time, each year, I failed that test. They kept telling me what's wrong with me, never once saying what was right. Never once asking, "How do you feel about this?" I was taught to respect adults, so I believed them. I was dumb, stupid, retarded. They said there was something wrong with me, so-o-o, I guess, there must be something wrong with me. I was broken.

In ninth grade, I was six feet tall and read at a sixth-grade level. So what do they do? They decide to teach me to read phonetically... by sound. HELLO. I can't hear sound. They were trying to teach a deaf person by sound. That's like trying to teach a blind person to read Braille by giving them a regular book. They were constantly telling me how stupid I was, and all that time they were the ignorant ones.

You may have a fresh start any moment you choose, for this thing we call failure is not the falling down, but the staying down.
—Mary Pickford

I could read lips, but with the teacher and the students talking simultaneously, I would freak out. It was like I was watching a ping-pong game, trying to follow which lips were moving.

I was unable to hear but not wanting anyone to know because that would make me different. I just couldn't accept the fact that I was deaf.

I kept getting into trouble, but not because I was bad. I just couldn't hear what they were telling me. They had no way to reach me. That's why today, it's so important for me to fight hard for education for the deaf.

They ignored the fact that I was hard of hearing because I could still communicate. I was about 8 years old when I got my first hearing aid. My parents just listened to the doctors and all they cared about was whether I could hear. But it wasn't about hearing. It was about under-standing. I needed a language. Because I couldn't hear as a child, I never had a decent vocabulary. Back then, the hearing aid was uncomfortable, and since I figured everyone probably heard the way I did, I stopped wearing it about three years later and did not get another one for over 20 years. I had friends but I felt so alone. Luckily, I never turned to drugs or alcohol. It's really hard to read lips when you're stoned.

I just made it out of high school with a 1.9 grade point average (Home Economics saved my life), and everything continued to go downhill. But I never quit. How could I? I was too busy trying to survive. I had been taught that I was a broken person and I needed to be fixed. I believe many of the accidents I've had were really a call for help. I still have a problem letting people help me.

> *Adversity is like the period of the rain. . . cold, comfortless, unfriendly to people and to animals; yet from that season have their birth the flower, the fruit, the date, the rose and the pomegranate.*
> —*Sir Walter Scott*

It seemed like everything I tried failed. I couldn't even sunbathe right. One day on Santa Monica beach while lying on the sand, a lifeguard (irony or what?) jeep drove over me. I stopped breathing. My heart stopped. I had died. But that horrible moment unexpectedly became my most glorious. I saw life after death. I felt a presence of love that I'd never felt before. When I was revived, that glorious feeling stayed with me. I knew there was an incredible power of love. It still keeps me going.

I realize now that not only the successes but the failures made me what I am today. My family refused to put me in an all-deaf school. If they had, I would have signed a lot more and I probably wouldn't be speaking as well as I do today. I was forced to struggle in a regular school. That struggle eventually made me stronger.

Because of my deafness, I pay closer attention to *how* people say things than what it is they say. Words might lie, but not the body.

Much of my comedy, my motivational speaking, my concern for children, the work I am now able to do for the deaf in the educational system, came out of the hard times of my life.

I was told so many times that I was a failure and I believed it. But it was later I realized that it was actually society's judgments that were created to make me think I was failing. The only thing I really ever failed was myself.

Now I know that you can't diagnose children with a single test score. It's important that before teachers and parents attempt to assess a child, they should ask her questions such as, "What are you thinking? What makes you happy? What makes you sad?"

Adults don't have all the answers. They just think they do. Parents need to be involved, listen to what their children have to say, and share their own experiences and feelings. You'd be surprised how relieved a child is to find that they're not the only one who feels that particular way. Communicate and be patient. Kids feel things they may not have the words for.

We've got to find out what a child enjoys and encourage it. Not everyone learns on the same terms. A person has to find out what they're good at, no matter what it is, and strive to become proficient. There are a lot of people who graduated with a 4.0 grade point average who are stuck in jobs that make them miserable. They never stopped to think what they wanted to do, only what they were told they were supposed to do. I graduated with a 1.9 and I'm a happy camper. Pretty amazing, huh?

Sometimes it's difficult to find out what your gifts or talents are. If you say, "I can't," you won't. But if you ask, "How can I?" you're moving in the right direction. As soon as you say, "I can't," your brain stops taking in information.

When we begin to take our failures non-seriously, it means we are ceasing to be afraid of them. It is of immense importance to learn to laugh at ourselves.
—Katherine Mansfield

Maybe you want to play an instrument but it doesn't seem to sink in. Don't quit trying. Look for a new angle. Maybe writing music. Maybe marketing it. Maybe become a D.J. Listen to your heart, not to people who don't know you. People told me not to try comedy, that I could only fail. Today I'm a successful comedienne and a trusted motivational speaker. I ask myself, how did I end up on the same stage with respected speakers like

Anthony Robbins and General Arnold Schwarzkopf? I realized I spent my whole life trying to figure out a way to communicate. Now I communicate for a living. After years of trying to understand hearing people, I'm speaking to hearing people and they understand me. At least I hope they do.

RED-LETTER REJECTS

"...we don't believe that you should offer it for publication.
It is diffuse and non-integral with neither very much plot development nor character development."
–From the rejection slip for William Faulkner's *Flags in the Dust*, which was rejected by 18 publishers.

Jimmy Breslin

"Remember the pain."

A news-reporting legend, Jimmy Breslin's street-savvy columns have graced the pages of New York's greatest papers. He was awarded the Pulitzer Prize, the George K. Polk, Meyer Berger and Damon Runyan awards. He has also written many books, including *The Gang That Couldn't Shoot Straight, Damon Runyon* and his memoir *I Want to Thank My Brain for Remembering Me*. The big things that Jimmy Breslin did were all based on his efforts to get the small things right.

I've made many mistakes and I have learned from them, but this business can make you crazy. Little details just killed me.

When I started in the business, I was at the *Long Island Press* in Jamaica, Queens. I didn't even know how to type. I still type with two fingers. I was 16 and the first job they gave me was writing the obituaries. The undertaker would phone in a death to the classified section of the newspaper. The classified guy took it down on a carboned pad. One part went to the composing room as a *paid death notice*, then the carbon was sent in a tube to the editorial department where you took the bare facts and created an obit of three paragraphs that would run in the paper. The first one I ever worked on was a man named Ruse who died in Queens Village. His remains were at Studsman Funeral Parlor. Just the fact that there were two names, two facts, got me in trouble from the start. I put all the information in and when I got to the last paragraph, I wrote that "Mr. Studsman will be interned tomorrow at the Cavalry Cemetery." I had mixed up the names and that's how it hit the paper. The next day, the editor came to me and said, "Congratulations, young Breslin. You're a professional newsman now. You just buried the undertaker." Getting the names straight is half the battle. If a name is in the paper and it's spelled right, the guy's got no complaint. From that I learned that you had to be so careful about the basics. It's been a tremendous help as well as a plague my entire life.

A life spent making mistakes is not only more honorable but more useful than a life spent doing nothing.
—George Bernard Shaw

The best training for a newspaper reporter is to cover a fire. A fire story gives you firemen fighting the blaze, the building, its owner and the inhabitants the firemen are attempting to save. It gives you the hospital end of it. There's so many facets to what most people would think as a simple fire story. And for me, it's the names. You get the names of the people that get out of the fire. Next, you get the names of the firemen. Then you get the names of the people at the hospital where the victims were taken.

When I got home after covering my first fire, I could not find one of those names in the files. I was stuck with trying out how to spell names like fireman George Smith. There's about five different ways to spell Smith. There was a J. Cox who owned the building. Was that spelled C-o-x or is it spelled C-o-c-k-s? I was putting in calls and couldn't find anyone. The firemen had gone home, the owner wasn't listed or lived out of town and the people at the hospital had finished their shift. At the end of the night, I was going crazy. I was stuck with names that I was sure I misspelled and I went to bed dying. Of course, some of the names were wrong and people tend to be particular about their last names. It's a killer. In those cases, you take a shot and do the best you can. The next time I covered a fire, I stayed on an hour after I might have left before. I would keep talking, going from one person to the other, getting the names right. It taught me that putting in a little extra time and effort saved a much bigger pain later. Details will make you or break you in the news reporting business. Now if I get the facts wrong, it's so devastating to me I'm sick for a week.

I've been fired who knows how many times, but I always figured it was just fear and jealousy. I wasn't such a nice fellow to do business with. A misbehaver. They all thought I was after their jobs...which I was. There came a point where those problems were forgotten.

The editors wanted me to do big things and everyone else had to get out of the way.

In news reporting, as in life, you can tell how well you're doing by how your feet feel. If you've walked a lot, gone up enough flights of stairs, run down enough leads, you'll know it. I would take half the telephones out of the newsrooms today. "Phoning it in" is an expression that really fits how a great many people do their job today. Getting dirty, getting involved, that's what's important.

Sometimes it's difficult to place yourself in someone else's shoes. When I was writing, a kid from a mob family talked to me and told me what he thought, which was too much. It was absolutely true and later he wanted me to stop the book. He thought he would be in real trouble. I went ahead and wrote it anyway. I didn't think the guy would actually get in trouble, but in that business, if you thought you were in trouble, you probably were. Whether the guy actually ended up in trouble or not, I should have considered that. If I had it to do over, I wouldn't have done it.

I once wrote a couple pieces about a bookmaker who killed a rich society guy. It was obvious to me that the bookmaker did it. I wrote the story and that summer at the beach, I ran into one of the clerks for the judge who was involved in the case. I found out that no one was sure if the guy had done it. In my stories, I had him guilty. I felt sick. But I had written the story honestly. I never mean to hurt anybody, but it happens.

The damage you do while you're trying to do good is sometimes unavoidable. But you have to keep moving ahead. The best advice I could give anyone is to get up in the morning and go to work. After the bombing of the World Trade Center, I was asked how people should act. I said, "Please, just get up and go to work." One of the survivors of

Accept failure as a normal part of living. View it as part of the process of exploring your world; make a note of its lessons and move on.

—Tom Hobson

the attack brought up the fact that the people who lost their lives were at their desks at nine in the morning or before. Our obligation is to honor their diligence and honesty of work by doing the same.

If you do something wrong, if you make a mistake, you've got to remember the pain. Remember how bad it felt. Don't go slobbering apologies around. Tell everybody what you did wrong. Trying to hide the mistakes only makes it worse. Look for the details that you might have been too f***in' lazy to find before and do a better job the next time. For me, I have no choice but to keep going on, to keep what I do as honest as possible. I never took failure or success to heart. I've done way, way more good than bad. Life is like writing a story. If you write something that turns out being wrong, you correct it and write it better tomorrow. But you never quit writing.

> *The elevator to success is out of order. You have to use the stairs. . .one step at a time.*
> —*Joe Girard*

FAULTY FINDINGS

"I think there is a world market for maybe five computers."

–Thomas Watson, chairman of IBM, 1943.

Ed *Asner*

"Sometimes, we have the answer before we know what the question is."

Television, film and stage actor Yitzak Edward Asner may be best known for his award-winning comedic and dramatic portrayals of journalist Lou Grant. Playing Grant on the classic comedy *The Mary Tyler Moore Show*, Asner won three Emmys. Asner next took his Lou Grant character on to the acclaimed series *Lou Grant*, winning two more Emmys. An additional two Emmys were garnered for his roles in *Rich Man, Poor Man* and *Roots*. He also has five Golden Globes on his mantle. Asner served as national president of the Screen Actors Guild for two terms and continues to be active in many humanitarian and political organizations. But Asner wasn't always a star and no Emmy or Golden Globe could shield him from bad reviews.

I look at my pictures as a kid and I can see how I reeked of insecurity. I was the youngest in the family, a momma's boy, deprived of my independence. I felt like the lowest man on the totem pole. I was not shoved out of the canoe so I could learn to swim.

During my sophomore year in high school, all the boys were pledging fraternities. There was only one other Jewish kid in school and he was in a fraternity. Even so, I didn't think I would be selected. And I wasn't. It didn't feel good at all.

> *I cannot give the formula for success, but I can give you the formula of failure—which is try to please everybody.*
> *—Herbert Bayard Swope*

In addition, I wasn't doing very well academically and as a defense mechanism I was becoming a class clown, a buffoon. Soon, for laughs, other kids began playing tricks and making fun of me. I finally couldn't take it anymore and decided "enough." I found myself alone and so I decided if I wanted to get anywhere in life, it would be up to me.

I started going out for everything. Football. Theater. Journalism. I did everything to keep busy. I got awards and showed everyone that I was more than competent. I eventually succeeded. I made All-City in football. In journalism, I received the Quill and Scroll. In theater, I received my thespian pin. I was drafted into the school's booster club. And I worked rigorously to get good grades.

In my junior year, I was rushed by another fraternity, one that I actually did not want to join. But I decided that it was time for me to try again, so I made myself available. When time came for them to vote, I was blackballed. I was blackballed because I was Jewish. They rushed me, yet they did not vote me in. Once again, I had put myself on the line, leaving myself vulnerable, and once again, I was hurt.

The wisest person is not the one who has the fewest failures but the one who turns failures to best account.
—*Richard R. Grant*

In my senior year, I actually did get into a fraternity and I discovered that I didn't even want to be there. I soon realized that sometimes being rejected is God's way of saying you wouldn't be happy there, anyway. Sometimes, we have the answer before we know what the question is.

But the biggest mistake I made was when I decided to play football on Kol Nidre [an important Jewish holiday]. The team and the coach said they needed me. I believed it. My principal asked my rabbi to give me special dispensation, but my rabbi refused. My father begged me not to play. Everyone else kept asking me to play. On the day of the game, my mother and my brothers conspired to sneak me out of the house so my father wouldn't find out.

Before the game, the coach made a speech to the team saying that they should "win this game for Eddie." I played and we won. But we would have won without me. I had a choice between right and wrong, and I chose wrong. Yes, I would have been despised if I hadn't played, but I would have done more for my people and my religion if I had not played. And I let my father down. It was to become a burden I would carry the rest of my life.

It was a mistake, but from it I learned a valuable lesson. I learned that you must do the right thing regardless of what others may want. I've tried to apply that in all areas of my life. Whenever a decision is imminent, I've tried to do what I know is right.

There have been times in my life when doing the right thing has caused me repercussions; when what I had chosen to do has flown in the face of powers. But because I know what I did or said was right, what others thought has not affected my thinking. And what others think does not change the fact that I'm doing the best that I can.

When I did a revival of *Born Yesterday* on Broadway in 1989, I worked really hard to make it work. We stayed open for five months. Not bad for a revival. *Born Yesterday* author, Garson Kanin, said I was the best Harry he ever had. Some reviewers thought differently. There seemed to be an anti-Hollywood attitude around then. It also seemed like they set out to eviscerate me, and to do it savagely.

Reviewer Frank Rich opened his review by saying he never liked the play to begin with. The reviewer for *The New Yorker* seemed bent on cutting out my guts. And every week in *The New Yorker* capsule reviews, they would repeat the worst elements of that criticism.

> *The reward of suffering is experience.*
> *—Aeschylus*

I felt very wounded. It wasn't easy to live with and it angered me. But I attempted to turn that anger into energy for my performance. Despite what the reviewers said, I just kept working on the role and it remains one of the proudest pieces of work I've ever done.

If you are struggling, work hard to find out what your strengths are. Be they physical. Be they cerebral. Be they scientific. When you find what they are, develop them as fully as you possibly can. When you use them, use them to do the right thing.

RED-LETTER REJECTS

Arthur Conan Doyle's *A Study in Scarlet*, the novel that introduced the world to Sherlock Holmes, was rejected by three publishers in 1897.

Pat Boone

"God is available."

Pat Boone is one of our country's most beloved singers; a television, movie and recording star; author and one of the most admired hosts of the Christian Television Ministry. He's even given evidence that there might be a bit of heavy metal rocker in those old white bucks. In the midst of his busy career, he and high school sweetheart, Shirley, raised four beautiful daughters. But it was as a business entrepreneur that he was once again reminded that adversity can be an opportunity for success.

During my own spiritually dry period in the 1960s, I had drifted into the Hollywood drinking and party scene. I was being led astray and it showed up in many ways. Even in family prayer times, I was just going though the motions.

Things started to go wrong, not only with my inner spirituality and family relationships but with my personal finances as well. I made a series of bad business commitments, and for a while it seemed certain that I'd lose everything and have to go into bankruptcy. For one thing, I had invested in the Oakland Oaks ABA basketball team, a colossal financial washout, an economic "black hole." One day, I received a terse letter from the Bank of America demanding immediate payment of $1.3 million. I just didn't have it and had no idea where I could get it. Only a miracle could save me from financial disaster.

> *You win only if you aren't afraid to lose.*
> —Rocky Aoki

Just after the demand from the bank, some friends took me aside at a Bible study and assured me that God wasn't going to let me go bankrupt. I began thanking God and rejoicing that He was going to pull me through this crisis. Within two days, a man I didn't even know flew in and bought the Oakland Oaks for $2 million. If he had waited just one more day, he could have bought the whole mess for half a million, and I'd have been bankrupt. Though certainly a miracle, there were still more lessons for me to learn.

If I were to say, 'God, why me?' about the bad things, then I should have said, 'God, why me?' about the good things that happened in my life.
—Arthur Ashe

In addition to the basketball deal, I had also become a general partner in a large and successful real estate company. The severe recession of 1970 threw us into a financial tailspin, and we found ourselves desperately struggling to reorganize and save the company under Chapter 12 of the bankruptcy law. Because of my legal status in the company, I was threatened with the entire $30 million liability—and that was at least $27 million more than I could have scraped together under any circumstances.

It was "SOS" time again, and for the second time, God spoke to me—this time, over the radio!

Driving alone one day, feeling utterly helpless in my latest financial catastrophe, I idly tuned across the radio dial and "happened" to hear a minister talking about giving. He said, "Every year in the United States and Canada, without fail, the insurance companies record about a 10 percent loss in crops. You can count on it—a 10 percent loss due to what they call acts of God, such as droughts, floods, blights and other natural disasters. One way or another, *God demands His tithe!"*

The preacher went on to say that according to a recent poll, farmers who tithed regularly fared a whole lot better, even when the weather was hostile, than those who gave nothing. And I thought, "Man, you're talking to me!"

I called my accountant and said, "John, we've got to get more serious about my giving. I want to give a tenth of every dollar I earn to God's work."

"Ten percent of the gross? That's something like 20 percent of your net income!"

I told him that I give about 10 percent to the agency that books me and another 10 percent to my manager. I'd better give 10 percent to God if I expect Him to show me the way out of my problems.

"You can't afford to."

"I can't afford *not* to."

We started The Pat Boone Foundation to give support to His Kingdom. I prayed with a new fervor. My partners prayed. We all worked harder than we had before.

At the end of the year, my accountant reported to me, "I don't know how this happened. You've paid all your expenses, you've reduced your debts, you've paid all your taxes and you've even started a pension fund—all this in spite of the fact that you've been giving 10 percent off the top."

"No," I corrected him, "it's *because* I gave 10 percent off the top."

While this was a money issue, there's no question in my mind that it works in all parts of my life. And giving doesn't necessarily mean money. It's being of service, donating your time, giving your love, helping others in any way you can.

Remember that your failures are the seeds of your most glorious successes. Be sad if you must, but don't despair.
—Unknown

I learned the hard way that you can't out-give God. He built some sort of giving principal into the universe, which assures us that He'll return far more than we've laid out. You can count on it. I do.

ACCIDENTAL ACHIEVEMENTS

Florida doctor John Gorrie thought in part that heat helped cause malaria, so in 1844 he built a small engine that cooled his malaria patients. While it failed to cure the malaria, it kept the patients' rooms comfortable despite the severe humidity and so he had created the forerunner to the modern air conditioner.

Venerable Grand Master Hsing Yun

"When we experience the difficulties of planting seeds and tilling the soil, the sweetness of harvest will come naturally."

Grand Master Hsing Yun is the founder of the Fo Guang Shan International Buddhist Order, with over five million followers worldwide. The Order emphasizes education and service and maintains public universities, libraries, free mobile medical clinics, children's homes, retirement homes and high schools. Master Yun has authored over 100 books, is an outspoken proponent of equality among all people and religious traditions and annually organizes conferences to bring together various Buddhist schools to promote dialogue between Buddhists and other major religious groups.

In order to be successful in our lives and careers, we need the help of many causes and conditions in the same way that trees and plants need sunshine, fresh air and water to flourish; buildings require materials such as timber, cement, steel and masonry to be constructed. When causes and conditions are smooth, it is easy to accomplish what we set out to do. When causes are not going our way, we face obstacles and difficulties at every turn in the course of our lives and careers.

Although setbacks and difficulties may defeat an ordinary person, they cannot overcome a capable young person. This because unfavorable causes and conditions motivate a person to develop his or her potential. They are the negative forces that actually help his or her progress. For example, when we are ill, we know we should care more about our health. When we suffer, we realize we should improve our situation by working hard.

In the world of nature, plum blossoms are often praised because they can withstand ice and snow, and the colder it gets the more fragrant they become. Pines and cypresses are admired by people because they can endure the frost and cold and grow greener as it gets colder.

Wherever we look, we can see many other examples of overcoming obstacles. A young person who suffers the discrimination and intimidation of others will work harder still and strive against the odds to progress. Just as a ball bounces higher when hit harder, we witness many physically challenged people overcoming their handicaps and becoming successful athletes, painters and writers.

> *I don't divide the world into the weak and the strong, or the successes and the failures... I divide the world into learners and non-learners.*
> —*Benjamin Barber*

Without the betrayal of Judas, the holiness of Jesus wouldn't be as apparent. On the path of life, when we encounter stumbling blocks, we may be tripped by them or we may use them as steppingstones for us to climb onto so we can see farther and wider.

Success and failure in life depend on whether we can overcome setbacks and turn them into conditions for progress. When there is no darkness, there is no brightness. Without crime, we cannot discover the good and the beautiful. When there is no filth, we cannot appreciate the cleanliness. Without differences, there will be no unity. When we experience the difficulties of planting seeds and tilling the soil, the sweetness of harvest will come naturally.

A person's accomplishments are built on blood, sweat, difficulties, disadvantages, tolerance and suffering. Greatness can only be achieved with much hardship and diligence. Therefore, being able to bear hardship is like taking tonics for our life.

People are not saints, so naturally we all have faults and err from time to time. It is not bad to make mistakes as long as we are willing to correct them. Those who refuse to admit and correct their faults are like a wall painted black. They refuse to add colors. We all make mistakes. But correcting the mistakes we make is the best virtue. No one wants to make mistakes, and mistakes are not necessarily bad. Learning

A man's life is interesting primarily when he has failed—I well know. For it's a sign that he tried to surpass himself.
—Georges Clemenceau

from our mistakes builds the foundation for success. All of us should face hardships with courage and thus, by our resolve, plant the seeds of strength for a future harvest.

Nature is based on harmony and it finds its balance through the harmonious functioning of its many parts. That which obstructs nature brings trouble to itself as it forces the basic harmony of life to decline into discord. The ancients used to say, "To oppose the flow of nature is to be mentally ill."

We should diligently correct our own faults, yet tolerate patiently the shortcomings of others. We should give others an opportunity to find a remedy, guiding them with kindness and wisdom so that they too can develop the right understanding. In confronting other's mistakes, we should try to exchange places with them. We should exhibit magnanimity rather than resentment, understanding rather than hatred, encouragement rather than scorn, care rather than negligence, unity rather than division. If we can do that, society will make favorable progress, and life will be much better.

There is an old Chinese saying: "Failure is the basis for success." When we treat every failure as a lesson, then we will be successful.

RED-LETTER REJECTS

Margaret Mitchell's classic novel, *Gone with the Wind,* was rejected by over 25 publishers. The general feeling was that the public was not interested in Civil War stories.

What is defeat? Nothing

but education. Nothing but the first step to something better.

—Wendell Phillips

10

Sam Donaldson

"At that moment of uncertainty, when things could go either way, I said to myself, '. . .they're going MY way.' "

Sam Donaldson's career as a news reporter has spanned four decades of American and world history. He's interviewed the most famous personalities of the century and reported on some of the most important events of our time. As a longtime White House correspondent, he was known for his opening salvo of "Now, hold on, Mr. President." As co-anchor with Cokie Roberts of ABC's *This Week*, Sam Donaldson still remains at the top of his game, but it was his earlier discouraging foray into primetime magazine news where he discovered that he might not be up to the challenge. That near disaster ended up being just the challenge he needed.

When I was 14, my mother sent me to a military institute. She was raising me alone and I was incorrigible, a wild kid. The first year there I was a sad rat. I was forever walking *tours* around the quadrangle. I didn't polish my brass. I would show up late for formation. I received lots of demerits, and for my less-than-appropriate behavior I had my butt beaten with rifle stocks and wire coat hangers.

I wanted to be on the other side of the equation. All at once a switch went off in me, and the next year I went back with a completely different attitude. I worked hard and by the end of the year I was one of only six or seven to be promoted to the highest rank—sergeant—for my third year. I'm not saying I was changed forever, but I had learned that it was in my power to change a bad situation.

> *If one does not fail at times, then one has not challenged himself.*
> —Dr. Porsche

In 1989, I joined Diane Sawyer as a co-host on a new ABC prime time magazine show called *Primetime Live.* I had just left the White House. All that time I had been a working reporter in the field doing what one would consider the traditional work of television news. I suddenly found myself on a magazine program and while it was television and it was news, it was as alien and foreign to me as I could ever imagine.

Some defeats are only installments to victory.
—Jacob Riis

I found that learning this type of format was excruciatingly difficult, and since I wasn't doing it well, I was clearly unhappy. And because I wasn't performing in the required fashion, people were obviously unhappy with me. Clearly, I wasn't working up to the level I should have been, but it wasn't just me. In every respect, the program itself wasn't doing well.

Television reviewer Tom Shales, in a *Washington Post* review, wrote, "*Primetime Live* is still having its shakedown cruise. After several weeks there seems to be one easy remedy for some of the show's ills: dump Sam. He's corny. He's hokey. He's out of his element. He's a klutz. How does the title, *Thursday Night with Diane Sawyer,* strike you? Just asking."

I felt terrible, but he was probably right. I wasn't a positive element at that point in the show. I would later end up thanking him for it.

Soon thereafter I was at a restaurant having dinner with Diane Sawyer and the executive producer, Rick Kaplan. We all acknowledged the program was failing. We agreed that if we couldn't fix it, it wasn't worth doing. We understood that if the program failed, not that we would never work again, but it would be a setback of monumental proportions for the news division and for all of us personally.

As many psychologists and the Alcoholics Anonymous program put it, I had hit "rock bottom." I mean, I was still making a princely sum and I knew where my next meal was coming from, but psychologically, with the considerable amount of time I had put into the business, it was clear that I was at some sort of a watershed. Part of me wanted to say, "I can't do this, Roone [Arledge, ABC News President]. Let me go back." I couldn't go back to being a White House correspondent. They already had an able successor. But I could be a Washington correspondent. Maybe Roone would say "yes."

Roone had a way about him where he would let you either hang yourself or save yourself. At that moment of uncertainty, when things could go either way, I said to myself, "…they're going MY way." So Rick, Diane and I made a decision. I would come back to Washington, the town that I knew, the town that I had worked in, the town where I understood the politics. I would anchor my portion of the show from Washington instead of trying to do it from New York. And it made a difference, especially with the kind of stories we chose to do. Along the way, we were learning how to put together a magazine show. And then, the Gulf War came along.

That was my forte. I knew these people. I knew them all. I knew Colin Powell. I knew Norman Schwarzkopf. I knew Dick Cheney. I knew George Herbert Walker Bush. I went over to the Gulf for the entire period of the war. What emerged from that was the real *Primetime Live*. It certainly wasn't all me, but instead of a drag, I had finally become a positive force for the show. And the program became wildly successful.

Our doubts are traitors,
And make us lose the good we oft
might win by fearing to attempt.
—William Shakespeare,
Measure For Measure

In 1995, I was diagnosed with stage-three melanoma. I was enjoying life and I didn't want it to end. You have to go ahead and lead your life as normally as you can. The very next year, David Brinkley retired, and it would have been easy for Roone to say, "Here's a guy who's 62 and has cancer and he's not going to be around much longer." But instead, he made me co-anchor with Cokie Roberts on *This Week*. He bet on me. It made sense for me to bet on myself.

I've been very fortunate, but if there is one lesson that I've learned, it's the one Churchill imparted: "Never, never, never, never, never give up." Everyone will have peaks and valleys. Once you reach a peak and think you've got it made, you can be certain that the next day or right around the corner, someone or something will arise to knock you in the head again. In other words, don't ever get so comfortable that you are not prepared for another set of adversities.

Mistakes are just successes waiting to be completed.
—Michael Nieves

ACCIDENTAL ACHIEVEMENTS

In 1913, Harry Brearley, in an attempt to make stronger iron for guns, found no use for much of the metal he generated. Months later, while looking through the scrap he had thrown out, he found that one of the discarded pieces had not rusted. That metal is today known as stainless steel.

Jeanie Buss

". . .what I thought was a waste was an investment in my future."

Jeanie Buss, executive vice president of business operations for the World Champion Los Angeles Lakers basketball team, was only 19 when she found herself in charge of the Los Angeles Strings of World Team Tennis. The team won two league championships and Buss went on to take over franchises in professional roller hockey and indoor soccer. She also headed one of the country's largest arenas, promoting concerts and various other sporting events. It took years of struggling with minor league franchises before Jeanie Buss would become one of the rare women in the high ranks of professional sports management.

When I was around 10 years old, my mother and father divorced. I could see the stress in my mom. I worried about her. Like all kids, I wished I could have made it better between my parents and, of course, there was nothing I could have done. My mother took care of my brothers and seemed to leave my sister and me to fend for ourselves. My father kind of disappeared. Whenever kids would ask where my father was, I had no idea what to say. I finally got to the point where it was easier just to tell them he was dead. My mother was so detached from what was going on with me that, when I had chicken pox in tenth grade, she never thought to contact my school to tell them that I was sick. Fact is, I could have ditched school completely and I don't think anyone would have noticed. I was out of school for two weeks and when I returned I found a pile of "F"s waiting for me. I was devastated. I hated being singled out like that, and it took me over a month to catch up with everyone.

No one seemed to be there for me. I craved adult attention, so without a parent to turn to, I looked to teachers as substitute parents. I found myself working harder than ever before. My "C"s became

"A"s. I grew more independent. I became more and more self-sufficient and, without knowing it at the time, what I was going through would stand me in good stead as I entered the world of business. At the age of 17, I started college and moved in with my dad.

Having Dr. Jerry Buss, the owner of a sports empire, as a father was both a blessing and a curse. It may seem like you're being handed something on a silver platter, but then you're expected to make that something work. When I was 19 and only a junior in college, my father named me general manager of the Los Angeles Strings, a member of the new indoor tennis league. My father made it clear that if I didn't stay in school, I wouldn't have the job.

Thank goodness I was naive. I believed if my father thought I could do it, I'd be able to handle it. It never dawned on me all the things I didn't know. I made so many mistakes. I thought I wasted so much time. Later on I would realize that what I thought was a waste was an investment in my future.

Thankfully, the first season was only four weeks long, so my mistakes didn't have enough time to cause devastating effects. In retrospect, would I have put a child of mine into the same situation my dad put me into? Probably not. But my dad knew this was just how I needed to build my experience. It took many years before I realized that my dad was right in not coddling me, even though at the time it was what I wanted. There were times that my dad explained what he was doing with me, but with me muddling through the problems, I just didn't hear him.

I became known as the promoter of *orphan sports*, meaning I had to promote events like indoor soccer, volleyball and roller hockey. I was in charge of the events that weren't big time and I thought of myself as *minor league*. It felt like there was no one else to do it, so I had to do the job. It's easy to promote someone like Madonna or the World Champion Lakers. Every ticket that we sold for an event like USA Volleyball vs. Japan, I earned. When I would get on the phone to ESPN to push indoor volleyball as the *next big thing*, the reality was that they had about a hundred other people on hold ready to talk about some other *next big thing*. It was so difficult because I took each hang-up personally. Looking back on it, I see that it was building up my reputation and my expertise. But at that point, I still found myself judging the worth, or lack of it, a little too quickly.

> There are no secrets to success. It is the result of preparation, hard work, and learning from failure.
> —Colin Powell

In the early '90s, roller hockey was invented. I say invented because the sport just did not exist before. I received a memo from my dad saying, "I decided we're going to have a team in this league. Handle it." The entire concept made no sense to me. I went to the league meetings to hear the plans and all I was thinking was, "Is there any way I could change my name so that no one would know I was involved?" They didn't actually show us anything because there was nothing for them to show. I literally had to promote a game that I had never seen. A game that no one had ever seen before. At least the concepts of indoor soccer or arena football were easily understood. But roller hockey? Hockey is played on ice. Here, there was no ice. There were no college roller hockey leagues. There were no stars to push.

In '92, they arranged a USA vs. Canada roller hockey tour to test markets. I did interviews, actually winging it, telling people how great this league was going to be. I felt I had nothing. I never took into consideration the fact that Wayne Gretzky was at the height of his popularity with the Los Angeles Kings and ice hockey was hot. We opened the doors for the exhibition game and 8,000 people showed up. Eight thousand fans for something that had never been seen. It was fantastic. The USA team won. The crowd went crazy. And I fell in love with the sport. When we announced that Los Angeles would have a team, it was like giving birth to a baby. We opened in Oakland in 1993. When the team came out for the very first time, I got a lump in my throat like I'd never had before. For five years, I had a great time. But undercapitalized, get-rich-quick owners hurt the league's reputation and we had to shut down. It broke my heart. I had associated the success or failure of the entire sport as a personal reflection on me. There was the constant,

"Will we make money, will we lose money, will we break even?" I put in a lot of worry hours.

From that point on, I became a businesswoman. I separated myself from the event. Either the event is good or the event is bad. It wasn't about me as a person. I learned not to get caught up in wins and losses. Only one team a year can win a championship. If you put all the emphasis on a championship year, then anything less becomes a failure. I'm concerned with the fans enjoying the game experience. From the minute they drive into the parking lot until they drive out, I ask myself one question, "Did the fan have a good time?" I realized it's more than just the game.

We stopped investing in minor league sports and I was given the position as alternative governor for the L.A. Lakers. That meant that for the first time I would attend the NBA owners' meetings. I had been a veteran of the minor league sports where every inch forward was followed by two inches back. It was always a struggle. Here I was, going to NBA meetings, the highly successful NBA with Michael Jordan, where I thought all they did was smoke cigars and pat each other on the back. How could they have the same stress that the small leagues had? Yet I found that the stress was just the same and I was prepared. If I hadn't had the years of experience working for those orphan leagues, with all the attended hours and heartache, I would have never been prepared for the big-time struggles of the NBA.

When I began to represent the Lakers, I had to deal with many of the same people who paid attention to what I had to say over the earlier years. Now I was in a more powerful position. I had developed a relationship with those people built on the time and effort I had invested during those pre-Laker days. When, in April of 1995, I walked into my first NBA meeting as one of three women, and the youngest of some 80 people there, the presidency of the Great Western Forum came open. I was selected to fill the position. That also happened to be the month *Playboy* magazine came out with my photos in it. What a trifecta!

No pressure,
no diamonds.
—Mary Case

We are the sum of our efforts.
—S. Young

When I took over the Forum, there were issues I had never dealt with before. Other arenas could be booked for half the cost. We had a union stagehand contract deal that had to be renegotiated so that we could compete. Threats against me followed. My attorney advised me to drive a rental car because someone might sabotage my own car. They thought they could intimidate me. It was scary for me, but still, I was successful in the negotiations. Did I need that kind of experience? I can't be sure, but I do know that it empowered me to believe that I could handle almost anything. Did my parents' divorce and my treatment actually help me become what I am today? Absolutely, and I have no complaints. I look back and see what my mom was going through and now I'm able to understand. Those circumstances helped make me stronger. Today I recognize that it all played a part in the passion I put into my work. It is so important to find what you're passionate about, whatever it is. When you do, commit to it and no matter how they try, don't let anyone talk you out of it.

OUTLANDISH OPINIONS

"The concept is interesting and well-formed, but in order to earn better than a 'C,' the idea must be feasible."

–Yale University management professor in response to Fred Smith's paper proposing reliable overnight delivery service.

Smith went on to found Federal Express Corp.

Dr. Howard House

"Mr. House, you're not serious about becoming a doctor."

Dr. Howard House transformed his one-person ear, nose and throat practice into the largest otologic and neurotologic center in the world. Dr. House led the way to major advances in the treatment of the middle and inner ear, establishing the use of cochlear implants and auditory brainstem implants for profoundly deaf patients. Dr. House has also been at the forefront of diagnosing and correcting hearing impairments in newborns. With colleagues calling his experiences *the hazards of howard*, you know that Dr. Howard House's long road of success was laden with more than his share of bumps and detours. And from many of those adverse situations came medical breakthroughs and life-saving circumstances.

My dad told me that if I wanted to be a dentist, I'd first have to become a medical doctor, because, as he said, "You cannot separate teeth from the rest of the body." I heeded his advice and became an M.D. I never became a dentist.

I'm dyslexic. As a student I had no idea that I had it, I just had to write down everything from every book I read until I had completely memorized it. Partly because of this, and partly because I spent so much time dating girls and playing tennis that when I attempted to get into medical school, my three years of college work had resulted in a 1.8 grade point average. My meeting with Dr. Paul McKibben at the University of Southern California School of Medicine was not exactly what I had hoped it would be.

Dr. McKibben said, "Mr. House, I understand you are interested in going to medical school here." I said, "Yes, sir." After looking at my transcript, Dr. McKibben's reaction was less than positive. It was both discouraging and humiliating. "Mr. House, you're not serious about becoming a doctor." I told him I was and he replied, "Our classes are very small, the courses are very hard, and we don't want to admit anyone unless they've got a chance of going the distance. Why do you think you've made such terrible grades?" I told him about playing tennis, being manager of the football team and being a member of the debating team. He wanted to know if I dated a lot, and I admitted I had. He took a long puff on his pipe and said, "Mr. House, when you go back to Whittier [College] in the fall, give up some of your activities and dates, and if you make better grades in your senior year, I'll have a place for you in next year's fall class."

When I was a young man I observed that nine out of ten things I did were failures. I didn't want to be a failure, so I did ten times more work.
—George Bernard Shaw

Amazingly, it seems that I had taken after my father, who applied for his dental education without even completing high school. Dad dropped out of school at the age of 13. At the age of 19, he went with my mother to the dentist where she received a gold crown at a cost of $5. Days later, when he realized how long he would have had to work at his parents' farm to make $5, he announced that he was heading for Indiana to enroll at Indiana Dental College. When he presented himself to the Dean as a prospective dental student, he learned that a precondition for admission was a high school diploma or its "equivalent." Dad immediately enrolled in high school. A year later, three decades before I was to meet USC's Dr. McKibben, Dad once again called on the Dean. This time, he must have realized that Dad's ambition was far beyond his academic record and accepted him into the dental school. My father, Milus Howard, went on to become a major figure in the history of modern dentistry.

Being a man of medicine, my father made me promise that I would not smoke until I was 21. If I kept to my promise, I would get a new car on my 21st birthday. When my birthday came and he asked if I had smoked, I admitted that I had puffed on a pipe or cigarette from time to time, but never inhaled. With that, my father declared,

"No new car." Then he added, "But you've just demonstrated that you have a quality above all others that is indispensable in a doctor, integrity. Therefore, I will cover the entire cost of your medical education."

With that powerful gift and the encouragement I received from Dr. McKibben, I went back to school and, working harder than I had ever worked before, raised my grade point average to 2.15. Immediately after graduation, I went to Dr. McKibben's office. He remembered me, "You're the one who had those terrible grades." He saw that I had improved my grades, and also remembered his commitment to me, but told me that the classes were full. He looked me squarely in the eyes and said, "What are you going to do now?"

Though I was bitterly disappointed, I didn't let on and said, "What I do now, Dr. McKibben, is up to you. You tell me what to do and I'll do it. I'll go back to college next year, and the next, and the year after that if necessary, because one of these days, I am going to be a doctor."

After a moment, McKibben said, "I'll take up your case with the admissions committee and we will decide what you should do this coming year and, if necessary, the year following."

After two weeks of anxiety and failed expectations, I received a letter from the Office of the Dean of USC School of Medicine. There had been a vacancy in the September class and I was finally in. What I was unaware of at the time was that McKibben *was* the committee. He was also the acting dean and the budget committee. There had been an opening all along, and Dr. McKibben had invented the no-vacancy story. He said that since doctors face crises on a day-to-day basis, he wanted to see how I would react to my own crisis. I had passed his test.

My first year in medical school was a nightmare. Besides my regular medical classes, beefing up on courses I had fallen

> *Notice the difference between what happens when a man says to himself, I have failed three times, and what happens when he says, I am a failure.*
> —S. I. Hayakawa

short of in college and having dyslexia, unbeknownst to me, I was also colorblind. The capacity to distinguish between colors was extremely important when trying to analyze elements under the microscope.

But I got through, much to the amazement of Dr. McKibben. Halfway through my second year, Dr. McKibben called me into his office to tell me that my grades were now in the top third of my class. I couldn't believe it. All that work had paid off. What was funny was that I was just thrilled to be there.

A few years after graduating, I began to focus on the ear and a condition known as otosclerosis. What happens is one of the bones in the ear, the stape, which is the smallest bone in the body, becomes fixed due to boney growth. It's the leading cause of progressive hearing loss at a young age. There were a number of unusual circumstances that led otologists to recognize possible solutions to the problem. Early in the 20th century, a traveling "medicine man," in an attempt to gather a crowd, offered $5 to any man who could stay in the ring with a professional boxer. A hearing-impaired farm boy got in the ring and was quickly knocked out. In falling, he banged his head against a ring post. When he regained consciousness, his first words were, "By God, I can hear!" Years before, a German medical journal published a study of a young man who, after a skull fracture, regained his lost hearing. What was happening was that the blow to the skull allowed sound to create waves in the inner ear fluid which, in turn, activated the hearing nerve. But because of lack of adequate magnification and antibiotics, successful surgery to duplicate the benefits of the *accidents* was still many years off. But the possibilities had already been born.

One of the greatest battles of my life was overcoming bias regarding technique. My brother, Dr. Bill House, was a genius. He wanted to focus his work on the inner ear and I put my ear institute clearly behind his efforts. He worked with cadavers to develop better ways to get to the inner ear to remove tumors safely, which had previously been impossible. Neurosurgeons used to go through the back of the head and the brain to reach those tumors, incurring a 40 percent mortality rate due to complications from the operation alone. Bill developed a procedure that decreased the mortality rate to one half of I percent. Neurosurgeons were livid. We were invading their territory. There was tremendous opposition.

Bill sat through an acoustic tumor procedure in which the patient died. He was near tears when he told me of it. The next acoustic tumor we saw, we decided to schedule it for Bill to handle at St. Vincent's Hospital, where most of our surgery occurred. The head of the neurosurgery department at USC, Ted Kersey, a good friend, was also head of St. Vincent's Hospital. Kersey raised hell. He demanded that Bill be prevented from doing the surgery. I called a meeting with the nuns who ran St. Vincent's. During the meeting Kersey stood up and said, "If you allow him to do this operation, I will resign." I jumped up and said, "If you don't allow Bill House to do this operation, I'll resign." It was *High Noon*. This would have meant losing an entire floor at St. Vincent's dedicated to our work. There was no doubt in my mind I had to say what I did. That operation had to be done. If not at St. Vincent's, we would find someplace else. The nuns went into executive session and 10 minutes later announced that Bill would be allowed to perform the surgery. Kersey resigned on the spot. The surgery was a success.

Perhaps the most divine intervention into a perilous situation happened in 1987 when I was in Leningrad along with my daughter Carolyn, her husband Dick and my friend, singer-actress Nanette Fabray. While walking through a shopping area, I experienced severe discomfort similar to what I had felt from my heart attack four years before. I slumped down on the curb as Dick and Nanette attempted to get the help of pedestrians. I was dying. I needed to get back to our hotel where medical care was available. The Russian pedestrians were unable to understand my friends' pleas. They tried to flag a cab, but again, with no grasp of English, the cab driver was unable to help. Finally, Nan saw three men standing at a corner talking in sign language. Using the few signs she had learned, which are quite international in nature, she made them understand the nature of my problem. The men stopped a car and explained to the driver what happened and where I

Few things are impracticable in themselves, and it is for want of application, rather than of means, that men fail.
—François, duc de La Rochefoucauld

should be taken. When you consider the pure mathematical improbability of this situation, it certainly seemed like divine intervention. The fact that Nan had a hearing problem and learned some sign language to help herself ended up becoming a life-giving gift to me. Communication through sign language had literally saved my life. Sometimes life is like that. What one might perceive as a handicap can otherwise turn out to be a blessing.

WRONG RATIONALES

"There is not the slightest indication that [nuclear energy] will ever be obtainable. It would mean that the atom would have to be shattered at will."
—Albert Einstein, 1932.

David Henry Hwang

"Every success comes with a little bit of poison and every failure comes with some great blessing."

David Henry Hwang, best known for his stage and film sensation, *M. Butterfly*, won the 1988 Tony Award for best play, establishing him as a major American playwright. *Time* magazine said that "the final scene of *M. Butterfly* is among the most forceful in the history of the American theater…he has the potential to become the first important dramatist of American public life since Arthur Miller, and maybe the best of them all." Hwang's first play, *F.O.B. (Fresh Off the Boat)*, won the 1981 Obie Award as the best new play of the season when Joseph Papp brought it off-Broadway in New York. Among a long list of credits, Hwang penned the book for Tim Rice's *Aida* and Philip Glass *The Vacation* for the Metropolitan Opera. Yet, it took his first stage flop to signal Hwang that he was really a writer.

When I was young, I had no idea what I would end up doing. I didn't have any interest in literature. I thought I might end up being a businessman or an engineer. Through high school, there was nothing I was particularly interested in. I watched a lot of TV. There were so many people in high school who seemed to know exactly what they wanted to do with their lives. I didn't have that. On some level, I envied the people who had that degree of confidence about what their life was going to be, unaware that it might not turn out that way. They seemed to have a calling or a sense of direction. I certainly wouldn't have admitted it then, but it did lead me to become withdrawn in high school.

In college, I was a classical violinist and became a jazz violinist, and figured if music or the other things didn't work out I'd probably go to law school. Around my sophomore year, I saw some plays and thought to myself that I might be able to do this. I don't know why.

So I wrote some plays in my spare time. A professor of mine took a look at them and told me that they were really bad...which they were. My problem was that I had the desire to write plays but knew nothing about the theater. I spent the next several years seeing and reading as many plays as I could. That became my education.

I was very lucky, very early. I wrote a play, *F.O.B. (Fresh Off the Boat)*, meant only to be done in the college dormitory. It was accepted in a national playwriting contest and ended up being produced in New York by Joseph Papp, who was arguably the most important American theatrical producer in the last half of the 20th century. The play won an Obie for best American play that year and Papp became a patron of mine. So I sort of fell into a writing career. Because it happened so quickly and relatively easily, I didn't really believe in myself. I thought I was a fake. I figured I was very clever in pulling one over on *The New York Times*. But I didn't actually think I deserved the success or that I was that talented or that good. I believed I just lucked into it.

Every success comes with a little bit of poison and every failure comes with some great blessing. Some of my most important experiences have come from what I considered failures. In my early 20s, I had done a number of off-Broadway plays that had been successful. I had my first failed play, *Rich Relations*, when I was 29. Everything I had done up to that time had been Asian-themed work, so I wanted to do a play that didn't have any Asian characters. I basically ended up doing an autobiographical play about my family and made them all white. I'd say it lacked cultural authenticity. Audiences and critics agreed. And because I had gotten out of the starting gate as a professional playwright while I was fairly young, my dedication to my craft had never really been tested. When I had a play that the audience and *The New York Times* didn't like, that all changed.

A smooth sea never made a skillful mariner.
—English Proverb

I think the fear of not having a hit show is always worse than the fact of not having a hit. The apprehension of whether it will be successful or not and what terrible thing may follow if it's not can be overwhelming. You end up dreaming all sorts of terrible scenarios. When I finally received negative reviews, I found that the reality was far less painful than what I imagined it might be. I realized, for the first time, that I would always be a writer. I learned that dedication to my craft went beyond a simple success or failure in the eyes of the world. To me, it was a great gift. That's why the failure of *Rich Relations* was important. I needed that experience to be able to evaluate my commitment to writing. Even though that play was not successful, working with non-Asian actors gave me a foundation when I did my next play, which would incorporate a mixed cast. That play turned out to be *M. Butterfly*, my most successful play to date. I don't know how consciously I used my failed experience in *M.*, but I did feel more comfortable and confident where one of the two leads was a non-Asian character.

> *Good people are good because they've come to wisdom through failure.*
> —William Saroyan

I decided, against my better judgment, to write a television miniseries for Hallmark. Unfortunately, it turned out badly. Based on the Chinese legend of the *Monkey King*, I had to figure how to both turn this story into a miniseries and turn the lead Chinese character into a Caucasian. I was, sort of, seduced by the owner of Hallmark and agreed to do it. It wasn't a good idea. He said they were going to get an interesting director out of China and shoot it there. I felt like it would be done with a measure of respect for the root culture. But that never happened. It taught me the importance of story. If I had written a script that I felt proud of, it wouldn't have mattered who they brought in to direct or where it was shot. I had created something that fell short and believed it could be salvaged by an interesting directorial approach. That approach is an ass-backward way to work and you would have thought I would have known that right up front. I guess I needed proof.

I always question how we're supposed to apply what we've learned from our past mistakes. Sometimes we learn the wrong things

If you can't make a mistake, you can't make anything.
—Marva Collins

from history. Sometimes, we fight the last war. I never say never, but I hope that I would apply the general lessons from an experience that went wrong in an intelligent manner.

Before I was able to do something with my life, I had to find out what I *wanted* to do. I didn't learn that academically. I learned from finding what entertained me. What I enjoyed. I felt that if I could do that, it would be incredibly exciting. If you find something you like, try it. You don't have to be good at it. But if you want to be good at it, then you have to do the work necessary to become good. That doesn't come in a lightning bolt from the sky. It comes from effort.

My mother used to say to me, "Just try to do one thing and be the best you can at it." It doesn't matter what that one thing might be, because no matter what it is, it will provide you with self-confidence and the ability to focus. And you can apply that to anything.

RED-LETTER REJECTS

Penniless and with little hope for his future, John Steinbeck struggled for years to get his work published, seeing rejection after rejection even after his first novel, *Cap of Gold*, was published. Steinbeck did not taste success until the acceptance of his fourth novel, *Tortilla Flat*.

Charles Joffe

"I realized that before you throw something away because you find it imperfect, you first look for what gold there may be. And when you find it, you mine it for all it's worth."

Producer Charles Joffe, president of Rollins and Joffe Management, has had a client list that included Woody Allen, Mike Nichols and Elaine May, Robin Williams, Billy Crystal and David Letterman. As Woody Allen's career moved forward, Rollins and Joffe moved right along with him. They produced every one of his films, working with him for over 42 years. In addition to producing Allen's films, Rollins and Joffe produced the film *Arthur* with Dudley Moore as well as many television shows. It was Charles Joffe's bad decision that resulted in sending his career down the road to success.

When I was beginning my career, I wanted to become an agent with the William Morris Agency. There I would learn the craft from the bottom up. They offered me $75 a week. Another agency, MCA, thought I knew much more about agenting than I actually did and offered me $100. I had wanted to go with William Morris but I took the money, ending up at MCA.

Instead of learning the business, I was thrown right into it. The first act I was assigned to was Dean Martin and Jerry Lewis, who were starting their first tour of one-nighters. At the time, they were the hottest act in show business; $10,000 a night. I didn't know what I was doing and was immediately intimidated. The first time I met Jerry Lewis, he said, "Where's your father?" I wasn't a good agent and I guess he might have seen that. We became friends, but I didn't know what I was doing. In addition, I could not bring myself to represent people I didn't like, and the standard line at any agency was, "Don't judge 'em, book 'em." I soon realized that it was a mistake for me to go with MCA and I hated the entire two years I was there. Finally, I was fired. Choosing MCA had been a mistake, yet that mistake actually led to the best thing that ever happened to me. If I didn't go with MCA, I might have never met Jack Rollins nor had the career I have had.

At the time, Jack was managing only one act. He would come in all the time touting this starving black folk singer. I never saw anyone believe in anybody the way Jack did in this kid. Jack was laughed at by all the agents. He was a joke. In those days, it was tough for blacks to work anywhere. But Jack kept saying this guy was an industry...a star. I never saw such dedication and I just fell in love with Jack. The folk singer was Harry Belafonte.

After I left MCA, I joined up with Jack. We weren't successful right away, but in time things began to happen.

Experience is the name everyone gives to their mistakes.
—Oscar Wilde

A lot of what Jack and I did in our business was based on risk. No contracts. We didn't bill commissions. We put the responsibility on the act. The only reason we drew up a contract was if the act was insecure. Our only contract was a verbal one. You keep working hard on your act and we'll keep working hard for you. There was never a problem.

Most comedians I see seem afraid to risk. They go up and do the same act every night, even if it's not great. Yet the purpose of doing the showcase clubs is to try new material and take a risk that it might bomb. In that way, they will grow and get better. A lot of them just aren't willing. They're afraid of not getting laughs, but there are ways to get around that. To make sure you don't completely die, you do half of your true blue material that you know will work and the rest of the time you try new material. If you don't risk, you'll never find the best in yourself. The idea is to go out there and risk some failure each time and keep trying new stuff until everything works; until all you get are laughs. When our comics worked out new material, a lot of which didn't work, we would all sit around afterward and look for ways to make it work.

Andy Kaufman really took risks. He would invent a whole new character for himself, never letting on that the character wasn't real. He could sit through an entire business meeting as a nightclub singer, never once breaking character. If he wanted to be himself, he would leave and come back later as the real Andy Kaufman. Andy made a commitment to what he was doing no matter what the audience's reaction was. With that type of dedication, risk and the willingness to take a chance of failing, you'll discover the best you can be.

I've come to believe that all my past failures and frustrations were actually laying the foundation for the understandings that have created the new level of living I now enjoy.
—Anthony Robbins

Though I wouldn't recommend taking enormous risks on big, paying nights, I remember one night we had Woody Allen booked in The Latin Casino, a huge club in New Jersey. He went in there the first night and did 40 minutes of new material that he had never tried before and he did great. He never wanted to use the same material twice. He played Vegas three times and each time he had a whole new act. Woody was always willing to take the risk because it always made him better.

In my mind, the development deals the networks make with comics are a terrible thing. They take you off the market and dry up your creativity. They don't allow you to try and be different or take a chance. Instead, they try to fit your comedy into a sitcom that someone else has written for someone else.

> *Every adversity,*
> *every failure, every*
> *heartache carries with it*
> *the seed of an equal or*
> *greater benefit.*
> *—Napoleon Hill*

I once made a mistake negotiating Woody's film deal by giving up video rights. At the time, I didn't think it was a big deal. We all know what kind of business video has become. Later, I felt horrible about it. I couldn't forget it. One day I said to Woody, "Is there anything I can do to make it up to you?" And Woody, desperate to let me off the hook said, "I was at that meeting. I was the one who gave it to them." I figured if Woody could let go of it, so could I. At the same time, I learned from the mistake and not only was I smarter for the next deal, but the original company came back and revised the deal to include the video rights.

When [Mike] Nichols and [Elaine] May came into our office and did their Second City bits, each of which lasted about 20 minutes, I couldn't figure out how they could do this in nightclubs. Nightclub comics were doing jokes. I couldn't see an audience going for 20-minute pieces that are more theatrical or improvisational. But Jack saw something and he worked with them. Soon after, I learned to trust Jack's opinion. I also realized that before you throw something away because you find it imperfect, you first look for what gold there may be. If you find any, you mine it for all it's worth.

ACCIDENTAL ACHIEVEMENTS

When taking a break, a Proctor and Gamble employee forgot to turn off a machine that stirred soap. When he returned, the soap mixture, having more bubbles than normal, was so light that it floated and was 99 $^{44}/_{100}$% pure. This became Ivory Soap™.

Syd Field

"If you are doing something that you know to be true to you, you must follow it."

Many Hollywood professionals consider Syd Field the pre-eminent authority in the art and craft of screenwriting. His internationally acclaimed best-selling books, including *Screenplay*, have established themselves as bibles of the film industry. A former advisor to the National Endowment of the Arts, Field has taught at UCLA, USC, University of California at Berkeley and Harvard; he has also conducted screenwriting workshops around the world. At present, he is creative consultant to the governments of Argentina, Austria, Brazil and Mexico. This man, who guides so many people in perfecting their craft, once thought himself a failure.

When I was growing up, I was very aware of success and failure. My father was always comparing me to my very successful older brother. "Are you going to be like your brother? Are you going be as smart as your brother?" I grew up in an environment of judgment. Good, bad, right, wrong. Because my brother was the pride and joy of the family, I simply made sure that I was everything my brother was not. I determined, at a very early age, that if my brother was a success, I was going to be the *opposite* of that, though I never called it "failure"...until I started writing.

Innovation is hard to schedule.
—Dan Fylstra

I started out as a documentary filmmaker and had all kinds of success with David Wolper Productions but still didn't consider myself a success. I had written nine original screenplays. Two of them were produced, four were optioned and three went nowhere, so I viewed myself as a failure. With the all-or-nothing message I received as a

Many a problem holds many an answer.
—Mel Kardos

child, to be a success meant I had to sell every single screenplay I wrote. That was my mindset.

Thankfully, one of my mentors, Waldo Salt, taught me differently. He was an extraordinary example of a man who reinvented himself. Prior to the Hollywood blacklist of the '50s, Salt had been a successful screenwriter, albeit writing for other people. Then the blacklist hit and he was forced to move to Europe. He realized that communism was not the great, idealistic environment that he had originally envisioned. He had to reinvent himself from the ground up. He spent a soul-searching year writing nothing. When he was eventually given an opportunity to write again, it was someone else's idea and it turned out terribly. He realized that if he was going to fail, he'd rather do it on his own terms. He decided to write a screenplay the way he wanted it to be written. He would take as long as he needed to write the best screenplay possible. That first script was *Midnight Cowboy*, for which he won the Academy Award. I told him about my screenwriting history and he thought it was very fruitful. Incredibly good. His words had quite an impact and I immediately changed my mindset. I began writing screenplays and the fact that they weren't all made didn't make those screenplays failures. Nor did it make me one. As soon as I made that distinction, I realized I had a choice in my life. I could view myself as a success or I could view myself as a failure. If I wanted to be a failure, I didn't have to do anything at all. Up to that point I had chosen nonsuccess over success.

What I learned from the great film editor Frank Santillo was that the things he tried that did not work always showed him what did work. I saw that the things I wrote really pointed me toward success.

I took a couple years off from writing and as a studio reader read over 2,000 screenplays and more than 100 novels. I found only 40 out of 2,000 that I could recommend. What made those screenplays better that the other 1,960? I realized that there was a craft to writing screenplays and it could be taught. I began to explore that medium and ride the horse in the direction it was going. I wrote up a presentation, which was to become my book, *Screenplay*, and sold it immediately. I no longer wanted to be a writer…I *was* a writer. Not the type of writer I first envisioned, but the one I was meant to be. I realized then that everything I did in my life led me to that moment.

Today, I don't believe people fail. They are actually accumulating all the things necessary to lead them to what will be successful. It's about your own belief system. If you do something that you know to be true for you, you must follow it. At some point, if you are open to it, you will understand what to do with your vision.

Henrik Ibsen, the father of modern theater, struggled but kept on working. He had completed two major plays before anyone recognized who he was and what he was doing. His homeland, Norway, was the last place to recognize his genius. But he knew that what he was doing was true to who he was. Failure was not in his vocabulary.

We are raised in a society that says to its children, "No, this is wrong. Don't do this." The information is negative, so we tend to break things down to right or wrong, good or bad. Any judgment that gets in the way of doing what you want to do is usually a self-imposed judgment. "Nobody bought it, so it must not be any good."

We have to make a distinction between an event and the interpretation we place on that event. The interpretation is what gets us into trouble. I grew up with the interpretation that I was not good enough based on an experience I had with my father when I was around 6 years old. I was painting a picture, which I loved to do. One day, I painted a picture of a tree on a desert island. The tree was as tall as a mountain. Because I saw mountains as purple, I decided to paint the tree purple. My father took one look at my painting and said to me, "Syd, you'll never, ever be an artist. Don't you know that trees are green?" I packed up my paints, put away my easel and never picked up a paintbrush again. Only now, thankfully, do I understand that my father's judgment had nothing to do with the worth of my own vision.

Every step of the journey is important. We may not realize it at the time, but in the overview of our life, where we find the answers, the answers come when we least expect it. You may try something that doesn't work, that leads you to something else that doesn't work, that leads you to something that finally does. When a writer says to me, "I can't get a scene to work," I try to get him to look at it from a different angle, take something out, put something else in, approach it from a different character's point of view. It's all about problem-solving.

> *Ever tried. Ever failed.*
> *No matter. Fail again.*
> *Fail better.*
> *—Samuel Beckett*

Accepting myself as who I am took quite a bit of work. Mostly it was about forgiveness of what I've done to myself and to others, forgiveness of what others have done to me and even forgiveness of what my father's father did to him to make him respond to me the way he did.

Youth is such a wonderful time to make mistakes. Don't get tied down thinking that in your teens and 20s you have to figure out what you're supposed to be doing. You can still make mistakes, fail and try things that don't work in order to get closer to what does work. Life is an adventure, a journey, a mystery. Just keep your eyes forward, your heart pure, and when you're ready, as Joseph Campbell says, "Follow your bliss."

INFERIOR INSIGHT

"But what...is it good for?"

–Engineer at the advanced computing systems division of IBM, 1968, commenting on the microchip.

Don't Quit!

When things go wrong, as they sometimes will,
When the road you're trudging seems all uphill,
When the funds are low and the debts are high,
And you want to smile, but you have to sigh,
When care is pressing you down a bit,
Rest if you must,
But Don't You Quit!

Life is strange with its twists and turns,
As every one of us sometimes learns,
And many a fellow turns about
When he might have won had he stuck it out.
Don't give up though the pace seems slow
You may succeed with another blow.

Often the goal is nearer than
It seems to a faint and faltering man.
Often the struggler has given up
When he might have captured the victor's cup.
And he learned too late when the night came down
How close he was to the golden crown.

Success is failure turned inside out
The silver tint of the clouds of doubt,
And you never can tell how close you are,
It may be near when it seems afar.
So stick to the fight when you're hardest hit.
It's when things seem the worst
That You Mustn't Quit!

Some credit this to ~ William Murray Angus; Some
to ~ Edgar A. Guest; While others say it was written
by ~ Adrienne Richards; Still others give credit to ~
Anonymous; Why don't you make up your own mind.

's *Failures and Successes*

About the Author

Steve Young is a multi-talented writer and motivational speaker. In addition to creating material for prime-time network television (so you know he's familiar with failure), his stories and articles have been published in magazines and national newspapers. He is winner of the 2000 Prism Award and has been nominated for the Humanitas Prize, both of which recognize his ability to blend entertainment with important social issues. His first children's book, *Winchell Mink...The Misadventure Begins* was recently published by HarperCollins. Mr. young lives in Los Angeles with his wife, Diana, and their children, Casey and Kelly.